Maskulinitas

Maskulinitas

Culture, Gender and Politics in Indonesia

Marshall Clark

Monash University Press
Caulfield

Monash University Press
MAI, Building H
Monash University
Victoria 3145, Australia
www.monash.edu.au/mai

All Monash University Press publications are subject to double blind peer review

National Library of Australia cataloguing-in-publication data:

Author: Clark, Marshall Alexander.

Title: Maskulinitas : culture, gender and politics in Indonesia / Marshall Clark.

ISBN: 9781876924768 (pbk.)

Series: Monash papers on Southeast Asia ; 71

Notes: Includes bibliographical references and index

Subjects: Social sciences--Indonesia
            Indonesia--Social conditions
            Indonesia--Politics and government.

Dewey Number: 300.9598

Cover design by Minnie Doron.
The illustration on the cover is a detail from a painting by Dyan Anggraini.
Printed by BPA Print Group, Melbourne, Australia - www.bpabooks.com

This book is dedicated to Colin Campbell

contents

acknowledgements

I have quite a few people to thank concerning this book—including almost every Indonesianist I have met, studied under or worked with. I want to express my deepest gratitude to my very first Indonesian *guru*, Colin Campbell, who initially opened my eyes to the wonder of Indonesia and the Indonesian language, culture and cuisine. My lecturers at the Australian National University, including Yohanni Johns, Ira Armstrong, Wendy Mukherjee, Soepomo and Anthony Johns, provided much food for thought with a rich array of cultural, literary and political explorations. Over the past decade, my PhD supervisors Virginia Matheson Hooker and Keith Foulcher were influential in sowing the intellectual seeds for the ideas presented here. Lauren Bain deserves special thanks for inspiring me to write about Indonesian men in particular; I want to thank Harry Aveling and Krishna Sen for suggesting I focus my scholarly energies and develop my post-doctoral thoughts and writings into a cohesive book on Indonesian masculinities.

I want to thank those who have given me the opportunity to present some of this material elsewhere: David T Hill at Murdoch University, George Quinn at the Australian National University, Ariel Heryanto at the University of Melbourne, Susan Blackburn at Monash University and conference organisers at Universitas Indonesia (Depok), University of California (Berkeley), Curtin University (Sarawak), Universitas Udayana (Denpasar) and University of Sydney. I want to thank my colleagues at the University of Tasmania, the Australian National University and Deakin University for conversation, advice and intellectual engagement, particularly Barbara Hatley, Pam Allen, Max Renyaan, Freddy Kalidjernih, Amrih Widodo, Yudi Latif, Bernhard Platzdasch, Ismet Fanany, Alistair Welsh, Cucu Juwita, Aaron Martins and Bart Ziino, who at a crucial stage single-handedly helped me overcome a serious case of writer's block.

My warmest thanks go to Don Emmerson, my ever-attentive host at the Walter H Shorenstein Asia-Pacific Research Center, Stanford University, California, whose remarkable insights into—and passion for—Indonesia were inspirational as I completed the penultimate draft of this manuscript. I would also like to warmly thank my other colleagues at Stanford, including Jim Hoesterey, Sudarno Sumarto, Christian von Luebke, Thitinan Pongsudhirak and last, but certainly not least, my most influential intellectual confidente, Juliet Pietsch.

Direct help in the revision of this book was expertly provided by Rachel Salmond. My thanks also to Wulan Dirgantoro for helpful assistance in gathering material for the cover design and to Dyan Anggraini for her willingness for me to use her artwork in this regard. I must also give my special thanks to several colleagues who read earlier drafts of one or more chapters of this book, if not the whole manuscript, including Joost Coté, Dirk Tomsa, Will Derks, Andy Fuller, Razif Bahari and Tom Boellstorff.

Several chapters of this book have already appeared in print, each of which has been extensively revised for publication here. Earlier versions of chapters 3 and 4 appeared in *Indonesia and the Malay World* and *Journal of Southeast Asian Studies* (Clark 2004a, 2004b) respectively. A preliminary portion of Chapter 5 appeared in *Popular culture in Indonesia: fluid identities in post-authoritarian politics*, edited by Ariel Heryanto (Clark 2008b). I am grateful to the editors and proprietors in each case for, first of all, editing and publishing the material, and secondly, for permission to republish.

I am also grateful to Binhad Nurrohmat for permission to publish translations of his poetry, just as I am indebted to to the Australian National University, University of Tasmania and Deakin University for supporting the research on which this book is based.

San Francisco, May 2010

about the author

Marshall Clark teaches the language, media, culture and politics of Indonesia and Southeast Asia at Deakin University, Melbourne, Australia. He is the author of Wayang Mbeling: Sastra Indonesia Menjelang Akhir Orde Baru (LSPP: Jakarta) (2008) as well as the editor and co-translator of Binhad Nurrohmat's Kuda Ranjang (Melibas: Jakarta) (2008).

When Pushkin said that the art of the theater was 'born in the public square,' the square he had in mind was that of 'the common people,' the square of bazaars, puppet theaters, taverns, that is the square of European cities in the thirteenth, fourteenth and subsequent centuries. He also had in mind the fact that the state and 'official' society (that is, the privileged classes), with their 'official' arts and sciences, were located by and large beyond the square. But the square in earlier (ancient) times itself constituted a state (and more—it constituted the entire state apparatus, with all its official organs), it was the highest court, the whole of science, the whole of art, the entire people participated in it.

—MM Bakhtin (1981:132)

The close relationship between politics and culture in Indonesia came to the fore in the weeks before the resignation of President Suharto in 1998. On the humid evening before the Black Thursday riots in Jakarta in May 1998, Pramoedya Ananta Toer, who had spent much of the 1980s and 1990s under house arrest, was participating in what can be regarded, in hindsight, as the 'Last Supper' of the Suharto era. The occasion was the launch of *Saman* (Utami 1998), the best-selling novel by Ayu Utami. A journalist and sometime photo-model, Ayu was a co-founder of the Alliance of Independent Journalists (Aliansi Journalis Independen), an underground journalist organisation that spoke out firmly against New Order censorship (Bodden & Hellwig 2007). The launch of *Saman*, held at the Teater Utan Kayu arts complex in a leafy part of Jakarta, had drawn a large crowd of students, activists, writers and literary critics. Ayu's novel had just won first prize in a literary contest under the auspices of the Jakarta Arts Council; its first edition had already sold out within two weeks of its release (Hatley 1999). The novel had generated a great deal of media interest, as well as heated public debate over its content and authorship. In terms of the novel's content, it highlights the oppressive nature and military power of the New Order and, according to Bodden and Hellwig, the novel's publication, in the midst of societal turmoil and political unrest, 'could not have been more timely' (Bodden & Hellwig 2007:1). It was so timely, in fact, that there was even a giddy rumour that *Saman*'s blatant political message was strong enough to bring down Suharto's New Order regime. Couldn't the publication of a powerful novel, some asked, have as much potential to topple Suharto as any student demonstration? There were so many rumours at the time that nobody seemed to mind when it did not turn out to be the case.

Although he was hard of hearing and now unable and unwilling to read works of literature, Pramoedya Ananta Toer's presence at the launch of *Saman*, at considerable personal risk, was a statement in itself. He was there as much out of respect for Ayu Utami as in defiance of the New Order, which appeared to be falling apart at the seams. In the chaos of the last months of the regime, Indonesia's extensive intelligence network could evidently no longer cope with the rising tide of anger. There were anecdotes of *intel* (undercover intelligence agents) being outed at student gatherings or demonstrations and dealt with violently. In an act of self-preservation, some police officers even took to wearing civilian clothes on their way home from work. Thus, it appeared that the time was ripe for the elderly Pramoedya to venture from his suburban prison and roam the streets, seemingly unnoticed and unknown.

To open proceedings at the book launch, Sitok Srengenge, a well-known Jakarta-based poet, read a proclamation signed by a number of leading writers, poets and playwrights. It denounced the military's shooting of four students at Trisakti University the day before. After a communal multi-faith prayer, the gathering sang a sombre rendition of *Hymne Darah Juang*, one of the student anthems popularised during the first half of 1998. The next few hours were spent in communion with Ayu discussing her novel *Saman*. Almost as a weary backlash against the highly charged political atmosphere of the previous few months, politics was avoided. Instead, animated discussion of literature, language, feminism, style and form proceeded well into the night, spilling out into the outdoor café nearby. The apparent avoidance of political debate was but a momentary lapse. In the previous month or so, the Indonesian arts scene had been highly political, as it had tended to be in the previous 30 years in a nation where the mass media had long suffered from strict censorship and self-censorship. This time, however, in the midst of the greatest political and economic turmoil Indonesia had experienced since the mid-1960s, the arts scene was on fire as never before.

The publication of Ayu's award-winning novel was just the icing on the cake, or rather the cherry on top of the icing. In the month before the launch of *Saman*, hundreds of Indonesian artists and performers had united under the banner of Ruwatan Bumi '98 (Earth Exorcism '98), a cultural movement designed to heal the nation's woes. Not unlike the Chinese 'cultural fever' that accompanied the democracy movement in Beijing in the late 1980s, the Ruwatan Bumi sought to use art as the medium to liberate the badly bruised political consciousness of the long-suffering Indonesian people.

Historically, *ruwatan*, or cultural exorcisms, are relatively common in Indonesia. In the ancient Javanese kingdoms, whenever the royal court was faced with a calamity of one form or another, all the court's writers, poets and puppeteers were sent out into the neighbouring villages to rid the kingdom of its defilement. According to Pemberton (1994), *ruwatan bumi* rites are still held sporadically in rural Java as a means of exorcising crop failure and epidemic illness. In 1998, a similar concept was in play. In the space of one month, from the start of April to the start of May 1998, more than 170 artistic performances occurred in almost every major Indonesian city. The performances included drama, rock music, video installations, pantomime, prayer, photography, *wayang* shadow-puppet theatre, poetry, avant-garde dance and installation art. Most performances were advertised through the Internet, email and the mass media, radically modernising what is essentially an ancient ritual. According to its manifesto on the Ruwatan Bumi website (which has long since disappeared),

> The Ruwatan Bumi is a number of small steps on the way to the path of a beautiful dream, the very beginning of a brave move to break free from the dead-end which has pinned down Indonesians. The Ruwatan Bumi rejects all the calamities that we have been burdened with. It is an effort to reinvigorate social cohesion, which can release the creative energies of the individual and society (Clark 1999a:39).

Another characteristic of the exorcism was pluralism. For the first time in living memory it appeared that Indonesia's artists had managed to forget their artistic and ideological differences and participate as a unified, yet diverse, cultural movement. Whilst more established cultural icons such as Emha Ainun Nadjib and author, activist and priest YB Mangunwijaya lent their considerable intellectual standing to publishing essays in the mass media, addressing student rallies and, in Emha's case, lobbying Suharto directly, the exorcism was also a chance for Indonesia's younger artists to come to the fore. Fringe artists and musicians, such as Jalu G Pratidina, Afrizal Malna, Erick Yusuf and Slamet Abdul Syukur, were suddenly prominent. Music drama was a common performance medium used by these four artists in particular, with dialogue at a minimum. For instance, Slamet Abdul Sykur's sublime 'Wanderer' involved Slamet playing a simple bamboo reed interspersed with the recorded sound of a woman making love. Later, poet and theatre director Afrizal Malna collaborated with choreographer Boi G Sakti in 'A panorama of father's Death', a minimalist performance incorporating dance, violins and poetry. As in many of the Ruwatan Bumi performances, sounds and movements often jangled and jarred, defying cohesion or comprehension. Yet one unifying element was an almost overpowering sadness, with each dancer and darkly robed foot soldier expressing an existential angst that words seemed unable to express.

Another Ruwatan Bumi performance without any coherent dialogue, Erick Yusuf's 'Bread and circuses', also used image and music to reflect the fragile state of Indonesia's collective psyche. In this unsettling drama, a soldier, a public servant and a *sarong*-clad villager sat at a table greedily devouring a meal of bread and Pepsi. In a metaphor for the crisis-hit nation, as soon as the food ran out, chaos took over. The public servant crouched into a foetal position, the soldier waved his gun around threateningly, and the villager circled the table gesticulating angrily for more food. Eventually, accompanied by a terrifying cacophony of synthesisers, each character was dragged off the stage to an unknown fate. According to Erick Yusuf:

> Indonesia's present problem is a problem of bread and circuses. As the people's access to their "daily bread" is hampered by the government's inability to provide economic equality, and as the circus comes to an end, it is only a matter of time before the people's anger will explode (Clark 1999a:40).

In Yogyakarta, Indonesia's 'student city', the Ruwatan Bumi performances were strongly oriented towards the *rakyat* (common people), in terms of both the performers themselves and their audiences. Popular pantomime artist Jemek Supardi brought his silent protest to the streets, attracting large crowds of shoppers and pedestrians, as well as photographers and journalists keen to document his latest antics. Jemek also boarded a train to Jakarta and performed, in full make-up, for a whole day. Back in Yogyakarta, the Girli street people performed drama skits beside the Code River. Elsewhere a group of prostitutes performed their own play, humorously bemoaning the lack of business since the onset of the monetary crisis. On buses, buskers sang songs they had written that vented their frustration and anger. For those unable to write their own songs, the songs of singer–songwriters with a social conscience, such as Iwan Fals and Franky Sahilatua, were particularly popular. In Jakarta unemployed actors and artists walked down bus aisles with outstretched hats reciting poetry, not only to criticise the government but also to pay for their next plate of rice.

Historically, traditional cultures have often been co-opted into making social or political comment and the period preceding Suharto's resignation was no exception. Throughout Java the traditional *wayang* shadow-puppet theatre thrived and Java's much-loved puppets were often used to present sharp satire. Many performances depicted stories from the *Ramayana* cycle of tales which tell of the kidnapping of beautiful Sinta, Prince Rama's wife-to-be, by the evil King Rahwana. The political allegory was clear, even to the most unassuming observer. Somehow the people of Indonesia had to try to rescue the kidnapped nation from the clutches of Indonesia's own evil king, commonly perceived as President Suharto. However, pro-government puppeteers, otherwise known as *dalang Golkar*, saw the common enemy as being a combination of the Asian economic crisis and the International Monetary Fund.

As with much of Indonesia's day-to-day politics, which are often regarded as an elaborate shadow play, the student struggle was interpreted by some in terms of the *wayang* cosmology. Two of the first students killed by the military in 1998, Moses Gatotkaca and Elang Lesmana, happened to be named after prominent *wayang* characters who suffered similar fates in the *Mahabharata* and *Ramayana* epics respectively, even though they fought for the 'good' side. For *wayang* aficionados, this added a certain nuance to the despondency that the nation sank into following their shocking deaths. There were other striking coincidences at the time, pregnant with symbolism. For example, it is well known that 20 May 1998 was a highly significant date for the anti-Suharto student movement. It was a national holiday, National Awakening Day, a date charged with historical significance. National Awakening Day marks the day in 1908 when student nationalist movements, which were dedicated to achieving independence from Dutch rule, were born. Eventually, at 11pm on 20 May, Suharto decided to resign from his position as President. What is not as well known is that 21 May was also a national holiday, marking the ascension of Jesus Christ. The question of whether Suharto deliberately chose 21 May to resign formally, as opposed to a less auspicious date, remains unanswered. Yet if, to paraphrase Shakespeare, the world is a stage and the last few months of the New Order were following a script to be played out, one could not ask for a more symbolic or more ironic denouement.

Shadow plays in the twilight of the New Order

Considering the deep and abiding appreciation for Indonesian cultures at all levels of society, it is understandable that many Indonesian artists have long been regarded as cultural prophets, their relevance rising exponentially at times of intense social and political turmoil. Take poets, for example. Traditionally, and more recently, poets have played an important role as commentators and critics in Indonesian society. Throughout the last century, the style and form of their poetry has been created, crafted and adapted to reflect and comment on issues of social or political import. Contemporary poets such as Chairil Anwar, Rendra and Emha Ainun Nadjib have become Indonesian culture heroes, their names readily associated with particular periods in Indonesia's history. Chairil Anwar emerged at the height of the Indonesian Revolution of the late 1940s; his poetry articulated the existential yearnings of a nationalist consciousness emerging from the long dark shadow of centuries of Dutch colonialism (Levertov 2000). Later, the New Order poetry of Rendra and Emha gave voice to the social, cultural and environmental losses concomitant with the New Order's unwavering pursuit of political stability, social peace and economic development (Aveling 2001a). As noted above, Rendra did not limit his social activism to writing poetry. He frequently joined demonstrations, and regularly spoke out in the nation's news media. He was banned from these activities from time to time and detained in a prison cell on more than one occasion.

Similarly, there were times when Emha was banned from performing poetry or speaking out on issues of human rights and social justice (Scherer 2006; van Erven 1992). For example, at the time that Rendra was being detained for protesting the government's closure of *Tempo* in 1994, Emha performed, one Thursday evening in Yogyakarta, a politically-charged poetry reading, accompanied by his lively *gamelan* back-up band, Kiai Kanjeng. The plan was to perform on two nights but the second performance was cancelled by the local authorities. One Aesopian joke too many and Emha, as Rendra had on numerous occasions, found almost overnight that he was on the wrong side of the local powers-that-be. Of course, it is a backhanded compliment that New Order pen-pushers—undoubtedly the intended target of his poetic activism—had taken offence. Ironically, several years later, in 1998 to be precise, Emha and a small number of intellectuals and religious figures were involved in several influential meetings with Suharto in the days before his resignation (Nadjib 1998). Because Emha was not publicly calling for Suharto's immediate resignation, his reputation among anti-Suharto activists as an opposition firebrand was significantly tarnished. Indeed, in the post-New Order era there has been a changing of the cultural guard. A new generation of young artists has emerged, many of them women, and, for various reasons, New Order era artists such as Emha and Rendra have been unable to recapture their earlier fame. Although Rendra passed away in August 2009, Emha at least still commands enormous respect and modest audiences, both within his particular artistic communities and internationally.

Generational change aside, one could argue that the Indonesian political imagination is inherently cultural. The conspicuous presence of a poet in the presidential inner sanctum, at such an intense point in Indonesia's political history as the days preceding a president's resignation, is testament to this. According to the editors of *The last days of President Suharto*, many reports indicated that throughout the 1990s Suharto was increasingly disinclined to listen to the advice of all but a small palace coterie of family members and cronies: 'Cabinet members were afraid even to approach him, let alone contradict or question his views' (Aspinall, Feith & van Klinken 1999:ii). Even if Emha was not calling for Suharto's resignation, he asserts that he subtly conveyed some of the public's restlessness. Ultimately, Emha's presence at the highest level of political power was a firm reminder that intellectuals and other opinion leaders were more than willing to engage in a conversation about the need for change, sooner rather than later. It was also an historical echo of the ubiquitous and often influential presence of poets, puppeteers and palace scribes within the palace walls of the ancient courts throughout the Indonesian archipelago.

Although some observers cynically claim that the New Order has simply recycled itself in the post-authoritarian era (Robison & Hadiz 2004), Indonesian artists continue to engage in a constant conversation about Indonesia. As Heryanto observes, 'While Indonesia has barely recovered from a decade of the economic and political crisis that began in 1997, its contemporary cultures (pop or otherwise) have been thriving as never before' (Heryanto 2008:5). This observation is not surprising. Historically, Indonesian cultures have always enjoyed a high degree of cultural cachet. Cultural expression has been consistently promoted at the highest levels of society and politics, often for political reasons (Hooker & Dick 1995). In the New Order era, the control of culture—which involved, primarily, promoting the state-sanctioned 'official' version of national culture—became a fundamental element of the government's social and political repression (Heryanto 2008).

As in the New Order heyday of Rendra and Emha, challenging the traditional myths and legends of Java has continued to play a part in the national conversation (Bain 2005; Campbell, M 2007; Christanty 2008; Hatley 2002b, 2007). Elsewhere, as in the New Order era, essayists and political commentators allude to the *wayang* to strengthen a particular argument. This retrospective turn is significant and, occurring as it does over ten years on from the demise of the New Order, somewhat surprising. As is well known, the myths of the shadow theatre originate from Javanese cultural tradition, based on a patrimonial hierarchy and patriarchal social traditions. Popular recourse to Javanese mythology might, therefore, indicate the national vision's return to a more masculinist and, consequently, conservative social and political order. In the New Order era, politicians, most of whom were men, made no apology for using the mythological narratives of Java for their own nefarious purposes. Ultimately, the ubiquitous masculinist mythology of the New Order, inspired by the reconstructed discourses of aristocratic Javanese court culture, was a key element in the patriarchal vision of the nation that had prevailed in Indonesia from 1966 to 1998.

The intriguing aspect of the post-New Order slant towards mythology and, thus, toward a patriarchal vision of the post-authoritarian nation is that Indonesia has experienced massive changes over the last decade, particularly in the area of gender mainstreaming initiatives and women's non-government organisation (NGO) activism (Budianta 2000, 2003). The fall of the New Order in 1998 saw the mushrooming of new women's organisations, many of which appeared in regional areas (Blackburn 2004). The post-New Order governments have conferred official positions upon many of the original women activists of the late New Order (Blackburn 2004) and increasing numbers of women have found employment in waged work (Ford 2003; Warouw 2008), even in traditionally male-dominated areas (Lahiri-Dutt & Robinson 2008; Nilan & Utari 2008). In the cultural sphere, women writers have begun to consistently challenge the state's normative gender roles (Bodden & Hellwig 2007). Indeed, some women writers have subverted mythological narratives as a means of questioning archetypes of masculine and feminine roles within the stereotypical New Order model of the harmonious family (Hatley 1999, 2007; Heraty 2000; Sears 2007a). Other women writers, however, have decided that the best way to challenge normative gender roles is to literally remove their protagonists from the claustrophobic confines of the Indonesian context, as observed by Bodden and Hellwig (2007). Thus a good number of women writers have created narratives 'in which Indonesians, and especially Indonesian women, travel outside the confines of Indonesia in order to situate themselves in a more global framework, suggesting that Indonesians need not see their identities as constituted only within the frame of the nation' (Bodden & Hellwig 2007:11).

Women writers are not the only ones to have attempted to challenge the state's patriarchal vision of the nation. Although male egos have been hurting from their exclusion from the post-1998 discourse on literature (Bodden & Hellwig 2007), some men have attempted to break through the masculinist sexual taboos and write about sexuality and gender identity, emphasising non-normative sexualities (Christanty 2008; Fathuri 2005; Murtagh 2007). Equally importantly, women writers are not the only ones who have attempted to develop their social critique from a space slightly removed from the frame of the nation. Pramoedya, for example, approached the theme of patriarchy and the theme of the Indonesian nation from an historical framework, encompassing the regional as much as the global. Thus, for Pramoedya, a life of railing against the indigenised mythologies of Java was as much about challenging the normative ideologies of the New Order nation-state as it was about warring against Javanese cultural traditions.

If we familiarise ourselves with the novels, interviews and personality of Pramoedya, we soon gain the distinct impression that for Pramoedya the myths of Java are just as imperialist in spirit as anything introduced by the Dutch. Pramoedya held a longstanding aversion to Javanism, which Benedict Anderson (1990b:219) styled as Pram 'crossing swords' with the ossified forms of his Javanese heritage. Pramoedya has argued that the Indies were ripe for colonial subjugation because the pre-colonial Javanese kingdoms had successfully sown the cultural seeds of feudalism, patrimonialism and social conservatism:

> Westerners came looking for spices in what is now Indonesia in the sixteenth century. They called it "East India" or later the "Dutch Indies". They never considered this area to be an independent culture. Even the present name means "Islands of India". During the colonial era, the countries in the area never considered themselves as strong and independent nations. Instead, they acted like servants of the West, mainly because of Javanism, a cultural attitude that eventually spread over all of what we now call Indonesia. Java was the center of colonial administrative power, hence the overwhelming influence of Javanism. From my personal experience, the impact of colonialism was that in the past, we—even I—felt inferior to people from the West...Javanism had only one principle—obedience and loyalty to the superior. That's why we were ripe for colonization. Understanding Javanism is crucial for understanding what became of us after 1965 (Vltchek & Indira 2006:53–5).

Pramoedya's comments here are as insightful as ever, even if many of the states in the region existed in relative autonomy from the Dutch until the early 1900s and colonial hegemony was not established in the Indies until almost a decade later. Understanding Javanism, particularly the ways in which Javanism has been reproduced, reinterpreted and subverted, gains potency when we consider how significant the role of Java and Javanism was to the New Order regime. Many commentators have observed that the New Order regime was heavily-Javacentric (Anderson 1990c; Liddle 1996; Magnis-Suseno 1999; Pemberton 1994). Suharto himself was an ethnic Javanese and he stacked his government with like-minded cronies and military supporters, most of whom were also from his ethnic group. In many ways, the Javacentric character of Suharto's regime was justified by the fact that the ethnic Javanese are numerically the largest ethnic group in the archipelago. Indonesia's first president, Sukarno, was also Javanese. The Dutch colonial government was situated in Batavia in West Java; that the postcolonial political and geographical capital remained in the same location ensured that the seat of power remained in Java.

In terms of political ideology, the New Order regime embodied Javanese aristocratic culture. In practice, this translated into a unique combination of traditional Javanese patrimonialism, deference and social stratification. As seen above, Pramoedya simply labels this cultural trifecta as 'Javanism'. Combined with other indigenous concepts/political mantras, such as *adat* (tradition), *musyawarah* (deliberation) and *mufakat* (consensus), Javanese notions, such as deference to one's superiors, ultimately became potent cultural–ideological instruments in the hands of the New Order government. Suharto's efforts to portray himself as a father figure emphasised the way in which ideal Indonesian citizens should see themselves—that is, as obedient members of a metaphoric family.

The Javacentric character of the New Order was further entrenched by Suharto's penchant for alluding to the world of the Javanese mythology. From very early on in his political career Suharto, like his predecessor, was quick to perceive the electoral value of linking the political imagination with collective myths. For instance, on 11 March 1966 Army Commander, Lieutenant General Suharto assumed power after intense pressure was placed on Indonesia's first president, Sukarno, to sign the 11 March Letter of Authority (*Supersemar*) (Elson 2001). Semar, of course, is the popular clown-god and *punakawan* or servant to the kings, commonly regarded as the representative and advocate of the common man. Suharto assiduously cultivated the symbolic link between himself and Semar, often making pilgrimages to 'Gua Semar' (Semar Cave) on the Dieng Plateau in Central Java. Yayasan Beasiswa Supersemar, a foundation intended to assist needy and deserving students with educational costs, was established in 1974. At the same time, apparently the fate of decolonised Portuguese Timor was sealed after a conversation in 'Gua Semar' in Dieng, when Suharto took Australian Prime Minister Gough Whitlam to tour the cave (McDonald 1980). Links with other heroes were also developed. In his biography (Roeder 1969), for example, there is a photo of Suharto posing in his presidential office in front of a large painting depicting Hanoman fighting Rahwana. Later in his career, when his popularity was waning, he felt the need to emphasise his Javaneseness and draw upon the *wayang* to reassert his links with the common people (Pausacker 2004). So in 1995 Suharto tacitly endorsed a wave of *wayang* performances led by a string of pro-government *dalang*. The majority of these performances starred the character of Semar. A similar pattern occurred at the height of the Asian economic crisis in 1997–98, when the government funded a number of pro-government shadow-theatre performances, this time starring Rama and Hanoman (Clark 2001). In this manner during the Suharto era, Javanese and non-Javanese alike became quite familiar with allusions to the *wayang* pantheon, even if they were not fans of the genre. The popular conception of Indonesian politics as shadow play, with an unseen *dalang* or mastermind orchestrating developments from behind a metaphoric screen, has persisted, particularly in the West.

In terms of political style, Suharto's presidential style was modelled on the values of the *gagah* (heroic) caste of warriors located in the upper echelons of the *wayang* world—the *satria*, or warriors, who were in turn models for the rulers of the aristocratic Javanese courts. Thus Suharto's presidency took on a dynastic quality, very much in the manner of his predecessor, Sukarno. Many commentators have observed that despite the differences between Indonesia's first two presidents, the main similarity between them is an essentially hierarchical political ideology derived from the Javanese cultural tradition. Anderson's essay on Javanese notions of power (1990a) explored the links between Sukarno and Javanese rulers, and Magnis-Suseno (1999) and Liddle (1996) have observed that Suharto projected an image of standing alone at the apex of government, like an idealised version of a traditional Javanese king. Like a king, he made all important political decisions, as far as outside observers such as Liddle could detect. As in the court scene of a *wayang* performance, Suharto usually received cabinet ministers and others as petitioners, rather than as colleagues. Consequently, the autocratic, kingly nature of Suharto's rule was a key motif of the New Order era, during which the central reality of the New Order's political system of governance was arguably 'government top down', with Suharto, like a Javanese ruler of centuries past, placed firmly at the top.

Many artists critical of Suharto and his regime focused their attention on capturing and reworking the highly stratified social structure of the *wayang* world, primarily for their own subversive purposes. Although there were many exceptions (Foulcher 1987; Hill 1984), most socially-engaged authors in the New Order era—that is, authors determined to engage with social issues yet keen to avoid the possibility of imprisonment, detention or bannings for criticising the ruling elite—soon turned their hand to surrealism, absurdism or the realms of myth (Foulcher 1995a). However, surrealist fiction and absurdist theatre—modes of representation usually lacking linear plots, identifiable characters, geographic locations, or a sense of history—more often than not confounded, confused and alienated readers (Maier 1999). This reluctance to use a realist mode of representation was, quite possibly, simply a form of self-preservation. With bills to pay and families to feed, many artists erred on the side of caution. The dangers associated with publishing or performing unmediated criticism of the Suharto regime were stark and well known. Ultimately for many ethnic Javanese or Balinese writers, strongly influenced by mythic narratives from a tender age, surrealism was the most expedient method to capture and critique New Order history (Tickell 1986). Indeed, it could almost be said that the insidious impact of censorship and self-censorship was such that a generation of writers had little option other than to draw upon the images, myths and tales of their childhood. Thus surrealism and mythology provided writers a canvas on which they could hone their literary craftsmanship, sharpen their political instincts and test their wits against the authorities within the permitted boundaries. Equally importantly, realist and non-realist writers who were both Indonesian and Javanese, such as Pramoedya, YB Mangunwijaya and Seno Gumira Ajidarma, used the Indonesian language as a means of participating in the national conversation, as well as a means of negotiating a break with their Javanese roots.

Some might argue that, historically, artists in Indonesia do little more than act as politically useful social safety valves, like pressure-cookers letting off a bit of steam. Perhaps to some extent this is true. But I would argue that most Indonesian cultural activists are political activists in their own right. After all, while journalists and political activists were muzzled, detained, kidnapped and murdered in the New Order era, many writers, poets and playwrights filled the gap. Of course, as argued above, a considerable number of artists and particularly writers were also censored and their activities curtailed (McGlynn 2000). On the whole, however, they were able to imaginatively convey much more of the underside to the New Order's master-narrative of economic success than journalists and their editors, who were forever fearful of losing their jobs or having their press licences revoked (Heryanto & Adi 2002; Hill 1995; Sen & Hill 2000). It is no coincidence, therefore, that the political relevance of Seno Gumira Ajidarma's best-known text stems from its arresting title, *Ketika jurnalisme dibungkam sastra harus bicara* (When journalism is muzzled literature must talk)[1] (Ajidarma 1997). In Seno's case, in the mid-1990s, his career as a journalist was dramatically muzzled when he was stood down from his job as editor of *Jakarta Jakarta* for publishing articles about East Timor (Bodden 1999; Clark 1999b; Heryanto & Adi 2002). *Jakarta Jakarta* has since closed down; to this day Seno has used fiction to reveal the truth about East Timor and many other issues of social and political relevance (Bodden 1999; Heryanto 2008).

Other Indonesian artists have also displayed a knack for embodying the cultural zeitgeist in a pithy book title or evocative line of poetry. Javanese poet Wiji Thukul is best remembered for his late-1990s thundering catchcry: 'Hanya ada satu kata—Lawan!' (There is only one word—Resist!). This line of poetry, like no other, perfectly captures the rebellious spirit of the times. It expresses the hopes, dreams and frustrations of a generation. The fact that Wiji disappeared in the last weeks of the New Order, never to be seen again, underlines Indonesian artists' surprising capacity to symbolically threaten and rupture the political status quo. Indeed, as in the case of Wiji Thukul, some have been regarded by the state apparatus as being too dangerous for their own good.

On other occasions writers and dissidents threw caution to the wind and Suharto was targeted directly. Pipit Rochijat's seditious *Baratayuda di Negeri Antah Berantah* (The Baratayuda in Never-Never Land) (1993) portrayed President Suharto as the butt of many a crude joke (Clark 2006; Widodo 1988). Consider also the case of Soebadio Sastrosatomo, the author of *Politik Dosomuko Rezim Orde Baru* (The politics of Dosomuko of the New Order Regime) (1998). Soebadio's monograph is based on a literalist reading of the *Ramayana*'s oppositional conflict between the evil ogre-king Rahwana (Dasamuka) and Prince Rama and the monkey army. As described earlier, there is strong evidence that Suharto likened himself to the monkey Hanoman fighting Rahwana (Dasamuka). Yet Soebadio undeniably represents Suharto as Dasamuka and the monkeys as ordinary Indonesians. Throughout the 23 pages of *Politik Dosomuko*, Soebadio is scathing in his attack on Suharto's 'evil' rule, claiming that throughout Suharto's presidency the Indonesian people were harshly oppressed. The dominant motif of Soebadio's highly polemical text is based upon the conceit that Suharto began and continued his rule of Indonesia in the same manner as Dasamuka had done in Alengka. Under the heading 'Dosomuko's political system', Soebadio bitterly claims that Dasamuka's ten faces represent ten aspects of Suharto's regime: the eradication of the *rakyat*'s sovereignty; the manipulation of the Pancasila as a means of political control; the neutralisation of the legal system; the repression of political parties and workers' unions; the emasculation of the parliament; the censorship of the mass media; the development of an economy rife with nepotism, corruption and collusion; the de-intellectualisation of the education system; the standardisation of culture;

and the violation of basic human rights. Marc Perlman (1999) has observed that Soebadio's 'blistering' comparison between Dasamuka and Suharto's regime would do many a *dalang* proud. Significantly, *Politik Dosomuko* appeared in February 1998 and was banned and withdrawn from sale on 22 April of the same year, a month before Suharto's resignation. Would it be too much to assert that this banning shows how seriously and personally such writing was taken by the President? At the very least it confirms the remarks of a 19th-century editor of Aesop: 'A tyrant cannot take notice of a Fable without putting on the cap that fits' (Joseph Jacobs, quoted in Patterson 1991:17).

As we shall see later in this book, some ethnic Javanese artists were reluctant to reacquaint themselves with the mythologies of Java, no matter how tempting it might have been to strike directly at the seat of power. The *wayang*, so the argument went, was simply too closely aligned with Suharto and his regime and all of the best *dalang* had long been co-opted by the government. Some younger writers, however, have conceptualised transformations of the mythologies of Java as much more than a means of merely conveying political satire. Of relevance to this book, complex issues such as the fluidity of gender identities have also been addressed in contemporary mythological transformations.

The ongoing reinterpretation of myth and questioning of dominant gender ideologies can also be seen as rich entry point into a fresh understanding of post-authoritarian Indonesia. The dovetailing movement of contemporary Indonesian artistic expression from traditional cultural expression to parodic reinterpretation to a depthless postmodern pastiche also provides us with a snapshot of the history of the Indonesian nation and of the changing status of the Indonesian masculine.

Key sections of this book will be devoted to delineating the subversive nature of contemporary artists challenging archetypal narratives of the heroic. Through this I aim to reveal the ways in which contemporary Java-based artists and dissidents have reinterpreted mythology and heroic narratives as a means of conceptualising alternative gendered identities as a whole, and alternative masculine identities in particular. But examining contemporary transformations of mythological narratives is not the key focus of this book. Rather, the key objective is to examine the ways in which cultural transformations and literary developments are constructing new Indonesian masculine identities, with or without recourse to traditional narratives. By analysing the cultural production of Java-based or ethnically Javanese artists and dissidents, this book foregrounds an ethnic identity long considered central to the project of Indonesian nationhood. In this way the voices and opinions of the cultural actors under discussion paradoxically write *back* to the centre of the nation from *within* the centre, thus making their conversation doubly potent.

Men and the masculine in Indonesia

Why examine men and the masculine in Indonesia, rather than women and the feminine? Despite the boom in men's studies internationally in the last 15 years or so, scholarship in Indonesian gender studies has, on the whole, been much slower than in other countries to incorporate the study of men and masculinities. In the West, interest in men's studies largely developed in the wake of Western feminism (Medrado, Lyra & Monteiro 2001). In Indonesia, feminism has taken much longer to gain a foothold, if it has done so at all. It was not until after the resignation of President Suharto in 1998, and the transition towards a more democratic social and political system, that a gender discourse hit centre stage and women's groups proliferated (Blackburn 2004; Budianta 2000, 2003; Robinson & Bessell 2002). Until recently, gender in Indonesia was widely regarded as a euphemism for 'women's issues' and the increasing work on gender among Western and Indonesian academics and activists has focused disproportionately on women (Oetomo 2000).

The delayed development of feminist scholarship and women's activism, and the inherent ambivalence towards women's groups, have meant that reflection on *kejantanan* (masculinity), *maskulinitas* (masculinities) and men's practices in Indonesia has also been delayed. As Blackburn (2004:30) argues, the women's movement still has a long way to go to gain influence over the political process:

> For one thing, it is hard for it to create a political constituency when it has had little experience in building a politically aware membership base. Failing to use its own members to act as an independent means of social influence, it is still too dependent on the state, which in turn is weak and preoccupied with matters other than the concerns of the women's movement.

Building Indonesian women's political capacity also requires much more work. For most Indonesian women, direct involvement in politics is daunting, as there are significant cultural and institutional barriers. While cultural barriers are likely to persist well into the future, at least some of the institutional barriers have been eased in the last few years. For example, during the 2004 parliamentary election Indonesian parties were for the first time required to nominate at least 30 percent of female candidates on their lists (Siregar 2006). However, the election law did not specify any sanctions for non-compliance so that many parties ignored the quota, further reinforcing the widely held impression that Indonesian politics is patriarchal by nature and political parties have little interest in the situation of women or in prioritising women's political education. Moreover, there continues to be a persistent social perception, inculcated through the New Order's patriarchal gender regime, that the feminine is a threat to male dominance, including, by extension, the state's dominance. Saparinah Sadli observes:

> While women are in the process of defining [a] new feminist paradigm, the establishment looks at this process as a threat. We have nothing to lose but they have everything to lose. Men could see that during the recent [economic] crisis women could find jobs more easily and better meet the demands of the market (Budianta 2000:109).

The inherent 'threat' of the feminine is not necessarily a new development. In stark contrast to the late colonial era when women were celebrated as comrades in the armed struggle for independence (Blackburn 2004; Martyn 2005), Suharto's military regime was 'built on an excessively masculine power obsessed with control and women's submission' (Wieringa 2003:72). The authoritative, masculinist and monolithic discourse of the Suharto era was intolerant of any perceived threats to the hetero-normative social order—so much so that, for some, orchestrated attacks against homosexual gatherings have been interpreted as evidence of both masculine and state insecurity (Boellstorff 2004). These are all issues that demand further debate and this book seeks to shed light on these questions and more.

Meanwhile, most, if not all, women's groups have been seeking to place issues such as women's rights, gender equity and gender justice at the top of the public agenda (Budianta 2000; Robinson & Bessell 2002; Sadli 2002). Elsewhere, efforts to understand the dramatic shift in women's employment in Indonesia towards waged work and the role of organised religion, particularly Islam, in the construction of attitudes towards employment are also quite recent and preliminary in scope (Ford & Parker 2008). As such, public debate on gender relations in Indonesia is, on the whole, a relatively new phenomenon—so new that some might be more inclined to think that gender refers to *gender*, a particular instrument in the traditional Javanese *gamelan* orchestra. For example, in a candid moment, Seno Gumira Ajidarma says 'I remember when I read the writing of one of the very first feminists, I even thought at first that gender meant "*gender*"' (Ajidarma 2002:138). Moreover, until recently the question of the gendered construction of Indonesian men has been almost completely ignored.

Several Western scholars, however, have helped broaden the understanding of gender in Indonesia by implying that there are many other gendered categories in addition to heterosexual femininity. Boellstorff (2005), for instance, has examined homosexual *gay* and *lesbi* (lesbians) in contemporary Indonesia, 'transgendered' categories such as *banci* or *waria* (those persons who regard themselves as belonging to a 'male-to-female, transvestite subject-position') and 'female-to-male transgendered persons' (known most often as *tomboi* or *hunter*). Oetomo (1996) and Blackwood and Wieringa (1999) have also written on same-sex relations in Indonesia. Others have discussed what have been called 'indigenous' homosexualities and transgenderisms, such as the *bissu* in Bugis culture in southern Sulawesi (Graham 2006, 2007; Pelras 1996) and the *warok* in the Ponorogo region of eastern Java (Wilson 1999).

Considering the exotic variety of what Boellstorff refers to as 'sexual/ gendered subject-positions' in contemporary Indonesia, it is not surprising that heterosexual masculinities are so little discussed. As Parker (2008) observes:

> I do not want to detract from the importance of their *gay*-ness or *lesbi*-ness to *gays* and *lesbis*, but I do want to bring some balance into the scholarly literature: at present we have the rather bizarre situation that we seem to have more explicit and sophisticated work on alternative sexualities than we do on hegemonic heterosexuality.

Nevertheless, if we scour the archives we find some notable exceptions to this absence of discussion about hegemonic heterosexuality, particularly about hegemonic masculinity. I have already mentioned the role of Anderson's 'The idea of power in Javanese culture' (1990a) in defining Javanese notions of male power. Anderson's *Mythology and the tolerance of the Javanese* (1965) also deserves special mention in this regard. Elsewhere, such is the fame of Clifford Geertz's discussion of Balinese men's practices in his 1972 article, 'Deep play: notes on the Balinese cockfight', that several websites are devoted to it. It has also been included in a more recent 'men's studies' anthology (Adams & Savran 2002). In terms of masculinities *per se*, the most interesting aspect of Geertz's article is the discussion of the ways in which different types of men are characterised in terms of fighting cocks. For example, 'a stingy man, who promises much, gives little, and begrudges that, is compared to a cock which, held by the tail, leaps at another without in fact engaging him', and 'a desperate man who makes a last, irrational effort to extricate himself from an impossible situation is likened to a dying cock who makes one final lunge at his tormentor to drag him along to a common destruction' (Geertz 2002:81).

Nevertheless, despite the seminal work of Anderson and Geertz, discussion of *kejantanan* and *maskulinitas* is unusual in Indonesia and 'the man question' is still to be asked. In contrast, according to Robinson, 'attention to "the woman question" is not new in Indonesia and discussion of rights is not alien to the political language of Indonesia' (Robinson 1997:159). The struggle for gender rights has been an ongoing social and political strategy of Indonesian women. This was particularly the case in the New Order era, as notions of proper behaviour for Indonesian women were closely attached to the state's political agenda and to notions of social control, order and stability. Consequently, the New Order state's gender ideologies and policies for women have attracted the attention of feminist scholars.

As Lauren Bain (2005:101) observes, 'One of the ways in which we can gain insight into the tensions and ambiguities inherent in gender ideology is through analyzing representations of gender in visual and other media'. We should not be surprised therefore that numerous essays and papers have been written about the representation of women and gender relations in film, soap opera, theatre and other media during the New Order. For instance, in one of her many discussions of the feminine in New Order cinema, Sen (1995) argues that in love stories and dramas—often called 'women's films'—women play substantial roles, often as strong and autonomous heroines. However, according to Sen, women's films perpetuate stereotyped gendered roles for women. Prominent among these is one of the New Order state's key gender ideologies, *kodrat wanita* (female nature):

> *Kodrat* implies both the nature and the destiny of women (*wanita*) and this seems to be the woman's function as mother, contained within the family sphere. Any movement of the woman beyond this sphere becomes an issue of contention within the dominant discourse of the narrative (Sen 1995:117).

In parallel to Sen's scholarship on gender in cinema, Barbara Hatley (1990; 1994) has critically investigated the participation and representation of New Order women in live theatre and performance. The repressive nature of *kodrat wanita* and stereotyped roles for women have also been among important themes in Hatley's work, but, as Bain (2005) points out, Hatley's work is an exception in the field of scholarship on women's participation in contemporary Indonesian theatre, and the absence of women from fields of theatre directing and writing in the New Order is often noted.

Since publication of Hatley's early work, Saraswati Sunindyo (1995) has examined gendered constructions in *sinetron* ('cinema electronic', or soap opera) as a means of revealing not only the pervasiveness of patriarchy in everyday life but also the ways in which it is strengthened by the state. In her analysis of several *sinetron* on the New Order's state-run television station, TVRI, Sunindyo argues that, through negative portrayals of 'career women', the state was able to enhance its patriarchal gender regime. In *Apa yang kau cari Adinda?* (What are you looking for, Adinda?), directed by Asrul Sani, and *Karina*, directed by Nano Riantiarno, the dominant gender discourse was inscribed: the two 'have a similar philosophy which is that a woman's place is at home with her family, and that even if she works outside the home, the family should have first priority in her life' (Sunindyo 1995:138).

A similar argument is presented by Brenner (1999), who asserts that print media reveal much about how Indonesian women and the family became the focus of national narratives of development and modernisation in the New Order. Through concerted media campaigns, images of the happy, middle-class family 'came to stand for a generic Indonesian moral and social order' and in images of domesticated mothers and wives 'the New Order woman signified the comforts of stability as well as the dangers that threatened the nation should that stability break down' (Brenner 1999:13–14). Control over the nation, it seemed, depended on control over the family and, more importantly, over women, who were portrayed as the linchpin of every family, at least according to the state's masculinist public discourse and media representations.

We should not forget the important role that Benedict Anderson's scholarship on gender in Indonesia has played. After all, according to Sears, Anderson's famous essay 'The idea of power in Javanese culture' (1990a) helped formulate the vision of Javanese masculinity which was to become a symbol of hegemonic masculinity and masculinist state power. As Sears (2007a:57) argues, 'In response to this gender construction, Javanese women were viewed as coarse: uncontrolled, possessing an excess of passion, lacking spiritual potency, and possessing an ability in the market that is denigrated by a disdain for business'. Of course, Sears also mentions Brenner's argument that these accepted gender ideologies are a complex product of other factors, including 'the patriarchal tendencies of the Dutch rule, of Islamic ideologies of male self-control, and of the repressive and non-repressive state apparatuses of the Indonesian government' (Sears 2007a:57). So we can't blame Anderson's gender constructions for everything. The trick is to find some middle ground, as this book attempts to do.

Such, briefly, are the aims and the social, cultural and political background for the present book. Chapter 1 will further contextualise the discussion of representations of *maskulinitas* in Indonesian cultures that follows in later chapters. The first half of the chapter will examine the gender issues that have been of concern to the state, the women's movement and feminist scholars. A further point of discussion will be the emerging global men's studies movement and its relevance to the Indonesian context. The second half of the chapter will introduce this book's analytical overlay of Bakhtinian cultural and literary theory. Inspired by Henk Maier's *We are playing relatives* (2004), Chapter 1, and indeed this book as a whole, allows Bakhtin's theoretical vocabulary to spice up proceedings, as a mild *sambal* sauce might add flavour and texture to an Indonesian meal. This chapter will elucidate Bakhtinian terminology, including concepts such as heteroglossia, dialogism and the carnivalesque. Chapter 1 also opens itself up to the possibility of indigenous referents for Bakhtinian concepts, as Maier's study does. Armed with these terms, I will reiterate my argument that Indonesian artists and dissidents are engaged in a constant dialogue between what Bakhtin would class as officialdom and the marketplace, or the state and the people.

A similar dialogic imperative underpins the discussion of *maskulinitas* and biography in the historical novels of Pramoedya Ananta Toer in Chapter 2. Just as Pramoedya's literary critique is a three-way conversation with Indonesia's younger generation and the colonial and neo-colonial powers of the Indonesian archipelago, my own analysis is part of an ongoing conversation about Pramoedya and his work. This chapter breaks new ground in the sense that it considers Pramoedya's best-known male protagonist, Minke, from various angles, including men's studies scholarship, Pramoedya's aversion to Java, and the recent biographical turn in cultural and literary studies. In Chapter 3 I revisit the subversive potential of Java. I argue that Ayu Utami's polyphonic reinterpretation of the Javanese epic theatrical and literary tradition offers an array of sophisticated alternatives to dominant Javanese constructions of the masculine, and the feminine for that matter. Sears (2007b:62) argues that 'Utami's novels suggest that the patriarchal vision of the postcolonial nation is doomed to failure'. Although my analysis is drawn from a masculine perspective—in contrast to Sears' feminist reading—my discussion tends to support Sears' conclusion, even if other chapters in this book suggest that patriarchy in Indonesia is still far from drawing its last breath.

Chapter 4 considers the resurgence of alternative constructions of masculinities in a period of regime change. In this chapter I begin to focus on cinema, investigating the difficulties of representing gay and other non-normative masculinities and the associated gendered dilemmas facing all young Indonesians in the post-authoritarian era. Examining several post-New Order films made by leading Jakarta-based filmmaker Rudi Soedjarwo, Chapter 5 explores Indonesia's ubiquitous culture of masculinised violence, both on the national stage and in the domestic sphere. This chapter suggests that not all cultural productions appearing in the post-New Order can be hailed as pro-feminist death knells of patriarchy; far from it. Indeed, the fact that Soedjarwo's films are so popular at the box office should be taken as a serious warning sign. This is because a significant proportion of Soedjarwo's films are violently misogynistic, homophobic and characterised by narratives where feminity is conflated with monstrosity and victimhood and *maskulinitas* is synonymous with violence, rape and murder. The fact that Indonesian horror—a genre in which Soedjarwo continues to experience great box-office success—is so resoundingly popular with Indonesian audiences of the post-authoritarian era suggests that Soedjarwo's films are merely the tip of the ice-berg, a cinematic microcosm of much broader cultural and societal trends.

Chapter 6 analyses a controversial literary storm in order to better understand poetic representations of contemporary masculinities and also contemporary responses to hypermasculine or transgressive cultural texts. This chapter suggests that fundamentalist religious groups are not the only groups who are inclined towards a kneejerk response to perceived affronts. I will argue that fellow artists and critics are also liable to take offence at perceived affronts to normative masculinity, as indicated by a string of literary furores. This chapter, as with all the chapters of this book, tells us something about masculinities in Indonesia; not everything, just something. I will leave it to others to assess my conclusions and the impact of cultural transformations and literary developments on the broader conversation about sex, gender and the state.

Notes

1　Unless noted otherwise, the Indonesian–English translations in this book are my own.

chapter one

The man question:
gender, recklessness and rage

The term "gender" is often used as a synonym for "women" or a euphemism for "feminism" or "feminist", with men not even discussed…rarely if ever is the construction of masculinity discussed, let alone questioned.

Dede Oetomo (2000:46)

In the post-New Order gender discourse there has been a much greater focus on men and masculinities, even if it is somewhat of a boutique industry. A number of factors might have led to the new level of interest. These include: an embattled and misogynistic response to the increasing social and economic emancipation of women; feelings of masculine disempowerment in the face of economic trends, such as the Asian economic crisis and, most recently, the global economic crisis; and a continuing renegotiation of nation, gender and hegemonic masculinities in the post-New Order period. There are suggestions that *maskulinitas* should be taken more into account. Indeed, with the increasing attention given to women and women's roles in Indonesia, there are also many indications that attention to the subject of men and masculine identity in Indonesia is increasingly relevant in a political sense. For instance, recent large-scale anti-pornography protests and demonstrations and the emergence of a booming men's lifestyle magazine industry can be easily associated with the emergence of new understandings of what *maskulinitas* can be in post-authoritarian Indonesia, and how it should be manifest most effectively in the context of a newly-democratising society.

In early 2006, Indonesian society and media were rocked by heated debates and violent demonstrations, especially from Muslim groups, over the rumoured gestation of an Indonesian version of the American *Playboy* magazine (Kitley 2008). Its actual birth in April 2006 was greeted by widespread anger and dismay. The demonstrations were characterised by flag and magazine burnings, anti-West placards, threats of legal action and, ultimately, the destruction of the *Playboy* magazine's Jakarta office. The office was moved to the predominantly Hindu island of Bali, and *Playboy* continues to be sold. By both Western and Indonesian standards, the first few editions were quite tame, with no nudity or partial nudity at all. Furthermore, in terms of cost, style and content, the magazine was quite up-market. Epitomising this deliberate marketing strategy, the leading article in the inaugural edition was an interview with Pramoedya Ananta Toer, who despite his fame throughout the Western world was never a household name in Indonesia. Some readers—Muslim and non-Muslim alike—complained that the magazine contained remarkably little in the way of titillation and that they felt ripped-off. Nevertheless, later in the year the editor of the magazine, Erwin Arnada, and the local *Playboy* licence holders, Ponti Carolus Pondian and Okke Gania, appeared at the South Jakarta District Court to face charges of publishing indecent materials (*SMH* 2006; Kitley 2008).

For much of 2006 the Indonesian parliament, attempting to appease both mainstream and hardline Islamic groups, seemed set to introduce a sweeping anti-pornography law (Allen 2007; Kitley 2008). Known as the *Rancangan Undang-Undang Anti Pornografi dan Pornoaksi* (RUU APP), the Anti Pornography and Pornoaction Bill proposed to legislate against the production, distribution and consumption of pornography in Indonesia. The bill also intended to regulate against instances of 'pornoaction', a neologism that encompasses a range of actions including the public representation of nudity, erotic dancing, kissing in public and the wearing of certain clothes. Significantly, for many years there have been existing laws in Indonesia designed to regulate pornography, yet these laws have rarely been enforced (Williams 2006). Regardless of this, supporters of the bill used the widespread availability of pornography, particularly pirated VCD and DVD 'blue films' originating from the West, Indonesia and elsewhere in Asia, as reason enough to introduce the new law. Although the proposed bill was officially withdrawn in late 2006, attempts to redraft the bill continued, until a watered-down version was finally ratified in late 2008 (Baskoro et al. 2008). The key point to make is that the momentum for the bill did not dissipate after the initial rejection, despite widespread protests and continued opposition across the country. Ultimately, the campaign to outlaw pornography embodies, as Robinson (2007) argues, a public contestation over gender relations and an assertion of 'popular front' Islamism and 'renovated' forms of *maskulinitas*, in jockeying for greater political leverage.

Ironically, despite the remarkable media focus on the anti-pornography legislation, risqué Indonesian men's magazines and cheap pornographic tabloids have proliferated since the late 1990s, without censure or meaningful criticism. These include the glossy and relatively expensive 'indigenous' *X Men's Magazine*, *Manly* and *Popular*. The market is subdivided into health-oriented titles, such as *Men's Health*, and magazines using similar names yet slightly different formats to other magazines originating in the United Kingdom, such as *FHM* and *Maxim*. Low-grade soft-porn tabloids have also emerged, complete with salacious titles such as *Dugem*, *Wild Girls*, *Exotica* and *Lipstick*. Nevertheless, in mid-February 2006, all men's magazines were discreetly taken off Indonesian bookshelves and roadside magazine stalls. With the increasingly vociferous calls for the banning of pornography and the intensifying anti-*Playboy* demonstrations, newsagents feared the financial cost of raids by over-eager local law enforcers. By the end of the year, things had returned to business as usual and these magazines are now widely available. Nevertheless, at the time, this pre-emptive strike was clearly a case of self-censorship. Yet, in my opinion, formed during several months of fieldwork in Indonesia in 2006, there was barely a whisper of protest. I would argue that the new crop of men's magazines in Indonesia and the persistent tensions between predominantly male producers, consumers and censorious local agents can be considered in terms of issues of male identity.

Concomitant with the anti-pornography debates, the emergence of new kinds of censorship might provide us with some implicit clues as to why the critical analysis of men *as men* has not yet occurred in Indonesian cultural and political discourse. Salient is the fact that many Indonesian writers, filmmakers and artists have endured decades of authoritarianism, censorship and self-censorship (McGlynn 2000). For Indonesia's artists growing up in the New Order, this has been the experience of their whole lives. So, rather than addressing what some may consider as typical concerns of male identity, including issues such as virility, male sexuality and homophobia, when Indonesian artists represent men, they are more often than not engaging in a conversation on broader issues, such as nationalism, colonialism, authoritarianism, the struggle for women's emancipation and the democratisation of Indonesian political culture. This book, therefore, deploys culture as a locus to examine not just politics, gender and masculinities in Indonesia but also a number of closely related themes. Besides the issues mentioned above, recurring themes discussed in this book include misogyny, misandry, violence, homophobia and freedom of expression.

Political Islam and colonial gender discourses

Because Indonesia is the largest Muslim nation in the world, Islam is another leitmotif occurring frequently within any discourse relating to *maskulinitas* in late and post-New Order Indonesia. Societal upheaval, coupled with ongoing economic disappointment and the resulting feelings of disempowerment and frustration, has driven many Indonesian men to seek solace in Islam. Not coincidentally, many hardline Islamic groups are increasingly suspicious of feminism and the recent proliferation of women's groups. As Platzdasch argues, 'conservatives generally view the call for self-determination by women as "un-Islamic", and as a threat to the integrity of the smallest unit and core of Muslim society, the family' (Platzdasch 2000:336). State and Islamic discourses have long worked together in Indonesia (Blackburn 2004; Blackwood 2005; Robinson 2008) and, in the post-authoritarian era, we can see the Islamic emphasis on the sanctity of the family and the valorisation of female domesticity continue to reinforce the New Order's patriarchal perspective on gender and sexuality.

The deeply conservative line on gender held by many Islamic leaders and publications has also led to a resurgence of polygamy in recent years. According to Blackburn, 'for some Islamic conservatives, polygamy is something to be proud of, the badge of a devout Muslim' (Blackburn 2004:134). Most Indonesian women, including many Muslim women who recognise that polygamy is sanctioned in the Koran, strongly disagree with this attitude. On the other hand, some women support it, even if they are deeply unhappy about their own husband taking a second or third wife. A spate of recent films depicting polygamous relationships—including Nia Dinata's *Berbagi suami* (Love for share) (2006), Hanung Bramantyo's *Ayat ayat cinta* (Verses of love) (2008) based on Habiburrahman El Shirazy's best-selling novel (2004), and Bramantyo's *Perempuan berkalung sorban* (Woman wearing a headscarf) (2009) based on a novel by Abidah El Khalieqy (2001)—suggests that interest in the topic is ongoing.

If we are to properly understand trends such as the resurgence of polygamy, the emergence of militant Islam, new kinds of censorship and the patriarchal legacies of the New Order, it is also helpful to examine earlier conservative colonial gender discourses. As Day (2002a:80) observes (referring to the scholarship of Gouda 1993; Locher-Scholten 1994; Stoler 1995; Enloe 1990), 'Colonialism, nationalism, and "modernity" subjected Southeast Asians to a conquering, middle-class European kind of masculinity that also engaged with the gender of Southeast Asian identities in significant ways'. In the Netherlands Indies at the beginning of the 20th century, for instance, European males were warned to avoid wearing light and cool clothes in the manner of 'the natives' and instead dress at all times in a 'civilised' fashion—with hats, shoes, socks, jackets, long trousers, etc—thus strengthening the dichotomy between 'imperial masculinity' (and 'imperial femininity') on the one hand and the masculinity (and feminity) of 'uncivilised' natives on the other.

According to Wieringa, in the Indonesian context 'the processes of colonization, with its attendant phenomena of the feminization and eroticization of the colonized have left deep scars, resulting in particular sensitivities' (Wieringa 2003:72). For instance, in the Dutch East Indies of the 1920s and 1930s there was a great deal of male anxiety and insecurity in the face of new European norms, such as the figure of the progressive, educated, Western-influenced modern woman. These notions were seen as threatening to established gender hierarchies and hegemonic understandings of women's nature and permissible social roles. Many male writers in the late colonial era, including Takdir Alisjahbana and Amijn Pane, denounced the new overly-Westernised freedom, which they believed brought moral degradation, sexual promiscuity and disaster upon their female protagonists (Hatley 2002a). These characteristics help us make sense of more recent patterns in postcolonial Indonesian literature. For instance, in texts of the 1970s and 1980s by male authors such as Umar Kayam, Ahmad Tohari and Linus Suryadi, 'nativist' images of female figures were a regular occurrence; they draw upon traditional, mythological archetypes of female compliance and subservience. In terms of the overarching political context at the time, the New Order state was aggressively promoting its ideology of a 'family-based' citizen-state, where women and girls were limited to dependent, subordinate wifely roles (Wieringa 2003). The other important aspect of this social conservatism was the need to curtail women and girls from indigenous female solidarity and autonomy. Thus the rhetorical castigation of feminism in the 1980s and 1990s was similar to the widespread fear associated with the threat of the Western-influenced 'modern woman' in the 1920s and 1930s. As Hatley (2002a:147) observes, in both periods 'the spectre of the West as a source of threat to male power looms large, and contributes significantly to ideological attempts at control and containment'.

As Day (2002a) argues, ex-President Suharto's postcolonial nation-state was as coercive, paternalistic and infantilising as the Netherlands Indies colonial state had been. A key element of these characteristics was the New Order ideology of a 'family-based' citizen-state, with the recurring symbolic identification of the people with the 'mother-as-nation' and the President as 'father-of-the-nation'. As explained by Ariel Heryanto, in the ideology of 'development' in New Order Indonesia, '[t]he presence of a Father of Development (*Bapak Pembangunan*) [explains] *Pembangunan* [development] as a unit of social activity with "familial" characteristics' (Heryanto 1988:21, quoted in Day 2002a:81 (with Day's interpolations)). Consequently, according to Day (2002a:81), the 'masculinisation' of postcolonial states in Southeast Asia, such as Indonesia, 'can also be traced to the reaction of males to the colonial experience and the process of modernization during the colonial and postcolonial eras'. Of course, Day also argues that there is no simple, teleological connection between colonial and postcolonial expressions of patriarchy in Southeast Asia. Yet it is clear, to Day at least, that 'Islam, Buddhism, Christianity, and colonialism generally have strengthened rather than weakened the role of hierarchy in the formation of Southeast Asian states, but this statement says little about the ambiguities and complexities of the overall process as far as gender is concerned' (Day 2002a:83). This book will, in its own modest way, discuss some of the 'ambiguities and complexities' of the cultural and political manifestations of this process, in the context of postcolonial Indonesia.

Men and masculinities in the global context

Given the comparatively inferior position of Indonesian women in a strongly patriarchal society—in which the norms of feminine subordination and submission are legitimised or sanctified by the ideologies of the state and the strictures of religion—it might seem a bit odd to concentrate on the position of men. But an argument can be made that if the subordinate status of Indonesian women is to be constructively highlighted and some sort of gender equality achieved, then surely the representations, subjectivities and practices of Indonesian men must be addressed.

According to two leading figures in international men's studies, Bob Pease and Keith Pringle, issues that impinge on women in the global context, such as unequal wages, gender-segregated jobs, the feminisation of poverty, inequalities in health and social care and gender-related violence, are central concerns of men's practices. As Pease and Pringle (2001:6) observe, 'Questioning dominant forms of masculinity and gender oppression in particular locations is a necessary step in addressing these global inequalities. If the global situation of women is to improve, men must change their subjectivities and practices'. This is especially so in contemporary Indonesia, where many hardline Islamic groups are already strongly suspicious of feminism and the recent proliferation of women's groups. We need, therefore, to avoid the possible marginalisation of an already threatened body of men. Nevertheless, other important questions also need to be asked. For example, how do we *enact* strategies that create positive, equality-oriented changes among men? How do we encourage men to loosen their connection with heterosexual dominance and patriarchy? These questions are central in much of the scholarship on men's studies, even if there are rarely any constructive answers beyond consciousness-raising and education. Australian writer Peter McMillan (1992:144) provides an eloquent solution:

> I believe that women do not want men to change, in the sense of becoming something that we are not. I believe that what they want is for men to evolve in the sense of becoming what we have the potential to become.

I do not necessarily see the need to urge Indonesian men to 'change' or to establish 'men's discovery groups' from Sabang to Merauke, following in the footsteps of the now passé men's mythopoeic movement in the West. Nevertheless, the analytical stance of this book is indeed along the lines of Pease and Pringle's call for 'questioning dominant forms of masculinity and gender oppression'. It aims to encourage the inclusion of men in the process of confronting gender inequality in Indonesia, not only for the sake of women, but for men as well. After all, as Pierre Bourdieu (2001) suggests, men are often just as subject to the patriarchal structures of gender domination as women. It can be added that older men are in a double bind. They are not only marginalised in a society where youth is highly valued but also regarded as patriarchal has-beens, suffering under the ultimate indignity—to be looked after by women in their old age. It is for this reason that I am, where possible, speaking of Indonesian *maskulinitas* or masculini*ties* across the age spectrum, rather than using the one single monolithic term, 'masculinity'.

I use the plural Indonesian term *maskulinitas* or the English gloss 'masculinities' here deliberately, in recognition of the shifting of the conceptual focus of masculinity to masculinities in international men's studies a decade ago, led by Connell, 'to encapsulate both the diversity and potential fluidity of the processes involved in men being men' (Pease & Pringle 2001:2). In Indonesia it is increasingly evident that the heavily Javacentric hegemonic 'ideal' model of masculine behaviour is exactly that—just a model. This is especially so with the increasing influence of Western feminism, the increase in grassroots women's activism, the outdated nature of the New Order's dominant patriarchal gender order, the increasing numbers of Indonesian women with tertiary qualifications and a desire for careers, and the large numbers of unemployed and underemployed men following the Asian economic crisis, the Bali bombings and, most recently, the global economic crisis. In non-Western countries such as Brazil, the debate on men and masculinities was instigated by similar socioeconomic factors, spearheaded by feminist activism (Medrado, Lyra & Monteiro 2001). In Indonesia, there has been no *debate* as such, but the heightened reactions to the anti-pornography bill and the introduction of an Indonesian *Playboy*, together with the ongoing boom in Indonesian men's magazines, indicate that change is afoot.

Debate on women and Indonesian femininities has occurred for well over a decade now. Of course, some Western critics would argue that the fight to change women's gender identities will remain almost impossible unless men begin to question their personal practices and the ideologies of masculinity which they embody (Pease & Pringle 2001). Similarly, the need to question ideologies and conceptualisations of the masculine has encouraged me to focus not only on representations of Indonesian men but also on the ideologies, institutions and cultures in Indonesia that help sustain gender inequality. An examination such as this is particularly important if we wish to see what sort of impact, if any, recent social and political developments have had on representations of men in a period of regime change. Because I do not want to mistake a synchronic variety of male images for diachronic change, my argument is a modest one, suggesting that changing images of men and masculinities in Indonesian cultural expression are not new phenomena. After all, from a historical perspective, there have always been images of men that challenge and subvert dominant hegemonic patterns of manliness. However, I will reiterate that recent social and political developments have ensured that the question of men in Indonesian gender studies has assumed a greater sense of urgency.

Theoretical approach

In *Rabelais and his world*, Mikhail Bakhtin (1984b) discusses the role of the carnival in European culture and how it is able to give us a much fuller appreciation of Renaissance literature. Bakhtin argues that the comic literature of the Middle Ages—parodies and satires of Greek mythology, biblical Scriptures and learned treatises—was infused with a carnival spirit and made wide use of carnival forms and images. The culture of the carnival, Bakhtin argues, is heterogenous. It melds myth, puppetry and folk humour with other literary forms, such as parody and satire. Bakhtin uses Rabelais' carnivalesque work to highlight the languages, styles and images of folk culture. Similarly, I would argue that Bakhtinian terms such as the carnivalesque (and closely related concepts, such as heteroglossia and dialogism) are eminently useful in highlighting the constant conversations on Indonesia's history, cultural identity, political imagination and male-centric model of nationalism.

According to Bakhtin, the carnivalesque primarily consisted of the logic of the 'inside out' (*à l'envers*), 'of a continual shifting from top to bottom, from front to rear, to numerous parodies and travesties, humiliations, profanations, comic crownings and uncrownings' (Bakhtin 1984b:11). There are other fundamental elements of the carnival, including festive or ambivalent laughter, licentiousness and the grotesque (the grotesque image of the body in particular). The spirit of the carnival is also critical, as it negates the fixedness of hierarchy, prevailing truths and authorities. But the carnival is not negative in spirit, as it also renews and revives. Thus the literature of the carnival was simultaneously subversive of official culture and authority and supportive of popular renewal. Bakhtin suggests that this ambivalence lies in the fundamental nature of the carnival festivities in contrast to the feasts of the official sphere:

> As opposed to the official feast, one might say that carnival celebrated temporary liberation from the prevailing truth and from established order; it marked the suspension of all hierarchical rank, privileges, norms, and prohibitions. Carnival was the true feast of time, the feast of becoming, change, and renewal. It was hostile to all that was immortalized and completed (Bakhtin 1984b:10).

In the Indonesian context, Bakhtin's concept of the carnival can be comfortably conveyed by the term *pasar*. The concept of the official feast, in Bakhtin's dialectic sense, does not have a precise parallel term. But, at a push, it can be covered by various indigenous referents, one of which, *sowan*, refers to the Javanese tradition of sons calling upon and treating their fathers with great formality and deference. We shall return to this notion in much more detail in the following chapter. Suffice it to say that Indonesia, like medieval Europe, has a longstanding dialectic between the officialdom of the aristocracy and authorities on the one hand and the earthy festivities of the *rakyat* on the other.

We can apply Bakhtin's trope of the carnival to the tensions between dominant masculinity and alternative masculine identities in contemporary Indonesia. For instance, in the New Order, the hegemonic masculine identity— that is, the masculine 'cultural ideal'—was as Javanese as Suharto himself. The aristocratic Javanese model of emotional self-restraint was widely deployed as an ideal pattern of masculine behavior (Aveling 2001b). Many Western scholars have made similar observations, most of them inspired by Anderson's essay on Javanese notions of power. According to Sears (2007a:57), 'The traditions of scholarship set in place in the 1960s and 1970s celebrated a certain vision of Javanese masculinity: as refined, mystical, spiritually potent, impractical, delicate, non-Islamic, controlled, and sexualised in a repressed way'. As I have explained, this model was based on traditional Javanese cultural attitudes of deference and obedience, ideals inspired, promoted and reified by the Javanese epic theatrical and literary tradition. Of course, the ways in which men and boys in Indonesia perceived and experienced manhood in the New Order were far more diverse and fluid than the ideal Javanese model, even within Java itself. Nevertheless, the New Order government, with its 'patriarchal symbolic order' (Sears 1996:18), was relentless in its adoption of hegemonic or archetypal images of Indonesian manhood deriving from the Javanese cultural sphere. Thus, like the culture of the carnival, artistic disruptions to dominant models of the masculine can also be regarded as political ruptures.

Images of alternative masculinities, or even revivals or renewals of archetypal masculine models, can also be considered as embodying much more than the carnival spirit. Reconceptualisations of masculine identities are also important components of an ongoing conversation—or 'dialogism' in Bakhtinian terminology—between artists, officialdom, and the people. As we shall see, in many cases artists have paradoxically allowed their fictional protagonists the freedom to speak for themselves, thus establishing a cacophony of voices, above and beyond the author's voice. Thus Bakhtinian concepts such as heteroglossia and polyphony appear to me to offer an exceptionally rich way to help us better understand not only the motivations of Indonesian artists but also their works, their insights into the Indonesian nation, and the Indonesian masculine.

This book examines representations of the masculine in Indonesian popular culture using Mikhail Bakhtin's key concepts of heteroglossia, dialogism and the carnivalesque as an analytical framework. In focusing on the popular cultural expression of the late New Order and the immediate post-authoritarian period in particular, Bakhtin's theories are eminently applicable to the Indonesian context.

According to Bakhtin's translator and editor, Michael Holquist, heteroglossia is the 'master trope' at the heart of all Bakhtin's other projects, including other categories often associated with his thought, such as dialogism, polyphony and the carnivalesque. These three categories, Holquist argues, are merely specific ways in which heteroglossia manifests itself. Bakhtin's 'master trope', as Booth observes, 'seems to rest on a vision of the world as essentially a collectivity of subjects who are themselves social in essence, not individuals in any usual sense of the word' (Booth 1984:xxi). Thus terms such as 'multi-voicedness' and 'multi-centeredness' are used to describe the world we live in and its subjects. Fundamental to this, the languages in which we speak are social languages, not private languages. As a result, our consciousnesses are as social as the languages we speak. Thus we are heteroglossic from an early age, having been forced to master a variety of social dialects and linguistic registers derived from our parents, ethnic group, class, religion and nation. Over time, we learn to accommodate more voices and more languages, ensuring that we speak a chorus of languages. Our individuality, therefore, is never entirely a private or autonomous individuality, an 'I'; rather, each of us is a 'we'. Human existence, then, is created *in* many languages and *by* many languages. In this sense our lives, like languages, are 'dialogical', where heteroglossia and polyphony are a part of life and, in Bakhtin's eyes, values to be pursued.

Bakhtin also argues that there are two opposing tendencies in heteroglossia. There are 'centrifugal' forces dispersing us outward into an ever greater and ever more chaotic variety of voices. Then there are various 'centripetal' forces that preserve us from overwhelming fluidity and variety. Based on the evidence presented in the introduction to this book, we can safely assume that Indonesia's continuous search for a definition of cultural identity is underpinned by a combination of centrifugal and centripetal forces. The contemporary resurgence of myth, and humorous parodies and satires of mythological narratives, is centripetal. These modernised tales draw the reader back to the heroic master-narratives of Indonesia's history and to the world of tradition, and to the aesthetics of aristocratic Java in particular. These tales also lead us back to Suharto and the ideologies of the heavily-Javanised New Order regime. But, in the hands of modern artists, most of whom are well-read, well-travelled and avid users of Facebook, email and SMS, the glorified culture of Indonesia's past is also undergoing inexorable transformation. In the cosmopolitan fiction and films of younger writers and filmmakers we see Bakhtin's 'centrifugal' culture of the carnival enacted on a daily basis. Material for one's latest poem, novel or movie is eclectic, sourced as much from the Internet as from one's recent all-expenses-paid tour to South Korea, California or Tasmania. However, these younger artists are just as likely to draw upon the languages, images and heroic narratives of Indonesia's regions. It is in this context that we can warmly embrace Bakhtin's argument that heteroglossia has the potential to be both centripetal and centrifugal.

This is not the first time Bakhtin's theories have been used as an analytical framework for understanding Indonesia and her culture. Henk Maier's groundbreaking study on literary culture in the Malay world (2004) quite impressively amplifies Bakhtin's concepts. Maier metaphorically doffs his cap to Bakhtin on several levels. First of all, Maier utilises Bakhtin's concept of dialogism, in the sense that his book aims to be part of a dialogue with the texts under analysis, as well as with the authors and fellow readers of those texts. Maier asserts that the relationship between text, writer and reader has long been intimate and fluid in the Malay world. Maier's own book seeks to reflect and perpetuate this dialogic system. I am not sure how successful Maier is in this aim. For instance, Maier gives the impression that he is not truly keen to engage intimately with either the authors of the texts or their readers. The readers most obviously include fellow scholars of modern Indonesian literature, few of whom are quoted or paraphrased. Of course, this very same flaneuristic attitude was adopted by Bakhtin himself, who rarely saw the need to quote his contemporaries at length, or indeed break up the flow of his writing with references and seemingly irrelevant footnotes or asides. In this sense, perhaps, the truly dialogic nature of Maier's text is that, in the spirit of Bakhtin, it engages in a communal dialogue with Bakhtin.

Although not on the scale of Maier's *We are playing relatives*, the book you are reading now is also an attempt to engage in dialogue with Indonesian artists, who, thanks to the wonders of the Internet and mobile phones, are in constant communication with each other. I believe Bakhtin's concept of dialogism also involves much more than an ongoing dialogue between text, writer and critic (complex as this is). In my opinion the spirit of dialogism, like the culture of the carnival, must also invoke a political conversation between the official serious culture of the state and the unofficial heterogenous culture of the marketplace. Despite market pressures of its own, the world of the critic or of the foreign academic, as in my case, should fit somewhere in between. After all, despite increasing pressures to seek out government largesse, the academic is to this day only one or two degrees removed from the Benjaminesque *homme de lettres*—the freelance writer or *flaneur* who lives by his pen. Just as the *flaneur*, pen and cigar in hand, contemplates the urban spectacle as a text, the foreign academic should also be in the thick of things *and* contemplative from a safe distance.

Maier identifies and praises heteroglossia. What, in Maier's view, is heteroglossia? In the context of Maier's book, it refers to the 'centrifugal' forces of diversity in the language of Malay/Indonesian literature, which persistently work against the unitary, 'centripetal' forces of the authorities and systematisers. I argue that a similar process is occurring in Indonesia today. Centrifugal forces appear to have the upper hand, especially when we consider the globalised nature of contemporary cultural flows and the cosmopolitan nature of the latest generation of Indonesian artists. Yet centripetal forces of the authorities and systematisers are still in play. Many artists still find their work eliciting unwelcome bureaucratic or critical attention, as I reveal in later chapters. Others complain of the new systematising forces at play in contemporary Indonesia, such as the court of public opinion, or, more worryingly, 'a hard-line literalist Muslim segment of the new Indonesian middle and upper middle classes' (Bodden 2007:98). Either way, contemporary Indonesian artistic expression is heteroglossic and continues to be riven by the centrifugal forces of the *pasar* or the *rakyat*, as well as by the centripetal forces of officialdom or religion.

Maier emphasises the open-ended 'dialogic' nature of the novel in the Malay world, as opposed to the closed and finalised 'monologic' nature of other art forms, such as epics, legends and poetry. This means that poetry is excluded from Maier's survey. According to Maier,

> The novel is an unfinished discursive institution and it is bound to remain so. It is the 'genre of becoming', never achieving fulfilment, closure, or finality; it can draw from every possible other genre, from every other text that is available, and by doing so it keeps rules and regulations of writing and reading wide open. It resists every form of restraint (Maier 2004:467).

This reification of the novel is based on Bakhtin's understanding of the novel as a dialogic genre and the lyric, the epic and poetry as monologic genres. Yet Millie observes in relation to the Malay context, 'while this rationale may be justifiable for some 20th century writing, I think that many Malay *syair* draw on the plurality of voices in Malay discourse in an open and often subversive way, and cannot therefore be regarded as monological' (Millie 2007:196). On the surface, Millie's critique certainly seems plausible. Besides the Malay *syair* Millie refers to, we could also mention the fundamentally heteroglossic nature of the Javanese epic theatrical and literary tradition, epitomised by the *wayang* shadow theatre and texts such as the 12th-century Javanese poem, *Bharatayuddha kakawin*. Millie's criticism points us, therefore, in the direction of the key question here: Is Maier's application of Bakhtin's concept of the novel, and the novel alone, as a dialogic genre missing much that would otherwise be worthy of scholarly attention? In order to answer this, we need to briefly return to Bakhtin's definition of the novel.

Holquist (1981:xxxi).notes:

> 'Novel' is the name Bakhtin gives to whatever force is at work within a given literary system to reveal the limits, the artificial constraints of that system. Literary systems are composed of canons, and 'novelization' is fundamentally anticanonical. It will not permit generic monologue. Always it will insist on the dialogue between what a given system will admit as literature and those texts that are otherwise excluded from such a definition of literature. What is more conventionally thought of as the novel is simply the most complex and distilled expression of this impulse.

Yet in the Indonesian context not all novels are dialogic, and many short stories, poems, films, pantomimes, legends and epics are anything but monologic. In Indonesia novels are far more likely than any other literary genre to be classed as canonical. This is despite the best efforts of those who have been arguing for years that, in Indonesia's thoroughly oral literary system, the novel form, dependent as it is on a culture of print literacy, is irrelevant and anachronistic (Derks 1996, 2002). Ironically, throughout Indonesian literary history the reification of the novel has ensured that the most popular genres—poetry and short stories—have been more or less excluded from the canon. There have been exceptions, of course, most notably the work of the larger-than-life poets Chairil Anwar and Rendra. More importantly, I would argue that Maier's implicit promotion of the novel as *the* pre-eminent dialogic genre is obscuring much that is important and deserving of analysis. First of all, everything Maier claims to be unique to the novel is characteristic of other genres of writing in Indonesia and, indeed, of many other genres of cultural expression. Secondly, in a Bakhtinian sense, there is much that is 'novel'—that is, irreverent and anti-canonical—about Indonesian poetry, cinema, theatre, advertising, music, mime, puppetry and other cultural expressions. Thirdly, if we consider that the best thing about the novel in the Malay world is that it is dialogic, then it is imperative that we unearth all that is dialogic in the many other genres of artistic expression in Indonesia.

Perhaps we need to pause for a moment to more carefully clarify our understanding of what is dialogic and, by the same token, monologic. I am not convinced that Bakhtin suggests that only novels can be considered as dialogic. Rather, in Bakhtin's perspective it is the overtly dialogic nature of the novel that fundamentally distinguishes the novel in principle and in spirit from other genres. Furthermore, in Bakhtin's eyes, whether a genre is dialogic or not is not even close to the heart of the matter. For example, in *Problems of Dostoevsky's poetics* (1984a), Bakhtin focuses on the novel genre not so much because it is dialogic, but rather because he is much more interested in a certain type of novel, the heteroglossic novel—that is, a novel that is organic, multi-voiced and multi-levelled, with a multitude of different languages, where the characters themselves entertain fully valid consciousnesses within their own worlds, paradoxically independent of the artistic designs of the omniscient author. According to Bakhtin, the heteroglossic novel is epitomised in the work of one of the most prominent Russian novelists of the 19th century, Fyodor Dostoevsky. It is in the context of unearthing Dostoevsky's heteroglossia that Bakhtin also entertains interconnected concepts such as polyphony and the carnivalesque. I return to each of these concepts thoughout this study.

Recklessness

In *We are playing relatives*, Maier uses *kacukan* and *sungguh*—referents to the chaotic world of the market and the authoritative world of the court respectively—to refer to the dialogic relationship between heteroglossia and monoglossia and between the dialogic and monologic. We could use the same terms to highlight the contrast between polyphonic novels and monologic novels, as well as the contrast between the open carnivalesque culture of the fairground and marketplace (*pasar*) and the refined closed culture of the state and court (*kraton*). Maier uses a passage from the *Hikayat Hang Tuah* as the source for his indigenous referents. I choose to use a passage from a similarly canonical text as a source for my own indigenous referents, a novelised metanarrative of the contemporary reality of the Malay world—Pramoedya's best-known novel, *Bumi manusia* (This earth of mankind).

Bumi manusia was published in 1980, soon after Pramoedya's release from a ten-year incarceration on the infamous island prison of Buru. The novel was an instant bestseller and was promptly banned. It was the first instalment of the Buru Quartet, a tetralogy of novels based on research Pramoedya had conducted before his imprisonment.[1] Set in turn-of-the-century Indonesia, the novels depict the emergence of nationalist resistance against Dutch colonial rule. The novels' protagonist is Minke, who finds himself torn between his Javanese background, his colonial Dutch liberal education and his desire for assimilation with the colonisers from which he is ultimately alienated.

In a pivotal scene in *Bumi manusia* Minke must *sowan*, or pay his respects to his father, who has just been promoted to the modest rank of *bupati*.[2] This passage is of great relevance as it introduces a clash as much within civilisations as between civilisations. On the one hand, Minke's father evokes the insular world of Java and all it encodes, including patriarchy, feudalism, tradition and hierarchy. In contrast, the errant son has emotionally and intellectually turned his back on his father and everything he represents. Minke is far more attuned to the brave new world of education, liberalism and nationalist awakening. The meeting between the two is a showdown and, for a reluctant Minke, it is deeply humiliating.

Minke's abasement begins before his father even says a word. In the same way that he had witnessed servants approach his parents and grandparents, Minke is obliged to crawl along the floor to bow at his father's feet, his hands raised and clasped together in obeisance. He curses under his breath, 'Ya Allah! you, my ancestors, you; what is the reason you created customs that would so humiliate your own descendents?' (Toer 1981:87).[3] Minke's torment is clearly documented:

> In making such obeisance it felt as if all the learning and science I had studied year after year was lost. Lost was the enthusiasm of my teachers in greeting the bright future of humanity. And who knows how many times I'd have to make such obeisances that night. Obeisance—the lauding of ancestors and persons of authority by humbling and abasing oneself! Level with the ground if possible! Uh! I will not allow my descendents to go through such degradation (Toer 1981:88).

Minke's humiliation is soon intensified. It becomes evident that Minke's father has become angered and ashamed by his son's seemingly wayward behaviour. He is dismayed by Minke's headlong rush to embrace the moral latitude of the colonial world while he simultaneously abandons his strict Javanese upbringing. He is particularly indignant at Minke's questionable choice of accommodation at the sprawling estate of Nyai Ontosoroh, a Dutch official's concubine. For Minke's father, his son's impropriety is deeply shameful. How could his son, an educated Muslim Javanese, possibly sleep under the same roof as a native woman indulging in the shame of interracial intercourse? This emotion, signified by the word *memalukan*, is acutely felt when Minke's father is forced to engage the services of a Dutch official to track down his son's whereabouts. As Minke is ordered to serve as the translator for the promotion ceremony, he is sternly warned not to cause his father any further shame (*jangan bikin malu*) in front of the Dutch officials and Javanese petty bureaucrats in attendance.

Throughout his meeting with his father Minke is consumed by indignation and rage. His heart hammers, his throat constricts and, with a passive exterior, he rails against his father's words. His hatred towards his father and everything he represents is all-consuming. Minke already lives on a different plane from his father's world of tradition and petty bureaucracy:

> Indeed the civil service reports were something that never attracted my interest: appointments, dismissals, transfers, pensions. Nothing to do with me! The world of *priyayi* bureaucracy was not my world. Who cared if the devil was appointed smallpox official or sacked dishonourably because of embezzlement? My world was not rank and position, wages and embezzlement. My world was this earth of mankind and its problems (Toer 1981:90).

His heart already set on the world beyond Java, Minke silently curses himself. Gnashing his teeth, he regards his father as an uneducated simpleton, one day a low-ranking public servant and the next a *bupati*, a 'mini-king' whose lineage is forever contaminated by the royal Javanese blood running through his veins. Yet insult is added to injury when Minke's father uses his ceremonial horse-whip to lay symbolic blows on Minke's body. His father asks Minke whether he needs to continue humiliating him in public with the whip, and Minke responds: '"Humiliate me with the horse whip in public," I answered recklessly, unable to stand such tyranny. "But it would be an honour if that order were to come from a father," I continued, still more recklessly' (Toer 1981:89).

Minke is responding in the only way he can, through faint praise, albeit reckless praise. Minke, it seems, is a provocateur. We must not forget, however, that in his father's presence Minke's position is one of powerlessness, speechlessness and helplessness. Consumed by rage, Minke becomes more determined than ever to abandon his family and his 'enslaving' roots. 'I could explode', he says, if he doesn't.

What might this mean, to 'explode'? Does he mean the well-known phenomenon of the Malay world of 'running *amok*', or *ngamuk* as the Javanese call it, which refers to random and explosive acts of murderous frenzy? In what direction might Minke unleash his rage, supposing he did 'explode'? Minke's father was not the sole root cause of his humiliation. After all, Minke's teachers, and the colonial government in general, had long denigrated the traditions of Java. Minke's selfhood was as much repressed by the colonial regime as by the figure and traditions of his father.

A crucial tension is developed in this scene between the external and internal man. Externally Minke is obeisant and impassive. Internally, he is running *amok*. The only visible sign of tension is a reckless sentence or two. Even if Pramoedya doesn't in this scene actually mention *amok*—a term which has become the obsession of psychiatrists, linguists and anthropologists alike—I would argue that *nekad* (recklessness) is the emotional precursor to the enraged state of running *amok*. In this sense *nekad* can be regarded as a form of interior *ngamuk*, an internalised mode of running *amok* without literal violence or bloodshed. This is, in effect, Minke's state of being during his meeting with his father and, indeed, for much of the Buru tetralogy. Humiliated, enraged and reckless, Minke has no outlet other than to react violently, albeit internally. Frustrated and mentally exhausted, after the meeting, Minke flops down in a chair.

Importantly, Minke's internalised combination of shame and rage is not just the result of his father's provocations. Minke's emotions are collective emotions. On one important level Minke is a reflection of his generation, the generation of educated natives striving to resist Dutch rule, whilst also weaning themselves off the crutches of nativism and tradition. Neither wholly native nor purely Dutch, many of the early nationalists are consumed by shame and rage in their pursuit of a national consciousness in the colonial context. They have no option other than to strike out in violence, sometimes externally, but most often internally.

This book examines the extent to which Minke's narrative of humiliation, shame, recklessness and rage is also the narrative of colonial and postcolonial Indonesia and, indeed, a metanarrative for the masculine in Indonesia, particularly in the New Order and post-New Order periods. It also argues that Minke, like any other literary hero, is much more than a free-floating signifier of a particular theory or category. Bakhtin's observation is pertinent in this respect: 'an individual cannot be completely incarnated into the flesh of existing sociohistorical categories' (Bakhtin 1981:37). Minke is his own man, full of humanity and endless possibilities. He is no shadow puppet or epic character whose fate has long been sealed, even if he feels from time to time as though he is being treated like one. Like the genre in which he appears—the novel—Minke is, however, deeply emblematic.

In Indonesia, much that appears in the genre of the novel is a disintegration of the supposed closedness, fixedness and distance of an epic cycle of tales such as the *Ramayana* or the *Mahabharata*. Similarly, Minke's humanity is in many ways a disintegration of the closedness, fixedness and distance of what we might assume about Indonesia and the Indonesian man. The same can be said for Minke's father, the other key protagonist in the passages discussed above. On the one hand, Minke's father could be viewed as the embodiment of the aristocratic Javanese world view. On the other, he is a flesh and blood individual, much more than a mere fleshing-out of the colonial *priyayi* male or the traditional Javanese father-figure. The author and the author's father also play a part in the many possible realities. Although it would be impossible to link each literary character with their real-life allusions, there are enough parallels between Minke, Pramoedya and Pramoedya's father to warrant further discussion.

Conclusion

Maier's use of *sungguh* and *kacukan* as referents to the authoritative world of the court and the chaotic world of the market respectively mirrors Bakhtin's division between the the 'high' culture of the state and the 'low' culture of the marketplace, the world of seriousness and the world of laughter. But these terms almost fit too neatly. Certainly they set up clearly and convincingly a horizontal trajectory of binary extremism common to the Indonesian archipelago: from court to the regions, from aristocracy to peasantry. Muddying the waters somewhat, this book aims to highlight the *political* nature of Bakhtin's dialogism and the differing emotions provoked by the constant conversation between the state or court on the one hand and the marketplace or peasantry on the other.

To write a study on Indonesian men in the contemporary era we must examine the metanarrative of Indonesia's history haunting Indonesia's present, as embodied by literary heroes such as Minke. This retrospective stance, if it can be labelled as such, is not an altogether innovative approach. As noted earlier, many scholars have commented on the deep similarities between the colonial era and the New Order (Anderson 1990a; Day & Foulcher 2002; Lev 1985). Similarly, some have regarded the experiences which accompanied the regime change of 1998 as complementary to the traumatic events and mass killings of alleged communists in 1965 (Heryanto 2006; Wulia 2008). Others have regarded the Islamist radicalism of the post-authoritarian period partly as a knee-jerk reaction to the harsh policies of the New Order, which was deeply suspicious of religious extremism (Barton 2005). These policies were, in many ways, a throwback to the colonial government's efforts to contain and neutralise Islam, which was quite correctly perceived as a potential anti-colonial rallying point.

Before directly exploring contemporary or post-New Order images of the masculine, I return in the next chapter to Pramoedya and the nationalist period. By expanding my discussion of Pramoedya's historical novels, I argue that we need to understand contemporary Indonesian men in terms of the historical metanarrative. Just as the post-Suharto era is very much an extension of the New Order in many ways, I argue that ethnic Javanese or Java-based artists, such as Pramoedya, have long grappled with the political and cultural continuities between Indonesia's colonial and postcolonial eras. For Pramoedya, images of historical heroes and anti-heroes, such as Minke and Ken Arok respectively, reveal as much about Indonesia's masculine heroes of the pre-colonial and nationalist era as they do about real-life cultural and political figures of the postcolonial era. It goes without saying that understanding masculine heroes of the pre-colonial and nationalist era can lead us to a better understanding of contemporary masculinities.

Notes

1   The other three novels are *Anak semua bangsa* (Child of all nations) (1980), *Jejak langkah* (Footsteps) (1985) and *Rumah kaca* (Glasshouse) (1988).

2   *Bupati* is the title given to a native Javanese official appointed by the Dutch colonial government to administer a region; most *bupati* could lay some claim to a noble lineage.

3   All translations from this novel are from Max Lane's translation of *Bumi manusia* (and *Anak semua bangsa*), entitled *Awakenings* (Toer 1981).

chapter two

Heroes and anti-heroes: images of the masculine in the historical novels of Pramoedya Ananta Toer

More broadly, Pramoedya gave me an inkling of how one might fruitfully link the shapes of literature with the political imagination.

Benedict Anderson (1990b:10)

The life and works of Pramoedya have inspired many scholars, chief among them Benedict Anderson, to analyse the relationship between culture and politics in the Indonesian archipelago. Indeed, there are a number of excellent postcolonial approaches to Pramoedya's fiction which highlight the links between Pramoedya and Indonesian history, society and politics (Bahari 2007b; Day 2002b; Foulcher 1995b; Hellwig 1994; Maier 2002). A combined analysis of postcoloniality and the masculine identity in Pramoedya's works has not, however, been considered, even though critical writing on Pramoedya has included a variety of gendered approaches. When discussing Pramoedya's writing, critics have generally applauded the effective versions of feminine subjectivity. A feminist approach to Pramoedya's texts should not be considered unconventional. In the field of Indonesian literary studies, explicit attention to gender has invariably been aimed at specifically understanding male authors' representations of the feminine or at the writings of women (Aveling 2001b; Bodden 1996, 2007; Campbell, M 2007; Hatley 1999, 2002b, 2002a; Hellwig 1992, 1994, 2007; Marching 2007, 2008; Paramaditha 2007; Sears 2007b). Apart from the odd exception (Anderson 1996; Cooper 2004; Murtagh 2007), there has been little critical acknowledgement of normative or non-normative men as gendered subjects in the study of modern Indonesian literature.

It is widely accepted that Pramoedya's primary literary vision has been of nationalism as a social force—a force stifled by the neo-colonialism of Suharto's regime (Vickers 2005). Yet Pramoedya stated in an interview (GoGwilt 1995) that issues such as gender and the role of Indonesian women have been of great concern to him, and this concern has been a consistent aspect of his fiction (Bahari 2007a). It reflects the interests of much writing in the Dutch colonial era, by Dutch and 'native' writers alike. In terms of gender and colonialism, the early texts of Indonesian literature shared the following characteristics: they reflected and challenged the gender norms of the Dutch colonial era; they engaged broadly with aspects of the social position of women; and they conflated issues relating to gender with broader concerns such as race and oppression (Coté 2005). Pramoedya's Buru tetralogy is significant in this regard. The four novels, narrating the birth of Indonesian nationalism, were not written or even conceived in the Dutch colonial era. Nevertheless, they were set in the Dutch East Indies between 1890 and 1920 and share thematic similarities with the texts described by Coté above. Indeed, the tetralogy has been celebrated for its articulation of the nexus between colonialism and patriarchy, and for the manner in which the native female characters have resisted this double colonisation. Although this chapter does not ignore the rich characterisation of these female characters, it examines them more in terms of how men's specificity is narrated.

This chapter argues that any serious discussion of representations of *maskulinitas* in Pramoedya's fiction cannot be divorced from discussions of Pramoedya's own biography. According to Foulcher (2005), most scholarship on modern Indonesian literature tends to focus on the text under discussion rather than the historical context underpinning the production and authorship of the text. Bearing this salutary caution in mind, I highlight in this chapter the close relationship between literary representations of the masculine, Pramoedya's biography and the historical context in which Pramoedya's texts were produced.

In terms of approach, the first half of this chapter consists of two concurrent steps: a literary analysis examining representations of men and the masculine in Pramoedya's historical novels; and a biographical focus on Pramoedya. Inspired by Tony Day's excellent article on Pramoedya's 'Javaneseness' (Day 2007), I discuss salient aspects relating to the examination of masculine subjectivities in Pramoedya's writing in the chapter's second half. These include the question of misandry, the influence of Javanese culture and literary traditions, and the autobiographical nature of Pramoedya's writings. It should be stated from the outset that these investigations are speculative and preliminary, and, in the spirit of dialogism, are merely designed to promote further discussion or debate.

Blurring the historical and the literary: Pramoedya's Minke

The literary analysis of men and the masculine in Pramoedya's novels that follows attempts to shed light on Minke, the narrator of much of Pramoedya's Buru tetralogy. At the beginning of the first novel, Minke is 18 years old and a student at the Surabaya Hogere Burgerschool. It soon becomes apparent that Minke is not his real name; it is a corruption of the English word 'monkey', which one of his Dutch teachers once used to refer to him in a derogatory manner and the unfortunate nickname stuck. For Minke, the only Javanese in his class, and indeed the whole school, his schooldays are a difficult time, as the Javanese are on the lowest rung of the colonial social ladder. *Bumi manusia* and its sequels describe Minke's experiences, initially as a schoolchild and, later, as a journalist, writer, lover, husband and nationalist in a colonial society.

An initial point of discussion is the argument that Minke does not appear to be nearly as successful or heroic as Tirto Adhi Suryo, the colonial era journalist and nationalist he has been modelled on. As Vickers (2005) observes, Tirto began his career as a journalist and political organiser in the shadow of Raden Ajeng Kartini, Indonesia's founding feminist. Like Kartini, Tirto was a Dutch-educated Javanese aristocrat from the Blora region (Coté 1998). Like Kartini, his education had provided him with a sense of personal enlightenment and a burning drive to help those around him who were less fortunate. One of Tirto's newspapers, *Daughters of the Indies*, was set up by a woman who helped set up the Kartini Schools for women in Bandung, in West Java (Vickers 2005). Tirto was also a prominent figure in the establishment of several nationalist organisations founded in the first three decades of the 20th century. Two of these, *Muhammadiyah* and *Nahdlatul Ulama*, were Islamic, as Tirto was keenly aware of the importance of Islam as an anti-colonial rallying point. As an educated journalist, fluent in Javanese, Dutch and Malay, Tirto was also highly conscious of the value of the medium of print and the strategic use of Malay to publicise opposition to the Dutch. According to Vickers (2005:57),

> Journalism gave the colonial power struggle an entirely new form and directed it towards a new aim. It was a struggle for emancipation that Tirto, supporter of the Kartini Schools, knew had to be fought for gender as well as racial and social equality.

Certainly in the Buru tetralogy Minke, like Tirto, was actually quite a risk-taker, socially, culturally, linguistically, romantically and politically. Minke's *nekad* bravado, however, is counterbalanced by his failings and disappointments in each of these areas. For example, among other tragedies, Minke lost his first wife, the beautiful Eurasian Annelies, the daughter of a Dutch philanderer, Herman Mellema, and his concubine, Nyai Ontosoroh, because of the systematic racial and legal inequalities that characterised the Dutch colonial regime at the turn of the 19th century. The process by which this occurs is tragic and convoluted. Six months after her marriage to Minke, Annelies' father dies. His son by his legal Dutch marriage, Maurits Mellema, lays claim to his late father's property in the Indies which includes the guardianship of his daughter. As Nyai Ontosoroh was never legally married to Herman Mellema, there is nothing that can be done to save Annelies from being extradited under Dutch law to the Netherlands in accordance to the court orders. As Foulcher (1981:4) observes, 'Minke is left deserted, shouting through his tears at the very end of the novel, *"Eropa! kau, guruku, begini macam perbuatanmu?"* [Europe, my teacher, is *this* what you have done?].' Ashamed, humiliated, *malu*, Minke's rage against his colonial masters is as repressed and ineffectual as the rage of his fellow nationalists.

Minke is also caught in the tension between his external and internal man by the bright and unforgiving glare of his Dutch education. Just before his fateful first marriage, Minke's mother's words are a pointed reproach: 'Hush! You who believe in everything that is Dutch' (Toer 1981:240). There is no doubt that Minke dutifully attended his classes with a wide-eyed naivety and he certainly married in haste. His affair and later marriage to the sickly Annelies was thrust upon him more by circumstance than by choice. Indeed, Minke's role in the tumultuous course of events was performed with little resistance, despite the sound advice of older and wiser confidants, such as Jean Marais and Télinga. In the sequels to the first novel, Minke's ambivalence towards those in his social milieu and his frustrating inability to truly break free from the shackles of personal and political failure only worsens. His shame and rage also become more deeply ingrained.

It could be argued that Minke's individualisation of emasculation, humiliation and anger is simply an aesthetic embodiment of Pramoedya's social-realist leanings. In a wider discussion on social-realist fiction in Indonesia in the early 1950s to mid-1960s and its dissenting and counter-discursive tendencies against official history, Razif Bahari (2003:67–8) observes:

> Rather than ennoble the individual, social realists esteem the virtues of the collective, and rather than deify the heroic, they celebrate the mundane and the quotidian. In this way, social realism places itself in what Paul Ricouer in another context calls the "sphere of the horrible"—the countermyths of poverty, isolation, and the like that the state sets out not only to forget but to annul.

Bahari is not making a direct reference to Minke. The allusion to Ricouer's 'sphere of the horrible' is, however, quite apt when we consider Pramoedya's literary oeuvre and his character Minke in particular. Yet we should not be tempted to just read Minke on the level of the symbolic. Indeed, it can be argued that there is no great difference between Pramoedya's social realism and the realism of the colonial era novel, either by Dutch authors or by those indigenous to the Indies. Furthermore, a purely symbolic reading of Minke may oversimplify matters, reducing complex literary and historical meanings to fit an ideological straightjacket, or, more commonly, to embody a narrative of the nation. Ironically, there are many scholarly arguments that Minke's embattled life as an early nationalist pioneer, a life that so often appears to be buffeted by forces beyond his control, is a metaphor for the nascent Indonesian nationalist movement (Bahari 2003; Maier 2004; Vickers 2005). This chapter, however, clears a space whereby Minke's *maskulinitas* can be rescued from symbolic readings and re-examined in terms of its rich literary, historical and biographical meanings.

A key point to make is that a biographical approach to understanding Minke and his embattled *maskulinitas* allows us to diverge from dominant scholarly views of Minke as a metaphor for the Indonesian nationalist movement. Certainly the highs and lows of Minke's personal story of nationalist awakening encapsulate, by and large, the twists and turns of Indonesia's emerging nationhood.[1] The personal trials and tribulations faced by Pramoedya, however, suggest that Minke's life story can also be read on another metafictional level. Minke's narrative can be viewed as a reflection on the manner in which Pramoedya himself was subjugated by the Dutch and then incarcerated by the neo-colonial New Order regime. The following section addresses this important parallel and leads us to further avenues of investigation, including the parallels between Minke and Pramoedya's nationalist father, Mastoer.

Minke, Pramoedya and Pramoedya's father

After fighting against the Dutch in the Indonesian war of independence, Pramoedya played a central role in the New Order period as a writer, historian and intellectual dissident. He also played a key role as an intellectual cultural arbiter in Lekra (People's Institute of Culture), a left-wing cultural organisation closely associated with the Indonesian Communist Party (PKI). Both organisations were subsequently outlawed in the New Order period and hundreds of thousands of communist activists were massacred, gaoled or exiled in the mid-1960s. Consequently, Pramoedya was arrested and incarcerated without trial on the remote island of Buru in eastern Indonesia for most of the New Order period. Minke experiences a similar fate. After the colonial administration loses patience with Minke's relentless pro-nationalist activism, he is exiled in 1912 to the island of Bacan, in the eastern part of the Indies. Eventually, years later he is released, but, as noted by Maier (2004:466), on his return to Java 'people neither remember nor recognize Minke'. Similarly, Pramoedya was released from Buru in 1979 and placed under house arrest in Jakarta. He too lived the rest of his life largely unrecognised.

While under house arrest, Pramoedya received a steady flow of visitors from the West. Interest from his fellow Indonesians, including the Indonesian media, was minimal. This had much to do with the fact that his publications were banned during the entire New Order period, either when they were published or soon after. Nevertheless, as with Minke who also worked under a highly censorious administration, there were efforts to circumvent these bans. For example, Pramoedya's banned publications were published in Indonesian by a Malaysian publisher, Wira Karya, and were widely available in translation in the 1980s. In Indonesia the bans on his body of work were not lifted until shortly after the resignation of Suharto in May 1998.

On yet another layer of significance, Minke can also be regarded as a significant reference to Pramoedya's own father, Mastoer. Pramoedya's father was born in Blora, a small town in northern coastal East Java, halfway between the port cities of Semarang and Surabaya. Blora is also the town in which Tirto Adhi Suryo and Pramoedya were born. According to Vickers (2005:4),

> Pramoedya wrote his novels to convey how his parents' generation grew to become nationalists. His father, a nationalist teacher, was born in the same year as the fictional Minke, and through Minke, Pramoedya examines his father's frustrations as a nationalist left powerless by the efficiency of the Dutch suppression of indigenous politicians, a powerlessness that led him to gambling as an outlet for his stymied political desires.

Pramoedya, like Tirto Adhi Suryo, Minke and his father, was subjugated, frustrated and incarcerated. He was imprisoned by the Dutch in the 1940s, then by the Sukarno government in the early 1960s and then arrested, gaoled and exiled from 1966 to 1979. As stated earlier, all his new novels were banned soon after release and a blanket ban was placed on all his earlier books. Thus the analysis of the life story of Minke in Pramoedya's *Bumi manusia* tetralogy can be understood as being closely related to the author's biography. Many other commentators have, after all, remarked on the semi-autobiographical nature of much of Pramoedya's writing. In these discussions Pramoedya's fictional narrators are unproblematically assumed to be none other than Pramoedya himself.[2]

Masculinity and Pramoedya's men

Minke's remarkable tale is highlighted by episodes of great disappointment, frustration and anguish and underpinned by a barely-hidden broken spirit. As this chapter has argued, this tale reflects the biographical circumstances of several real-life Indonesian men. This close association between the fictional and historical realms also problematises any efforts to generate simple understandings of men and the masculine in the writings of Indonesia's leading novelist. However, a few preliminary observations can be made.

In terms of understanding literary signifiers of *maskulinitas* in Indonesia, it can be argued that the behaviour and experiences of the key male protagonist and narrator of Pramoedya's Buru tetralogy is not necessarily a critique or embodiment of any particular form of Indonesian *maskulinitas* as such. This is entirely due to the fact that Minke is envisioned as being much more than a mere embodiment of a particular strain of *maskulinitas*, be it Javanese masculinity or the masculinity of Indonesian nationalism, usually epitomised by the *pemuda*, the heroic young man of the anti-colonial revolutionary era. Through the *pemuda* we can see, in Tony Day's words, 'the important role of violent male prowess in creating an aura of male beauty around the postcolonial state' (Day 2002a:235). Day goes on to provide his readers with an ample quote from Benedict Anderson, who offers 'an evocation of the thrilling masculinity of the militarized, liberated, re-"masculinised" *pemuda* (revolutionary youth) of Java during October 1945':

> For the pemuda it was a time of improvisation and exhilaration. Underneath the anarchic spontaneity of their movement, giving it power and conviction, were the fundamental impulses of every revolution. Liberty was merdeka, not a political concept of independence or freedom, but an experience of personal liberation. For many it was a release from the disciplined structures of the occupation period… as these disintegrated in the October days. For others it was liberation from the apparent fatality of their lives…The pemuda rode free on buses, trains, and trams. They forced Japanese soldiers to kneel before them in the dirt. They scrawled their terse slogans on doors and walls. They emptied the tills of unguarded banks, and opened warehouses to the people of the kampong. They attacked tanks with sharpened bamboo spears and homemade gasoline bombs. And they killed—Dutchmen, Englishmen, Japanese, Eurasians, Chinese, sometimes their fellow-Indonesians (Anderson 1972:185, quoted in Day 2002a:235–6).

Certainly, as a literary figure, Minke does embody aspects of both the Javanese male and the nationalist *pemuda* who fought against the colonial power. Minke's social and political activism preceded the revolutionary youth by several decades, yet he was just as committed to improvising in whatever way he could to release himself and his people from the 'disciplined structures' of his own period. As Pramoedya would be the first to attest, Minke's anti-colonial writings foreshadowed the 'terse slogans' scrawled on doors and walls in 1945 and his words, as they appeared in the censorious colonial press, were in a symbolic sense just as sharp as the sharpened bamboo spears of the *pemuda*. In terms of being a Javanese male, Minke has a distinguished pedigree. He was born and bred in Java. As the son of a *bupati*, he is a product of the Javanese aristocracy. He is a speaker of fluent Javanese. Yet he embraces his European education and rails with a passion against everything that Java and his parents symbolise, including hierarchy, feudalism, patriarchy, insularity and superstition. In many ways Minke is an outsider within the world of rural Java. This state of being arises partly from his upper-class socioeconomic background. Much more significant, however, is the impact of his Dutch education in the cosmopolitan port city of Surabaya. This social, cultural and economic distance is reinforced by Minke's exposure to a world beyond Java and by his eventual use of Dutch and Malay.

Minke's enigmatic friendship with the charismatic Nyai Ontosoroh, another outsider in the colonial context, and his marriage to her daughter Annelies, is yet another confirmation of Minke's desire to distance himself for good from the world of Java and all it represents. The shameful failure of this first marriage is due to the blatant inequalities of colonialism and the ensuing embitterment encourages Minke's sense of himself as a man to merge with the aims of the nationalist *pemuda*. Yet Minke's personal and political alignment with the nationalist cause is by no means straightforward or heroic. In *Bumi manusia* he experiences more than his fair share of anger, frustration, marginalisation and disappointment. Things get much worse over the course of the quartet's later novels. Eventually, after threats and intimidation, an embittered Minke is exiled by the colonial administration to Bacan and, soon after his return, 'he dies as a forgotten man' (Maier 2004:466).

As mentioned earlier, there are sound arguments for Minke to be read on the symbolic level, either as a personal embodiment of Indonesian nationalism or as an aesthetic representation of Pramoedya's underlying social-realist literary leanings. This chapter, however, argues that Minke is also a complex embodiment of several real-life nationalist figures, including Tirto Adhi Suryo, Pramoedya's father and Pramoedya himself. This biographical focus helps us avoid the temptation to misread Minke as a free-floating signifier of a particular dominant form of Indonesian *maskulinitas*, such as the refined and self-restrained Javanese male or the heroic and unencumbered *pemuda*.

Misandry and Java

Attempting to understand the embattled nature of Minke's life story could lead us in at least two different directions, both deserving examination. On the one hand, it is tempting to read the seemingly negative representation of Minke's *maskulinitas* as an expression of misandry. On the other hand, Pramoedya's ambivalent portrayal of Minke might simply be an unwitting expression of Pramoedya's inherent Javanese world view, engendered by his exposure to pre-modern Javanese texts, mythologies and folktales.

The first question that needs to be addressed is: exactly how pervasive is misandry? Misandry is still a rarely mentioned word, even in the burgeoning men's studies field. In a candid moment the authors of *Spreading misandry* (Nathanson & Young 2001) have admitted that they are not even sure how the word is pronounced (Hamilton 2001). The pervasiveness of misandry in Western culture and society is still open to conjecture and debate. Feminist activists have been battling for so long to highlight and address misogyny that, outside the men's movement, any discourse on misandry appears to have slipped under the radar. What is clear is that in *Spreading misandry*, the first book on the subject, there is no mention of the existence or absence of misandry in non-Western societies such as Indonesia.[3]

I would argue that it is hard to systematically gauge the pervasiveness of misandry in Indonesia, either through face-to-face interactions or through media representations. Heider (1991) has observed that many melodramas in New Order cinema depict weak and foolish male characters in contrast to strong and autonomous women. This alone might not necessarily be a negative thing. However, this pattern does take on negative undertones when contrasted with traditional representations of archetypal male figures. These might include the rural *jago* (bandits) operating in the shadow of the Dutch colonial state, but whose genealogy goes back to the pre-colonial political system (Nordholt & van Till 1999), or traditional masculine mythological heroes, such as the mighty *satria* or warrior-knights Arjuna, Bima and Gatotkaca of the *Mahabharata* cycle of tales.

Hegemonic masculinity might also be defined in terms of the men appearing in contemporary cigarette commercials (Ajidarma 2005). Depending on the brand being advertised, these men are pictured climbing cliffs, hang-gliding, flying kites, racing buffaloes, driving jeeps, tending to animals and so on. These male archetypes are rarely portrayed as weak and foolish. In fact, these icons are consistently associated with virtues of action, heroism, discipline, valour, decisiveness, intelligence and romantic conquest and, to this day, they are positively regarded as models of Indonesian masculine behaviour.

Meanwhile, other advertisements appear to be implicitly misandric. A Hexos commercial featuring a man screaming hysterically at the sight of a cockroach clearly denigrates men by exploiting a stereotype of women. A Frozz advertisement portraying a woman wordlessly snatching a lolly out of the hand of a hapless man is also cynical. A video clip promoting a popular soap opera of the early 2000s, *Jay anak metropolitan* (Jay the metropolitan boy), features the meek male characters appearing either as clowns or as objects of ridicule and derision. In their interactions with men, women are often portrayed as sensible, virtuous or wronged. In the same vein, a significant number of advertisements feature attractive and intelligent women in a dominant or motherly role, while men and boys in the same advertisements are often portrayed as sick, foolish or in need of guidance.

As observed by Medrado, Lyra and Monteiro (2001:170), 'commercials are a very condensed form of information and tend to express selectively the social contexts from which and towards they are pointed'. It is quite possible, therefore, to use a selection of advertisements to support one particular argument over another. Indeed, if we were to closely examine the diversity of images of men in Indonesian television advertising, we could just as easily argue that a culture of misogyny is dominant. As I have shown elsewhere, although a tentative argument can be made for the possible existence of a culture of misandry in post-New Order Indonesia, the same argument can be used to prove that its sexist counterpart, misogyny, may in fact be more pervasive (Clark 2004c). Watch commercial TV nonstop over a day or two in Indonesia and you will soon see that, although there are negative portrayals of men in certain commercials, more often than not men are portrayed in a positive manner, especially when they are depicted in the public sphere. Women, on the other hand, are still thoroughly domesticated. When women do appear in a public setting, instances of sexploitation and objectification are common. Advertisers appear to have determined that smoking cigarettes and playing sport remain primarily male activities, while cooking dinner, cleaning clothes and servicing men's sexual needs remain the province of women. Of course, advertisers are quite aware that consumer behaviour is gendered; in Indonesia most sportspeople and smokers are men, and, until women's activism provokes significant changes in behaviour, women are much more likely than men to purchase and use detergent or laundry powder.

Perhaps it is time now to return to our discussion of Pramoedya. The presence, or rather lack, of a misandric attitude in the Buru tetralogy is intriguing. The key reason for its absence is that Pramoedya's positive portrayals of women are often linked with his positive attitude towards his mother. Asked to comment on the feminist aspects of his Buru tetralogy, Pramoedya responded: 'In my view, women deliver everything. In the back of my mind is always my mother—my mother as teacher, educator, and bearer of ideas' (GoGwilt 1995:12–13). Yet it is well known that Pramoedya's relationship with his father was ambivalent, to say the least. Vickers traces this ambivalence to his father's inability to resist the waves of Dutch repression from the 1930s onwards:

> Some of the nationalists did agree to compromise [with the Dutch government] but many, such as Pramoedya's father, became disillusioned with the lack of progress. Pramoedya records the bitterness this period raised, the arguments over whether or not to cooperate with the authorities, and the resulting ambivalence he felt towards his father (Vickers 2005:83).

Pramoedya's autobiographical 'Dia yang menyerah' (The vanquished) (1952) is perhaps the record Vickers alludes to. The prickly relationship between father and son is also reflected in the Buru tetralogy in the anguished exchanges between Minke and his distant father, whom he comes to hate. Consider too the quiet desperation experienced by the male narrator of Pramoedya's *Bukan pasar malam* (Not a night market) (1999b), a bleak novel addressing the death of Pramoedya's father. The bewildered soldier of 'Blora' in *Subuh* (Dawn) (Toer 1999c), returning to his home town, is also a revelation. The narrator's father is portrayed as a marginal figure, resigned to spending his days in genteel poverty, reading and reciting ancient Javanese texts under the shade of a tree, not unlike Pramoedya's own father. Most damningly, he is completely uninterested in the progress of the nationalist cause.

Nevertheless, searching for examples of misandry, hostility or contempt towards males in Pramoedya's fiction might prove ultimately unhelpful. Although there are many flawed male characters in Pramoedya's work, this is not necessarily an indication of misandry. First of all, Pramoedya was not writing in the context of a post-feminist West, where misandry is both hegemonic and ubiquitous. Secondly, because the figure of the male in Javanese culture is so central, dominant and hegemonic, Pramoedya probably felt that there was no need to make a positive case for them. Interviews also suggest that Pramoedya acutely felt the need to make a case for Indonesian women. Thirdly, Pramoedya's flawed men can be considered simply as portrayals of men as real men—humans with failings, not infallible paragons.

There is also the issue of Pramoedya's relationship with his father to consider. After all, Pramoedya almost never spoke to his father, and vice versa (Toer, KS 2006). How could this not have some impact on Pramoedya's portrayal of men and on the representation of father figures in particular? Nevertheless, it should also be mentioned as a note of caution, that to view Pramoedya's relationship with his father as the source of his negative portrayals of men would be more of a behaviourist psychological approach than a biographical approach. The latter is ostensibly the stance of this chapter. The psychological approach suggests that Pramoedya's negative representations of men, particularly of father figures, were inspired by influences from his formative years, such as family relationships, which left a permanent psychological imprint. A biographical approach attempts to understand a text in terms of the context in which the text was produced. The distinction between the two approaches is subtle and important. Yet it could be argued that a biographical approach must also take into consideration the formative years of an author's life, not just the phase in which the writer was most productive. It is also important to appreciate that Pramoedya's self-acknowledged failings as a father might have played an important role in his bleak representation of fatherhood, particularly in his later writings. These failings were, no doubt, accentuated by the crippling effects of divorce, economic hardship and years of imprisonment, among other things.

In contrast to the argument outlined above, Day (2007) argues that the literary aesthetics of Java are the determining forces shaping Pramoedya's fiction. This includes the influence of the Javanese epic theatrical and literary tradition, epitomised by the *wayang* shadow theatre and texts such as the 12th-century Javanese poem, *Bharatayuddha kakawin*. This argument is mounted even though Pramoedya has on many occasions expressed his contempt for the characters and tales of the *wayang*, and, indeed, almost all things Javanese.[4] Day highlights the fact that Pramoedya was born and bred in Java and was undoubtedly exposed to the Javanese epic theatrical and literary tradition. Analysing one of Pramoedya's most famous short stories, 'Dendam' (Revenge) (1999d), Day goes on to suggest that the Javanese literary influence is deeply rooted and unmistakable. This is not an entirely new argument. Johns (1972) has presented a similar case, arguing that Pramoedya is thoroughly Javanese in his cultural attitudes, despite finding much in his traditional culture repellent. This ambivalence, Johns also suggests, is the source of much of the emotional intensity of Pramoedya's body of work. Furthermore, both Johns and Aveling (Aveling 1975b) have highlighted the similarities between the lead characters of one of Pramoedya's earliest novels, *Perburuan* (The fugitive) (1994) and several warrior archetypes of the Javanese shadow theatre. In addition, Aveling outlines other mythic parallels, including the manner in which *Perburuan* is structured in the traditional set format of a shadow play.

Extrapolating from Day's argument, and the observations of Johns and Aveling, it could be suggested that Minke's struggles were modelled on and reflect the flawed yet masculine heroism of archetypal *wayang* warriors such as Rama, Arjuna, Bima and Gatotkaca. Perhaps the semantics behind Minke's name, which was earlier noted to be a corruption of 'monkey', suggests an important link between Minke and Hanoman, the heroic monkey general of the *Ramayana* cycle of tales. Hanoman is instrumental in rescuing the kidnapped Sinta from the evil ogre Rahwana. Similarly, Minke battles doggedly on behalf of his kidnapped nation, the colonised Indies, by resisting the injustices and repression of his colonial antagonists. Hanoman is said to be 'besides a messenger and a querulous fellow, also a beast of science and a poet, and is immoderately inquisitive to boot. The creature also loves music' (Resink 1975:229). Minke is, likewise, a keen scholar and writer; he is intensely curious and, under Nyai Ontosoroh's influence, he comes to admire classical music. In the *Ramayana*, Hanoman acts as an emissary for Rama, who asks him to locate Sinta in Rahwana's kingdom. As a journalist and writer Minke also acts as a go-between, revealing the suffering and injustice experienced by the downtrodden of Java to the colonial elite within Java and, by extension, in the Netherlands. Minke's personal victories, obstacles and failures, in love and in war, echo Hanoman's tortuous path to success, which is characterised by deprivation, capture and torture, eventually resulting in the rescue of Sinta. Even the physical whiteness of Hanoman, an albino, is symbolically echoed by Minke, who often wears a white suit and is enchanted by all things European.

The parallels between Hanoman and Minke, just a few of which have been outlined, are resonant and have the potential to take our understanding of the tetralogy to a much richer depth. Nevertheless, it could be argued that, if we are to conduct a literary analysis of the tetralogy that emphasises the biographical, advocating the Javaneseness of Pramoedya's writing goes against the grain. To conduct such an analysis, we must ignore most of what Pramoedya has ever said about his own work, about Java and about Javanese *sastra*. In spite of Pramoedya's withering attitude towards his own ethnic group, the imprint of Java on his writing is unmistakable, as Day and others have argued. Whether Pramoedya approved of Java or not, Java is a fundamental element of his biographical makeup.

Thus we must ask: is there any biographical basis to support the possibility that Pramoedya deliberately, or even subconsciously, inscribed parallels between Minke and Hanoman? I have two points to support this path of analysis. First, Pramoedya has admitted:

> I am an Indonesian citizen, ethnically speaking a Javanese. That explains that I have been raised by Javanese literature which is dominated by the literature of the shadow play, both oral and written, which tells of the Javanised Mahabharata and Ramayana (Toer 1997:228).

Secondly, when I asked Pramoedya directly about his attitude towards the *wayang* and its potential to convey the grievances of the average Indonesian, his answer was typically withering: 'Ya, tetapi siapa rakyat dalam dunia wayang? Punakawan dan monyet!' (Yes, but who are the common people in the wayang world? Clowns and monkeys!).[5] Can these two statements combined be classed as evidence to help hypothesise a connection between Minke and Hanoman? Pramoedya's comments certainly do not help us understand how Minke's characterisation was related to what was happening to Pramoedya at the time the Buru tetralogy was conceived, researched and written. But they do suggest, at the very least, that Pramoedya has a modest understanding of the shadow theatre, as well as an acute awareness of where an Indonesian everyman might be symbolically located in the *wayang*'s hierarchical pantheon. In this sense, it is not beyond the realms of possibility that Pramoedya drew on the personality and epic deeds of a mythical monkey to enrich the characterisation of a young Indonesian nationalist, no matter how distasteful alluding to a mythological archetype may have been for him.

Admittedly, as with the temptation to search for elements of misandry in Pramoedya's fiction, the 'Javanese heritage' argument outlined above also requires a degree of caution. For instance, despite the apparent parallels between Minke and warriors of the Javanese shadow theatre, Keeler argues that the success of Minke's characterisation lies precisely in the fact that he does *not* appear to be based on a shadow-play stereotype:

> Of course, a novelist, like a puppeteer, is often evaluated for the ability to get the speech right, to have an ear for ways particular people at particular times might express themselves. But novelists are not supposed to traffic in stereotypes: it is the ability to create rounded, unique individuals that usually wins a novelist praise. Pramoedya's main character in the *Buru Quartet*, Minke, is a strongly delineated, because unusual and complex, character (Keeler 2004:204).

Whether Minke is 'strongly delineated' because he is not based on a *wayang* stereotype is unclear. On the contrary, it can be easily argued that many stock standard *wayang* figures, including Hanoman, also convey 'unusual and complex' characters. Keeler himself observes that 'many [of the characters in shadow plays] are so familiar and highly individuated that they have the vivid, living qualities of characters in a novel' (Keeler 2004:204). Either way, if we are to comprehensively delineate Minke's *maskulinitas*, the influence of literary tropes and conventions of Java and Pramoedya's ambivalent attitude towards the characters and tales of the *wayang*, we need much more detailed biographical research.

Ken Arok and Suharto

Finally, and this returns us to earlier points in this chapter, we can view many of Pramoedya's textual representations of the masculine as incisive reflections of particular historical figures. In reiterating this point, it is worth considering the parallels between the real-life President Suharto and the 'antihero' of Pramoedya's *Arok dedes* (1999a), the legendary 13th-century bandit usurper to the throne, Ken Arok. This provocative association has also given rise to a great deal of discussion within Indonesian literary circles. Pramoedya's own biography, whether we like it or not, also unavoidably colours our analysis of the parallels.

As is well known, Pramoedya's own life story was interconnected with and interjected by Suharto's rise and fall. Pramoedya paid a great price for his art and Suharto quite possibly made sure of it personally. The exiled Pramoedya even received a famous letter from Suharto offering him advice and suggesting he learn from the error of his ways. Yet Pramoedya never shied from pouring scorn on many false narratives of the Indonesian nation, in particular on the transfer of political power between Indonesia's first President, Sukarno, and the second, Suharto. *Arok dedes* reveals the collective tragedy, trauma and violence associated with Suharto's rise to power.

Of course, Pramoedya's tale is not a direct representation of this recent historical experience. *Arok dedes* is, as is so clearly stated on the book's back cover, an allegory. It details so-called historical events dating back to the 13th century as a means of reflecting on the experience of the present. The central conceit is that, just as the uneducated scoundrel Ken Arok violently usurped the throne in 13th-century Java, the poorly educated commoner, General Suharto, wrested control of the Indonesian Presidency by equally questionable means. That the name 'Arok' is defined in the novel as 'Developer' is extremely significant in this respect, as Suharto was often called Bapak Pembangunan (Father of Development). In Pramoedya's novel, Ken Arok murdered in cold blood Gandring, the man who was assigned to make him a powerful wavy-bladed *keris* (dagger). After using the *keris* on the king, he planted the weapon on an innocent man, Kebo Ijo, who was then promptly executed. Similarly, Suharto's rise to power was accompanied by the anti-communist massacres of 1965–66, when more than 500,000 communists and communist sympathisers were killed or detained, many without trial. Pramoedya, like the incumbent President Sukarno and the hundreds of thousands who were murdered or imprisoned, was treated in much the same way as Kebo Ijo. As mentioned previously, Pramoedya was imprisoned on the isolated Buru Island for 13 years because of his alleged communist leanings. Similarly, Sukarno, who was also deemed to be too sympathetic to the communist cause, was hurriedly removed from the centre of power, and, after his death in 1970, was buried in an isolated part of Java. Although to my knowledge no-one has accused Suharto of patricide (either literally or figuratively), Pramoedya's novel indisputably implies that Sukarno was ungraciously and violently usurped.

Conclusion

As has been argued by many scholars, Pramoedya's Buru tetralogy narrates the birth of the Indonesian nation. In this sense, the shortcomings of Minke can tell us much about the nationalist movement led by journalists such as Tirto Adhi Suryo. This chapter has argued that Minke's personal and political failings and his ostensibly embattled *maskulinitas* reflect the struggles of Pramoedya's father and of Pramoedya himself, who in real life angrily railed against the neo-colonialism of the New Order regime. Ironically, he did so after he had fought in the war of independence against the Dutch, which puts the phrase 'double colonisation' into a new and biographical light.

This chapter has also examined Minke's lived *maskulinitas* in terms of misandry, a concept belatedly popularised in recent international men's studies scholarship. This avenue of investigation is inspired by the well-known fact that Pramoedya's relationship with his father was ambivalent, to say the least. This might have been a factor underpinning Pramoedya's ample portrayals of flawed male characters and of flawed father-figures in particular in all his writings. However, considering that Pramoedya wrote most of his fiction well before the development of feminism and the rise of men's studies, this argument draws a long bow indeed. Pramoedya's desire to develop a redemptive case for Indonesian women was probably far more compelling than any desire to develop positive portrayals of men. A keen sense of his own failings as a father may also have influenced his portrayal of men.

Equally problematic is this chapter's argument that Pramoedya's representations of the masculine quite possibly owe a great deal to the warrior archetypes of epic Javanese cultural and literary expression, such as the *wayang* shadow theatre. Pramoedya was quite cynical towards most things Javanese and he responded intellectually to the shadow theatre with distaste. Nevertheless, as it stands, this argument is worth exploring further. A fresh examination of Pramoedya's Javaneseness has the potential to open up our understanding of Pramoedya's writing and his biography in new directions.

Finally, a masculine reading of Pramoedya's other men can provide us with a reminder that Pramoedya responded in his work to tangible events and real people from his own life. Therefore, if the male protagonist of Pramoedya's *Arok dedes* is portrayed as a cunning and murderous village thug, an analysis examining representations of men and the masculine should not be divorced from external events. For example, it might be tempting to read the characterisation of Arok as a general comment on 13th-century rural Javanese males and bandits, or perhaps even as a metaphorical comment on contemporary Indonesian masculinities. To do so would be telling only half the story. Instead we must view Pramoedya's Arok as a brutally honest portrayal of the ultimate patriarchal and patricidal figure of recent Indonesian history, the so-called Bapak Pembangunan, Suharto. In this sense Pramoedya intimates in his work Suharto's unjust treatment of President Sukarno and of Pramoedya himself. We cannot, therefore, separate Pramoedya's literary figures from Indonesia's national history.

On another level, we can read Arok simply as a particularly cruel and Machiavellian literary character; such is the fine line between the literary and the historical in Pramoedya's fiction. The boundary between fact and fiction has constantly been blurred in modern Indonesian literature, not to mention in pre-modern cultural formations in Indonesia and, indeed, literature throughout the world. The following chapter examines further the manner in which Indonesian artists have allowed the worlds of fact and fiction to overlap, simultaneously revealing a polyphonic array of new gendered identities.

Notes

1   In this regard, it would be quite interesting to compare Minke with other characters in the *Bumi manusia* tetralogy. Nyai Ontosoroh, for instance, has also been viewed as a metaphor for the nation: 'her story is the story of Indonesia, which is about the struggle to overcome various kinds of domination in a particular colonial space: the race-based hierarchy imposed by the whites, the ancient familial patriarchy of the Javanese and the ideology of the submission of the lower orders' (Mohamad 2002:184).

2   Consider, for instance, Barbara Hatley's account of a visit to Blora (Hatley 1980) and Harry Aveling's introductions to Pramoedya's *A heap of ashes* and *The girl from the coast* (Aveling 1975b, 1991).

3   Indeed, in the field of men's studies as a whole, comparative studies have been lacking. As a means of addressing this situation, significant writers in the field emphasise the need for in-depth ethnographic work, albeit located in 'global history' (Pease & Pringle 2001). This book is a modest response to that call.

4   Later in his life, Pramoedya occasionally enjoyed listening to the relatively 'unrefined' *gamelan* of regional and coastal Java (Personal communication, Jakarta, 5 April 1998).

5   Personal communication, Jakarta, 5 April 1998.

chapter three

Reinventing masculine archetypes:
the polyphonic fiction of Ayu Utami

Demons, foreign and local, portrayed as sensitive and thoughtful conversationalists, constitute one pole of Ayu's subversion of standard male stereotypes. Another is the reinterpretation of the knightly 'hero'. Wis or Saman, the undoubted hero of the novel, displays enormous courage and tenacity in defending the dispossessed community of rubber tappers, culminating in brutal torture by the military on their behalf. But in physique and personal style he is the antithesis of the strong, virile *satria* (warrior), magnetically attractive to women but coolly resistant to their seductive wiles. Saman is small, thin and not particularly prepossessing.

Barbara Hatley (2002:135)

In a review of Seno Gumira Ajidarma's *Wisanggeni sang buronan* (Wisanggeni the Outlaw) (2000), Radhar Panca Dahana (2000) comments that Seno's novel about the *wayang* hero Wisanggeni is a combination of racy martial arts action, deep philosophical musings, easy-reading entertainment, comedy and lyric poetry. Seno's vivid literary poetics are modelled on a number of different sources, including the *wayang* comics of RA Kosasih, the ancient court texts of Central Javanese palace scribes, the improvisation of jazz musicians and, most importantly in *Wisanggeni sang buronan*, Danarto's fine line drawings of Wisanggeni and the *wayang* world. When Seno first wrote the novel, as a series of narratives in 1984 in a now defunct current affairs magazine, *Zaman*, he wrote in response to Danarto's sketches. Seno felt that each of Danarto's finely-wrought masterpieces brought the *wayang* characters and their world to life, humanising and exoticising them at the same time. Emphasising the radical nature of Danarto's sketches, Dahana (2000) labels them as 'life-like, contemporary, and going against the *pakem*'. Although these drawings play a significant role in the novel, it is their counter-hegemonic ideological stance that has the greatest impact—a stance most obviously displayed in the way that they simultaneously embrace the *wayang* tradition and reinvent it with a twist.

Consequently, Seno's novel has much in common with the postcolonial project of canonical counter-discourse. This is a process whereby, in the words of Gilbert and Tompkins, 'the post-colonial writer unveils and dismantles the

basic assumptions of a specific canonical text by developing a "counter" text
that preserves many of the identifying signifiers of the original while altering,
often allegorically, its structures of power' (Gilbert & Tompkins 1996:16).
Seno is not alone in his desire to borrow, appropriate and humanise Wisanggeni
and his world as a means of writing back to the New Order regime. Arya (Aji)
Dipayana, the scriptwriter of *Wisanggeni berkelabat* (Wisanggeni appears), a
theatre production presented by Teater Tetas in Solo in October 2000, also uses
the characters and plots of the *wayang*, particularly the Wisanggeni legend,
to counter the New Order regime and its protean gender archetypes. Aji, like
Seno before him, wrote an earlier version of his text in the 1980s, resurrecting
it over a decade later in the aftermath of the New Order. Ayu Utami's highly
acclaimed novel, *Saman* (1998), also draws upon the character of Wisanggeni;
it too entails a critical re-writing project that is revisionist, counter-discursive
and unequivocally gendered.

Why, one might ask, has each of these young writers drawn upon Wisanggeni in
their attempts to destabilise the power structures of the *wayang* and all it has come
to symbolise in contemporary Indonesia? Is Wisanggeni not a shadow-theatre
warrior in the mould of Rama, Arjuna, Bima and Gatotkaca, past favourites of
villagers and presidents alike? In many ways Wisanggeni is no different from
the host of *wayang* characters inhabiting a typical puppeteer's *wayang* box.
Even though Wisanggeni is a member of the younger generation of the Pandawa,
which includes warriors such as Antasena, Antareja, Gatotkaca and Abimanyu,
he is as much a symbol of the feudalism of Java and the New Order regime as
any other *wayang* puppet. According to Pamudji (2000), in the *wayang* cosmos,
there aren't any 'students' as such, because 'younger generation' figures such as
Wisanggeni, Antasena, Gatutkaca, or Abimanyu are just the latest generation of
New Order nepotists, like their 'Suharto-era' fathers, including Arjuna, Bima etc.
In other words, even the next generation of Pandawa heroes cannot be allowed to
represent the pro-Reformasi students. They are just as nepotistic as their parents'
generation, which was often used as a symbolic representation of the New Order
elite. To be fair, Pamudji also observes that some *wayang* performances at the
turn of the millennium, such as Ki Anom Suroto's performance of *Wisanggeni
gugat* (Wisanggeni accuses) in Solo, appear significantly reformist in content
and presentation. Nevertheless, he claims that performances such as these are
still based on a feudalistic moral ethos (Pamudji 2000).

In many ways Wisanggeni can be set apart from a significant number of his
fellow puppets, and from certain groups of the Javanese and the feudalistic
ethos of the *Mahabharata*. By exploring the ways in which Wisanggeni has
appeared as a social bandit or outlaw hero in literary form, this chapter focuses
particularly on the manner in which his latest appearances re-establish the

prominent role of the *wayang* in the Indonesian literary and cultural psyche. This chapter also reiterates the strong desire of Indonesia's leading writers to write back against the social and political power structures depicted in the *wayang*. This is a form of counter-discourse that is as much creative as it is gendered and political. Ultimately, my analysis shows that, even as the shadow theatre and all it has come to stand for is borrowed and given greater legitimacy in literary form, Indonesia's latest generation of writers are not interested in merely contemporising traditional cultural expression. Their interest is rather the oppositional and gendered reinterpretation of myth.

This chapter is divided into three sections: a summary of the Wisanggeni legend; a close analysis of the manner in which the Wisanggeni legend is appropriated in the first half of Ayu Utami's *Saman*; and a gendered analysis of the second half of *Saman*'s polyphonic move beyond the state's *dalang*-like monologue. Ultimately, this chapter argues that late-New Order literary appropriations of the *wayang* mythology have inscribed ambiguous and contradictory images of *maskulinitas*, rather than the permanent, popular and heroic male archetypes of the *wayang*.

The Wisanggeni legend

Bambang Wisanggeni is one of several *Mahabharata* characters indigenous to Java and, almost for this reason alone, he enjoys great popularity. In the *wayang* tradition of Central Java, Wisanggeni, which literally means 'fiery poison', is the son of Arjuna and Dewi Dresanala (Drestanala, Darsenala or Dersanala), who is the daughter of Batara Brahma, the God of Fire. Dewi Dresanala, a heavenly goddess, is one of the many women Arjuna knew intimately during his seven years as King of Heaven. Wisanggeni has his father's good looks and superior intelligence, as well as the supernatural powers of both of his parents. In one of several versions of his childhood, Wisanggeni spent his formative years as a fugitive under the sea, in the care of Dewa Baruna, the God of the Ocean, and Antaboga, a minor deity with the head of a dragon, the body of a man and the tale of a snake. Aware of the immense challenges Wisanggeni would face as an adult, Dewa Baruna and Antaboga ensure that Wisanggeni is provided with a powerful arsenal of magical powers and weaponry. A popular lighthearted tale involving Wisanggeni is *Wisanggeni takon bapa* (Wisanggeni Seeks His Father). In his travels to find his father he comes across a number of sacred weapons that had gone missing. These included the sacred text of Kalimasada, which was intended for his uncle Yudhistira, the arrows Pasopati, Saratoma and Ardha Dadali, and the magical *keris*, Pulanggeni, which were all intended for Arjuna. Later, all of these weapons are crucial in helping the Pandawa achieve victory in the great war of the Baratayuda.

Wisanggeni is outspoken, garrulous, honest, principled and well-intentioned. His upward-facing countenance betrays his extreme self-confidence and an almost arrogant belief in his supreme powers as a fighter and a warrior. His arrogance is fully justified, as he is invincible on the battlefield. When engaged in mortal combat, as a matter of principle he continues fighting his adversaries until their death, only sparing their life if they admit their mistake in challenging him. He has a shrill and excitable voice and, upon the death of each of his adversaries, he is known to spontaneously break into a *tajungan*, an energetic victory dance. Such quirky behaviour, together with his irrepressible energy, his dry sense of humour and his status as a high-principled rebel and outlaw, have ensured that Wisanggeni has a cult following amongst Javanese devotees of the *wayang*. Wisanggeni's feisty dynamism is reflected not only in his deliberate usage of *ngoko* (Low Javanese) in all social situations, but also in his unique aesthetic form. Physically he is small, slender and refined, almost petite. His slight frame adds to his quicksilver nature, especially during battle scenes where he proves to be an extremely agile power-packed dynamo.

Wisanggeni also has a keen sense of survival, forged early in his life. In a fit of rage his grandfather, Batara Brahma, who strongly opposed the union between his daughter, Dewi Dresanala, and Arjuna, threw the newborn Wisanggeni into the boiling-hot Candradimuka cauldron. The baby, however, not only survived but also thrived, magically turning into a young man. The many gods who witnessed this event, such as Dewa Baruna and Antaboga, rewarded Wisanggeni by giving him a host of magic weapons and talismans. These weapons prove essential, as Wisanggeni is constantly forced to fight for his life against a stream of deadly emissaries acting upon the orders of Batara Guru, the supreme god, who cannot countenance Wisanggeni's potentially disruptive existence. Later, in his passionate yearning to leave the underwater kingdoms of Dewa Baruna and Antaboga in order to search for his mother and father and in his unquestioning willingness to uphold righteousness by defending himself and crushing evil, he also displays an unwavering sense of duty.

Despite his popularity as an outlaw and a rebel, Wisanggeni has always remained a peripheral figure in the shadow theatre of Central Java; he is overshadowed by the exploits of his famous father, uncles, cousins and half-brothers. Unlike the other great *satria* heroes of the *wayang*, Wisanggeni does not participate in the climax of the *Mahabharata*. In the Central Javanese *wayang* shadow-theatre version of the *Mahabharata*, the scheming Kresna ensures that Wisanggeni and his equally invincible half-brothers, Antasena and Antareja, surrender and ascend to the Heavens before the onset of the Baratayuda. According to popular understanding, if Wisanggeni and his half-brothers were to participate in the Baratayuda, the Pandawa would almost certainly win. But if this victory were to be achieved with Wisanggeni's help, the personal cost to the Pandawa clan would be too severe.

As is the case with other outlaw heroes throughout the world, although Wisanggeni carries out deeds of considerable cunning and immense bravery, usually associated with traditional heroes of the *wayang* such as Arjuna, Bima or Gatotkaca, his valiant feats are tempered by the shadow of ambivalence. The ambivalence of Wisanggeni's status derives from the fact that, despite his heroics, he is also an outlaw, a fugitive living outside and against the rule of the gods. By opposing the will of the gods and by refusing to use the polite registers of Javanese—*kromo* or *kromo inggil*—he is at once a representation of the dissatisfaction of the common people who sympathise with him as well as someone set apart from and opposing the members of other groups, because he is an outlaw. It is for this reason, one may assume, that Wisanggeni, unlike Arjuna, Bima, Gatotkaca, Semar and others, may well have been suppressed, like the people he represents, in the sense that he was not as actively adopted and promoted by either Sukarno or Suharto or the extremely influential pro-government shadow puppeteers of the New Order. This did not mean that Wisanggeni rarely appeared on a *wayang* screen. On the contrary, Wisanggeni has remained one of the most popular *wayang* characters of Java; as noted, between 1998 and 2000 two critically acclaimed novels and one drama production have attempted to reinvent him. Wisanggeni clearly has stood the test of time; he has re-emerged phoenix-like from the ashes of the heavily-Javanised New Order regime, as a people's outlaw. This attests to the latent 'Indonesianness' of the mythic energy embedded in the Wisanggeni legend and the depth of the dissatisfaction of the many Indonesian people represented by his slender frame.

As observed by Sidel (1999), bandits and gangsters in the Philippines have often enjoyed great popularity, appearing as local heroes of the poor and the downtrodden, their criminality becoming 'a form of societal "resistance" to injustices unpunished—or perpetrated—by predatory agents of capital and the state'. Hobsbawm (1959) has referred to Robin Hood-like figures as 'social bandits', while Seal (1996) argues that the bandit or 'outlaw hero' is a particular type of folk hero whose tradition can be traced as a cultural constant persisting through time and space, available to be called into use whenever the particular local circumstances and pressures are appropriate. Wisanggeni is a folk hero of Indonesia who has been called upon, metaphorically, from time to time, particularly, it seems, in the twilight years of the New Order. In the following discussion of Ayu Utami's *Saman*, it will become evident that the unsung folk heroes of Indonesia, who may appear in the form of intellectually handicapped teenagers, lapsed Catholic priests or promiscuous expatriate dancers, do indeed have much to say and do, ultimately challenging and appropriating the state's *dalang*-like monologue.

Wis, Upi and Oedipus in Ayu Utami's *Saman*

Much has already been said and written about Ayu Utami's award-winning first novel and about Ayu. Critics such as Sapardi Djoko Damono (*Kompas* 1998b) and Faruk (1998) have praised *Saman* for its unusual structure, its poetic, innovative language, its powerful and unusual themes, the breadth of its vision and its aesthetic and thematic beauty. Other leading literary luminaries such as Umar Kayam (*Kompas* 1998a) and YB Mangunwijaya (1998) praised *Saman* for its rich symbolism, its emancipatory populist spirit and its illuminating representation of the consciousness of contemporary Indonesian urban youth. Some have argued that the emergence of Ayu's novel, coinciding with the resignation of President Suharto and the collapse of the New Order regime, spearheads a new generation of socially and politically engaged Indonesian literary expresssion, usually labelled as *sastra reformasi* (literature of the Pro-reform era) (*Kompas* 1998b). Meanwhile, Hatley (1999) celebrates the fact that, whilst the dominant female image in New Order literature appears to be one of 'modesty, restraint and domesticity', all social and sexual mores are questioned and broken in *Saman*, ultimately subverting the feminine ideal espoused by the dominant ideology and standard literary characterisation of New Order Indonesia.

Critics have hitherto failed to approach *Saman* in terms of its retelling and reinterpreting of myth and mythical characters. A mythopoeic approach to *Saman* may have held little attraction, because Ayu does not profess to be a great follower of the shadow theatre and claims modestly that her knowledge of *wayang* characters and plots is hardly sophisticated. Nevertheless, the allusions to the *wayang* world in *Saman* are many and intriguing.

For many readers, the leading characters in *Saman* are not immediately recognisable as reinterpretations of mythological characters. Yet those well-versed in the characters and tales of the *wayang* soon recognise the parallels. First of all, the choice of Wis as the name for the leading male character and, secondly, the way that Wis bravely challenges the powers-that-be in South Sumatra and breaks the mould of religious and sexual conservatism, leaves little doubt about his mythological ancestry. Like the popular Wisanggeni of the *wayang* world, Wis is both saviour and devil incarnate—a man seeking social and political justice, a man who is extremely caring yet dangerous; his placid exterior hides a soul consumed by inner turmoil. Wis carries the same allegorical message and weight as the rebellious Wisanggeni, but it could be argued that in one sense he is much more fully envisioned, in a fresh and contemporary fashion. The following discussion explores the parallels and differences between the mythological hero Wisanggeni and Ayu Utami's fictional hero, Wis. It establishes the important position of Wis in *Saman* which serves as a key point of departure to explore the ways in which the gendered transformations of mythology underscore the novel's broad thematic scope.

Wis's struggle to trace and develop the full depths of his own identity as a young pastor and social activist in New Order Indonesia mirrors and transforms the mythical Wisanggeni's personal quest. Like Wisanggeni, from an early age Wis displays a keen awareness of and affinity with all things mystical. As a boy he resolutely avoids the forest behind his parents' house in Perabumulih, South Sumatra, as he is afraid that ghosts and snakes live there and is told that it is inhabited by demons, goblins and fairies. Upon his induction as a Catholic priest, he approaches one of the senior priests, Romo Daru, to talk about the possibility of serving in his home town. They discuss this, yet Wis ultimately feels disappointed, as the elderly priest ends the discussion before Wis gets the opportunity to speak of a matter far more intimate, 'the spirits that had been in their presence, spirits they had both felt, spirits that flew in the air or walked the earth' (Utami 2005:45).[1] Later he spends some time alone in his old house in Perabumulih and senses the spirits of his three stillborn brothers and sisters. After turning off the lights, closing his eyes and fearlessly tuning himself into the spiritual domain, he hears them speaking to him and, although their sentences are incomprehensible, he excitedly feels as though he is able to communicate with them. Wis appears comfortable with immersing himself in the spiritual realm in this way.

As noted earlier, the mythological Wisanggeni refused to remain in the relative safety of Dewa Baruna's underwater kingdom and sought his mother and father on the earth and in the heavens, confronting many challenges along the way. Similarly, upon his induction Wis refuses a posting to the predominantly Catholic island of Siberut and presses for a posting to predominantly Muslim Perabumulih, where he intends to search for traces of his mother. In an intriguing reversal of the *Wisanggeni takon bapa* tale, Wis, rather than searching for his father, takes leave from his father and seeks traces of his late mother. This reinterpretation of Wisanggeni's search ultimately becomes a key premise for understanding not only the dynamic mythopoeic tapestry of Ayu Utami's novel but also the rich depth of its sociopolitical message.

Accompanying Wis's search for his mother are another tale and another challenge—the re-enactment of the Oedipus myth. The child who fantasises about killing his father and marrying his mother, thus repeating the offence of Oedipus, is here aligned with Wis and his search for what his mother lost and his ambivalent attitude towards his father and all that he stands for. Sigmund Freud turned Sophocles' version of the ancient Greek myth of Oedipus into an exploration of repressed desire; in Ayu Utami's hands the mythic dimensions of Freud's psychoanalytical explorations are given greater intensity. Freud took Sophocles' narrative as evidence that every male child sexually desires his mother, but rejects this desire out of fear of retaliation from his father, whom he hates because he is a competitor for his mother's love. The child then develops castration anxiety, as he fears that his father will harm his genital organs, the source of his lustful feelings. Whilst the complexity of Wis's background and motivations would be severely diminished by creating a single and reductive link to an Oedipal trauma such as this, Wis's ambivalent relationship with his father, Sudoyo, appears to become a dominant influence both in his childhood and in his later life, with significant ramifications.

Wis's father is a hardworking bank manager who attends church regularly. He also sternly warns Wis about the dangers of venturing into the forest behind their house, scaring him with a sermon on the dangers of Satan and Lucifer and the deadly habits of snakes. The Freudian undertones here are portentous, with the image of the snake both phallic and sexual. Elsewhere, Wis's father is depicted as taking pleasure in seeing his mother vomiting from morning sickness and, after his mother's two unsuccessful pregnancies ending in mystery and tears, not to mention the possibility of a mysterious male lover, the ashamed Wis finds that he is unable to speak to his father about his thoughts and feelings. In a word, his emotional life has been scarred by a deep sense of *malu*. Even after Sudoyo is transferred to Jakarta and Wis's mother dies, Wis is unable to forge a particularly close relationship with his father. Distraught, he is haunted and enraged by the image of his mother silently crying and uncontrollably shaking. At the time Wis senses the great pain that his mother was experiencing in leaving behind the spirits of the children she had lost. It was only later, after his mother died and after his intense jealousy and anger had subsided, that he could begin to imagine the bitter sense of betrayal and loss that his mother had experienced.

Ironically, in the New Order context, it was men like Sudoyo who were easily associated with the archetypal masculine hero, Wisanggeni's mythological father, Arjuna. Arjuna, one of the most popular warrior characters of the *wayang* world, has long been held up as a perfect model for the Indonesian 'everyman'. Anderson (1965:13) explains:

> What is one to say of Ardjuna? Unequalled warrior on the battlefield, yet physically delicate and beautiful as a girl, tender-hearted yet iron-willed, a hero whose wives and mistresses are legion yet who is capable of the most extreme

discipline and self-denial, a satria with a deep feeling for family loyalty who yet forces himself to kill his own half-brother, he is, to the older generation of Javanese, the epitome of the whole man. In contrast to Judistira, he is joyfully at home in the world. His amorous adventures never cease to delight the Javanese, yet in a strange way he is in complete contrast to Don Juan. So great is his physical beauty and refinement, that princesses and maid-servants alike hurry to offer themselves to him. It is they who are honoured, not Ardjuna. And in contrast to Wrekudara he represents the physical grace and gentleness of heart which generations of Javanese have so highly prized.

Sudoyo can be considered as an Arjuna-like warrior, willing to defend, or at least preserve, the state's emphasis upon order, stability and economic rationalism for the sake of national unity and development. An economics graduate from Universitas Gadjah Mada, one of Indonesia's most prestigious universities, Sudoyo is depicted as a hardworking, religious, morally upright citizen and a caring husband, on the whole. In short, he is the epitome of the New Order regime's conceptualisation of the ideal Indonesian man—an individual, as explained by Reeve (1996), who guards against base passions that could lead to error, a citizen who finds his fulfilment and identity through the vast interdependent community of the nation. This conceptualisation, called an 'integralistic' view, 'puts duties before rights, and places the obligation on the individual to act according to values of harmony and the general good' (Reeve 1996:127). Nevertheless, for the sake of his career, Sudoyo appeared to coldly sacrifice his wife's intense maternal need to be close to her lost children. The consequences were disastrous; his wife soon passed away and Wis's sense of *malu* soon turned into internalised rage. It is no surprise that Wis shows little interest in following in his father's footsteps as a banker. Although he has no qualms about asking his father for cash transfers, Wis is at best ambivalent towards his father's chosen path.

The relationship between Wis and his mother is equally problematic and, from the perspective of this relationship, one could argue that *Saman* is a profoundly Oedipal novel. By opting for celibacy and the life of the cloth and immediately seeking out traces of his late mother in South Sumatra, Wis betrays not only an incredibly warm tenderness for his mother but also any ability to sustain a fulfilling relationship with a woman. This condition is highlighted when, soon after arriving in South Sumatra, Wis befriends Upi, who in many ways represents what Wis once lost and, indeed, what he is searching for. As Hatley (1999:457) observes, the appearance of the physically disfigured, intellectually handicapped and unintelligible Upi somehow convinces Wis that he had truly encountered the long-lost and sought-after traces of the maternal. Nevertheless, as will be discussed in greater detail shortly, in many ways Upi remains a mystery for Wis. Of course, Wis's mother, like Upi, is also an enigma. She is said to be warm, attractive and a loving wife and parent, her aura as radiant as the sun. Like Dewi Dresanala, Wis's mother is also from another dimension altogether:

> His mother, a Javanese woman of noble origin, was a figure who could not always be described in rational terms. She often seemed not to be in places she was or to be in places she wasn't. At such moments it was difficult to engage her in conversation because she didn't listen to people around her. Sometimes her silence would be brought to an end by a visit to a place that nobody knew, a space that didn't exist anywhere: an emptiness (Utami 2005:46).

When she loses several children in mysterious circumstances, the incomprehensible side to her nature and her mystical qualities become even more dominant. For example, six or seven months into her second pregnancy, Wis's mother is unable to explain why her baby disappears without trace. Even more mysteriously, months later, one morning during his mother's third pregnancy, Wis hears the sharp cries of a newborn child and the sound of his mother singing soothing lullabies. Yet, when Wis opens the door to his mother's bedroom, there is no sign of a baby and no sign of his mother's five-month pregnancy: 'as if it had been absorbed into the atmosphere' (Utami 2005:52).

In many ways Upi's identity remains as blank and mysterious as Wis's mother. Nobody other than her mother knows her proper name; her fellow villagers call her Eti, Ance, Yanti, Meri and Susi, and it is explained that, like a dog, she answers to any name that ends with 'i', such as Pleki, Boni and Dogi. Like Wis's mother, a 'mythology' has been developed as a means of understanding her. Intersecting with the mysticism surrounding Wis's mother's child-bearing experiences, Upi's father thinks that Upi failed to develop normally because he killed a turtle during her mother's pregnancy. Many think that Upi, like Wis's mother, is possessed; her habit of masturbating in public, not to mention her tendency to become more sexually precocious immediately preceding menstruation, embodies the male apprehension of female power in Indonesia, particularly uncontrolled sexuality (discussed further in Chapter 5). Clearly, the similarities between Upi and Wis's mother are not insignificant. In a classic Oedipal correlation, not only is Upi attracted to Wis, but a shocked Wis vigorously rejects Upi's amorous advances, preferring to concentrate his energy on his social and spiritual mission, which includes building Upi a solid shelter and lobbying tirelessly for the rights of the local rubber tappers. Despite growing pressure to abandon his attempts to help the local villagers, Wis is unable to completely deny the significance of the villagers or his relationship with Upi. By rejecting the villagers and, thus, Upi, he would also be unconsciously rejecting his mother *in* Upi—evident in Upi's naive charm, her unpredictability, and most importantly, the incomprehensible elements of her nature.

From Wis's male perspective—the dominant narrative voice of the first half of *Saman*—both his mother and Upi embody the monstrous or uncanny, humanising the mystery of the heavenly Dewi Dresanala. However, as argued by Aisenberg (1994:82), 'if *women* are doing the viewing and defining, then their sexuality is no longer "other," and losing its "otherness," no longer uncanny'. Much of the remainder of Ayu Utami's novel is indeed based upon women doing the viewing and defining and, even more importantly, involves a far more eclectic, ironic and self-conscious approach to mythology. As opposed to Wis's convincing, yet unintended, evocation of the centrality of the male Oedipus myth and the Wisanggeni outlaw legend, the expatriate Indonesian women in the second half of the novel present an arresting case for the development of an array of female narratives comparable to the Oedipus and Wisanggeni outlaw myths—narratives that not only validate women, but also allow them to develop into heroines in their own right.

The masculine and feminine beyond Wisanggeni

Although the first half of *Saman* appears to be underscored by some of the more established mythical paradigms of both the Indonesian and the Western world, the second half of the novel is equally interesting because it is a radical exploration of inherited mythical models. In its depiction of Wis in his new life as Saman, a technology-savvy expatriate NGO activist, the second half of *Saman* is both a continuation and a reworking of the Wisanggeni legend. In the depiction of young and assertive female characters, such as Shakuntala, overcoming societal taboos and forging their own social and mythological identity in an international context, *Saman* is not a mere repetition of the Wisanggeni legend, but rather a counter-discursive feminist re-creation of it.

In terms of the reinterpreting the Wisanggeni legend alone, the second half of *Saman* is quite radical. Ayu not only explores what it might be like for a 'real' Wisanggeni in the real world, but also what it might be like post-Wisanggeni: how does the *Mahabharata* fare without him?; what if the setting of the *Mahabharata* was not Indonesia at all, but contemporary New York?; and what if the stars of the show were not archetypal masculine warriors in the mould of the *satria* but much more marginal characters such as Drupadi, Cangik or Cakil? It is in the exploration of these notions that Ayu's achievement is not only to rewrite ancient myths, but also to challenge contemporary myths of the New Order era, especially myths that have hitherto fed the patriarchal vision of the Indonesian nation. The second half of the novel queries the superior role of the Indonesian male; Shakuntala's assertion of personal and creative autonomy plants the seeds for a significant feminist revision of New Order Indonesia's patriarchal conceptualisation of women.

Shakuntala, also known as Tala, is one of a group of four Indonesian women whose friendship provides the second key narrative focus of the novel. She recounts the experiences of the different members of the group. As a narrator, she has much in common with a shadow puppeteer, energetically introducing and focusing upon one of the women, then moving on to the next in quick succession, all the time moving between prose, conversation, poetry and internal dialogue. A sublime storyteller, Shakuntala deftly combines her own thoughts and fantasies with snippets of conversation among the women, as they discuss anything from their school experiences together to intimate details of sex. Most importantly for the purpose of this discussion, Shakuntala places a great deal of emphasis on the world of dreams, myths and fairytales, at one point asking 'What is the difference between dreams and reality?' (Utami 2005:113). One could even argue that her interpretation of the world of myth is crucial as a means of developing, maintaining and asserting her own keen sense of autonomy. Her highly personal appropriation of myth and mythical characters lends weight to the argument that the term 'archetype' must be redefined as the 'tendency to form and reform images in relation to certain kinds of repeated experience', thus varying from culture to culture and person to person, rather than having an eternal and universal form (Leuter & Rupprecht 1985:13–14). Thus, although Shakuntala may compare herself with a *wayang* character such as Arjuna, who is, as we have seen, quite heavily laden with a good deal of social and cultural baggage, she does not necessarily take on the full archetypal weight of such a character.

In a sense the eclectic nature of Shakuntala's private mythologising perhaps ensures that she cannot be reductively linked with any particular mythical archetype. In effect Shakuntala denies from the outset the possibility of deconstructing and reconstructing mythical prototypes in the manner of Wis. Consider the following sequence, characterised by an extreme fluidity of gender positions, where Shakuntala links herself with no fewer than four *wayang* characters:

> I'm an expert at imitation. Sometimes I'm the Ramayana monkey-king Sugriwa, complete with low guttural growl. Other times I'm Cangik, whose slow, sluggish voice somehow seems to suit the flabby skin around her armpits. When I was a teenager I always used to dance as Arjuna in the *wayang orang* and all the girls would idolize me because, without realizing it, they saw no signs of femininity in me. But I was also Drupadi, who ignites the passion of all five Pandawa brothers (Utami 2005:112).

The lack of boundaries and the fluidity of gender positions identified in this passage are highly significant. Although her ancestry is Javanese, Shakuntala does not by any means limit her private mythologising to the Javanese archetypes; elsewhere she draws upon Western myths and fairytales. For example, when her father sends her to a new school in a new city, Shakuntala compares the setting to a wild forest; when she leaves home for school each day she leaves a trail of bread in order to find her way home, just as in the Brothers Grimm tale of Hansel and Gretel. She also believes that she, like Hansel and Gretel, has a cruel father.

It is evident that Shakuntala's imagination was active from a young age; besides imagining herself as a fairy or nymph, she fantasises about *wayang* ogre-giants (*raksasa* and *buto*), so much so that she reveals that she had her first sexual experience with an ogre and was sent away from home for having a romantic relationship with one. Freudian critics see ogres in Western folk tales and children's stories as always embodiments, in part, of the male children's fear and resentment of their fathers (Hourihan 1997). Bettelheim (1976:190), for example, describes the giant ogre in *Jack and the Beanstalk* as the 'oedipal father' and argues that, in cutting down the beanstalk and killing the giant, Jack frees himself from a view of the father as destructive and devouring. According to Hourihan, however, the felling of the ogre evokes a far richer set of personal, social and political meanings than Bettelheim allows. A similar argument can be made in the context of understanding *Saman*. For example, while it is clear that Shakuntala despises her father, she certainly has no desire to kill any ogres. On the contrary, she seeks them out as a means of liberating herself, both personally and sexually. On a political level, her intimacy with ogres is an image of rebellion arguably against feudal oppression and certainly against unjust authority. Consider the following passage:

> I am descended from the nymphs. I lived in a women's compound where all the children danced. All around the compound were hills inhabited by giants: the ogre with a protruding jaw, the ogre with flaming hair, the green ogre, the eggplant-nose ogre, the carrot-nose ogre, the radish-nose ogre. *Ferocious ogres.* They were both the enemies of and butt of jokes by the knights, who dismissed them scornfully as weird, insignificant fugitives. But I fell in love with one of them.
>
> Because the ogres would be killed as vermin if they set foot inside the compound, which was behind the knight's quarters, I used to meet him secretly under the *kepuh* tree. We wound about each other like a royal serpent Naganini making love to a common snake. But the gardener caught us and told my father. He gave orders for the knights to capture my lover and I was exiled to this town (Utami 2005:114–15).

What is the significance of Shakuntala's attraction to these ogres outside her dormitory? In answering this question, a brief overview of widely-held understandings of *buta* (ogres) or *raksasa* (giants) is perhaps beneficial. Nowadays it is a common sight to see shadow-theatre screens lit up with the battles and skirmishes between warrior-knights such as Arjuna and ogres such as Cakil and his cohorts. Brandon (1993) suggests that the ogres were introduced into the *wayang* in order to be incidental figures, to add variety, but because of their popularity and dramatic usefulness, they gradually became stock figures of major importance. Sears (1996a) discusses the ways in which ogres and ogre kingdoms were introduced into the plots of *wayang* performances at about the time that the Dutch became heavily involved in the internal affairs of the Central Javanese kingdoms of the late 18th century. Humorously resembling the Dutch, the ogres were at the time portrayed as bad-tempered, threatening, impatient and uncouth, often with clumsy Javanese. What is certain is that the ogres' aims were more often than not to usurp the *wayang* kingdoms, kill the warriors and kidnap the *wayang* princesses. Likewise, the aims of the shadow-theatre warriors were generally to protect their kingdoms, kill the ogres and rescue the kidnapped princesses. Nowadays almost every *wayang* performance includes scenes with ogres; it would not be an exaggeration to claim that the inevitable triumph of the warriors over the ogres dramatises the aggressive mastery of Indonesia's patriarchy. Shakuntala's enactment of rapprochement between the princess and her opponents is, therefore, highly subversive, rejecting not only the dominant role of the warrior, but also the passive role of the princess, not to mention the ogres. Thus Shakuntala's creation of a kind of private mythology is as much a form of personal empowerment as it is a radical move to forge new possibilities of narrative, space and voice for women.

The way in which Shakuntala conceptualises these ogres is highly suggestive. Initially it appears that she is convinced she is communing with ogres originating from India. Yet later, in a bizarre scene resonating with the fantasy of magic realism, it becomes apparent that Shakuntala's conceptualisation of ogre-giants is perhaps much closer to the designs of the shadow puppeteers and poets of the late 18th century Javanese courts—that is, the ogres may in fact be Dutch colonisers, priests and sailors who have somehow slipped inexplicably into the 20th century through a rip in the space–time continuum. Confronted by a naked Shakuntala dancing out in the open, the Dutch 'ogres' still believe that they are in the 17th century. Later, when Shakuntala plans to relocate to the Netherlands, this ogre metaphor expands to include Westerners in general, an association not developed in the earlier references to ogres. These images are powerful and resonate deeply, not only with feminist concerns but also with postcolonial issues. Despite enduring tensions, feminist and postcolonial theory has followed what the authors of *The empire writes back* call 'a path of convergent evolution' (Ashcroft, Griffiths & Tiffin 1995:249). As explained by Leela Gandhi,

> Both bodies of thought [feminist and postcolonial] have concerned themselves with the study and defence of marginalised 'Others' within repressive structures of domination and, in so doing, both have followed a remarkably similar theoretical

trajectory. Feminist and postcolonial theory alike began with an attempt to simply invert prevailing hierarchies of gender/culture/race, and they have progressively welcomed the poststructuralist invitation to refuse the binary oppositions upon which the patriarchal/colonial authority constructs itself (Gandhi 1998:82–3).

In her representation of Western men as ogres or giants and the West as the origin of ogres (Utami 2005:126), Shakuntala objectifies the West, inscribing it as an exoticised and uncanny Other in opposition to the female Indonesian Self. Thus the familiar imperial hierarchy of the coloniser as Self and the colonised as Other, as well as the standard patriarchal norms encountered throughout the world, whether in Bali or New York, are interrogated.

Shakuntala's narrative ensures that the Indonesian woman is no longer destined to remain a voiceless bare-breasted handmaiden tempting unwary Europeans, as portrayed in *Saman* in the magic realist colonial-era transcription of 1625 presented by one of the Dutch ogres. Instead, after a brief sexual encounter, we find a typically precocious Shakuntala engaging this Dutchman in conversation, questioning his racist attitudes, informing him (ironically) of the strength of 'Eastern' values and reminding him of the lax moral standards of his own kind. In the sense that Shakuntala presents an entirely different reality from the 17th-century Dutchman's reality, her narrative helps complete an incomplete story. It should be noted that, in keeping with Shakuntala's rebellious nature, her narrative is by no means intended as a completion in itself; her final comment in this striking passage is an ironic effacement of her previous comments: 'And East–West is surely a strange concept, since we were discussing decency while stark naked' (Utami 2005:128).

As a consequence, the key to understanding the full symbolic significance of Shakuntala's encounters with her Dutch ogre may not be so much in what she says to them but rather in the symbolic act of loving them, at least in a sexual sense. From a postcolonial perspective, Shakuntala's encounters exploit the Dutch, regaining a sense of self through romantically fighting back from the colonial margins. From a mythopoeic perspective, her allegorical enactment of rapprochement between the princess and the ogres, all the while precluding the involvement of the warrior archetype, is an important statement in itself. Indeed Shakuntala's engagement with the mythical realms supports Leila Chudori's observation that Ayu Utami's novel is strongly imbued with feminism, not as an explicitly stated argument or an intellectual idea but as a lived reality (Hatley 1999:456). According to Chudori (1998), the greatest achievement of *Saman* is that of 'fulfilling our most basic desires: that of making a woman a human being'. By drawing upon the world of myths and *raksasa*, a predominantly male domain, Shakuntala's lived reality is all the more empowering, as it is experienced in spite of what Hatley (1999:458) calls 'the old restrictions and taboos' that have held back Indonesian women for so long. In effect, by inscribing herself as a 'princess' and a 'heroine' in her own radically reinterpreted mythological paradigm, Shakuntala's narrative is liberating and empowering, imaginatively appropriating and reinterpreting *wayang* archetypes in order to forge new narrative possibilities for Indonesian women.

Conclusion

Wisanggeni is regarded as one of several mythological embodiments of the *rakyat* of Indonesia. It could be usefully argued that he, as the rebellious son of Arjuna, represents the *wayang* equivalent of the post-Suharto generation. However, in Ayu Utami's *Saman*, Wisanggeni's power of advocacy is limited and his acts of resistance are met with stiff opposition; ultimately, his greatest act of resistance is to withdraw and let fate run its course. In *Saman*, where the mythology of the Wisanggeni legend is reworked to such a degree that few, if any, critics have noted the link, Wis realises, as did Wisanggeni, that he cannot continue his fight against the powers-that-be and must flee not only South Sumatra but also Indonesia.

By taking on a new life in the United States as Saman, Wis gives up the narrative focus and thus allows the ideological direction of Ayu's mythological reinterpretation to shift. Consequently, one of the women intersecting with Saman's life story, the promiscuous outsider, Shakuntala, is handed the reins of the narrative. It is at this point that Ayu, like Seno before her, breaks free from the ideological chains of the *wayang* and all it stands for. This does not mean that the *wayang* is completely rejected. On the contrary, a fictional overcoming of the *wayang* entails an even greater interaction between the two discursive domains. For example, Shakuntala embraces an eclectic array of mythological beings, including fairies, Hansel and Gretel, and a number of the more peripheral *wayang* characters, such as Sugriwa, Dewi Drupadi and Cangik. Furthermore, she falls in love with the *wayang*'s ogre-giants, who are perceived as both mythological and human entities.

Ultimately, by shifting narrative focus and style between Wis, Shakuntala and several other characters, such as Saman, his lover Yasmin and a Dutch ogre, Ayu Utami's polyphonic novel allegorically embodies what one might suggest is a postmodern *dalang*, presenting various voices in the one narrative monologue, where each voice differs from and challenges the other, ultimately deferring any real sense of narrative cohesion or unity in favour of an emphasis on egalitarianism and autonomous perspective. The ultimate hope of such an ideologically-motivated narrative technique is that more 'post-Wisanggeni' characters will emerge, or even 'post-*wayang*' characters, such as Saman and Shakuntala.

Significantly, Shakuntala never treats herself too seriously and constantly laughs at the *wayang*. She chooses and adapts mythological archetypes freely and lightheartedly, always ensuring that what she embraces fits in with her lived reality of feminism, a reality she struggled to achieve during the New Order, when the paternalistic aspects of Indonesia's patriarchal society still dominated. Finally, through the voices and lives of her organic characters, the *dalang*-like Ayu appears to be suggesting that it is perhaps time for new 'post-*wayang*' Wisanggenis to be given a greater voice, in the mould of her Saman and Shakuntala. In the ten years since *Saman* appeared, this literary vision has become a reality and many young women writers have followed Ayu's example. In the next chapter the beginnings of a similar scenario are seen to unfold during the same period in Indonesia's history, this time in the field of cinema.

Notes

1   All translations from this novel are from Pamela Allen's translation entitled *Saman: a Novel* (2005).

chapter four

Alternative masculinities: the landmark film of Indonesia's Generation X

> Male privilege is also a trap, and it has its negative side in the permanent tension and contention, sometimes verging on the absurd, imposed on every man by the duty to assert his manliness in all circumstances…*Manliness*, understood as sexual or social reproductive capacity, but also as the capacity to fight and to exercise violence (especially in acts of revenge), is first and foremost a *duty*.

Pierre Bourdieu (2001:50–1)

Although there is a substantial body of scholarship on the role of hegemonic constructions of gender in postcolonial Indonesia (Blackburn 2004; Sears 1996b; Suryakusuma 2004), there has been no rigorous assessment of representations of men, men's practices or masculinities in Indonesian cinema, where male filmmakers and male protagonists are dominant and influential. Reflecting feminist emphases, gendered analyses of Indonesian cinema have primarily focused on women (Heider 1991; Sen 1994, 1995, 2005). While the scholarly impulse has hitherto focused on the feminine or other issues of social and political importance, portrayals of men or *maskulinitas* in cinema have been seen as unproblematic. As though it is the norm, *Maskulinitas* has not been discussed or analysed. Consequently, there has been hardly any critical analysis of images of men *as men* in recent Indonesian cinema. This chapter attempts to redress this curious scholarly lacuna in the field of Indonesian cinema and gender studies.

The approach here revolves around two key emphases: a synopsis and discussion of the content and significance of the landmark film *Kuldesak* (Cul-de-sac) (1998), which I believe was responsible for kickstarting the careers of a significant number of Indonesia's most influential Generation X filmmakers; and a gendered analysis of the main thematic strands of *Kuldesak*, which examines the contrast and conflict between the film's various models of heterosexual and homosexual masculinity and femininity.

Kuldesak: a cinematic cul-de-sac

Kuldesak began production in 1996 at the height of the New Order regime, but money soon ran out after the onset of the Asian economic crisis in 1997. Like several other films in production at the time—including Garin Nugroho's *Daun di atas bantal* (Leaves on a pillow) (1998), Marselli Soemarno's *Sri* (2000) and Slamet Rahardjo Djarot's *Telegram* (2001)—production came to a standstill until after Suharto's resignation. The production of *Kuldesak* was already under a cloud long before this. None of the directors were members of the Indonesian film union, nor did they have the required permit from the Ministry of Information (now defunct). Eventually a permit was issued mid-shoot and financial help came in the form of a grant from the Hubert Bals Fund of the Rotterdam Film Festival. Even so, the cast and crew donated their services and film equipment was supplied for free by PT Samuelson Nusantara and PT Elang Perkasa (*Kompas* 1998c). In November 1998, six months after the resignation of President Suharto, *Kuldesak* was screened for more than three months in the high-class cinemas of the Studio 21 Group. This in itself was an important development, because this leading movie-theatre chain had a strong preference for screening American films in the preceding ten years. The preference for Western films, together with the strict rules and regulations for film production and the popularity of *sinetron* soap operas, had all but extinguished the Indonesian film industry (van Heeren 2002a). According to Sen and Hill (2000:137), the number of companies making film features for cinemas fell from 95 in 1991 to just 13 in 1994. The situation had become even worse by 1998.

Kuldesak was eventually viewed by 140,000 people (Muhammad, A 2002); it had up-beat reviews in major newspapers and magazines, such as *Kompas* and *Tempo* and anecdotal evidence suggests that the film was well received. One filmgoer observed that the young audience was so excited and expectant after a long wait in a queue that, when the film was finally shown, the theatre was too raucous for anyone to hear anything.[1] However, not all responses were positive. According to one of the filmmakers, Mira Lesmana, 'Many of the older film-makers hated *Kuldesak*. They said it was too American' (Muhammad, A 2002).

The film is divided into four separate strands, with a different director responsible for the production of each strand. The directors were Nan T. Achnas, Mira Lesmana, Rizal Mantovani and Riri Riza, with Sentot Sahid responsible for the film's overall editing. The film begins with the story of Dina (Oppie Andaresta), who works in a cinema in Jakarta, and her friendship with a gay couple, Budi (Harry Suharyadi) and Yanto. Dina has a problematic relationship with a television celebrity, Max Mollo (Dik Doang), and Budi later copes with being abandoned by Yanto, who decides to head back to his village after a number of homophobic attacks. The second strand of the film portrays Aksan (Wong Aksan) and his friend Aladin (Din), who decide that the only way they can make a film is to rob the safe of Aksan's father's VCD store. Their plan is foiled by the appearance of three drunken youths who want to steal a VCD. In the ensuing mayhem Aksan is shot. The third strand of the movie depicts the rape and kidnapping of Lina (Bianca Adinegoro), a secretary for a psychotic crime boss, Yakob Gamarhada (Torro Margens). Lina eventually escapes and kills Gamarhada and his henchmen. The fourth strand of the movie details the last few hours of a teenage rebel, Andre (Ryan Hidayat), who commits suicide after hearing of the death of Kurt Cobain, lead singer of the American grunge band, Nirvana. Although each strand of the film is set in Jakarta in 1994, there appears to be only one point at which all four strands meet—halfway through the film, in a scene set in a cinema where the movie showing in the background is, paradoxically, *Kuldesak*.

In terms of content, *Kuldesak* is a movie distinguished by its focus on the alienation of Jakarta's bourgeois urban youth and the vulnerability of the Indonesian male subject. In many ways *Kuldesak* represents Indonesian men negatively. Unlike the women, most of the men are not real people at all; they are, on the whole, simply wooden caricatures who represent various models of *maskulinitas*. Each strand of the movie portrays at least two or three male characters in lead roles, but in each strand the viewer is confronted with a collage of 'deviant masculinities' rather than 'real men' or, at least, men trying to be real men. Significantly, it is the real men who are constantly under attack and they are often their own worst enemies.

This notion is depicted quite dramatically in one of the movie's most surreal scenes, the dream of the wannabe filmmaker, Aksan. In his dream Aksan is chased and attacked by a movie camera accompanied by a few marauding rolls of film. When he wakes up, we soon learn that this is not the first time he has had this dream. In fact, his friend Aladin, who works in Aksan's father's VCD store, reiterates his belief that this recurring dream is a sign that Aksan must follow his ambition to make a movie—not just any movie, but a movie that will be truly Indonesian, winning international acclaim.

From consideration of the gender components of the protagonists' looks and behaviour, it becomes quite clear at this point that Aksan is the masculine centre, under attack not only from his subconscious self but also from his sidekick, Aladin. In contrast to Aksan's straightforward behaviour and placid exterior, Aladin's almost constant babble is in every respect prissy, nagging and deviant. Later, when he grabs the gun from the youths trying to break into the VCD store, his hands shake, he points the gun wildly and he stutters and shrieks, exaggerating his hysterical, effeminate personality. Like the camp Ceki, who was actually holding the gun in the first place, Aladin's sexual orientation is ambiguous; one of the girls even suggests that the two guys were 'up to something'. Aladin's defensive assertion that he is 'a real man' only serves to emphasise his sexual insecurity. Ceki, meanwhile, is also a male. Yet his catty and asexual repartee with his two vampish female partners in crime, not to mention his timid reaction to being disarmed, foppish hairstyle and camp fashion sense, suggests that he represents the movie's masculine centre no more than Aladin does.

This particular strand of the film's perspective is focused on Aksan, not the effeminate and possibly gay characters of Aladin and Ceki. Certainly Aladin dominates the dialogue, yet, even as Aladin babbles on, the camera's gaze is sympathetically on Aksan on a number of occasions, with Aladin out of focus. The lifeless Aksan, however, has nothing much to say or do. Perhaps this is precisely the problem with Indonesian men, as the filmmakers seem to suggest. Caught between archetypal yet unrealistic ideals, such as the Arjunas of the past and impossible Western post-feminist images of the sensitive New Age guy, so-called 'men' such as Aksan are hesitant and unconvincing. Nevertheless, the privileging of Aksan's perspective reflects a dominant motif of the movie—the hierarchy between heterosexual masculinity and its deviant Other, which consists of gays, madmen, freaks, villains and the sexually precocious women accompanying Ceki in the hold-up. Some critics found the *berlebihan* (over-the-top) aspect of these characters acutely annoying, as it only served to highlight the shallowness and triviality of the characters' attitudes and actions rather than the seriousness of the film's themes (*Kompas* 1998c). Nevertheless, contrary to critical opprobrium, *Kuldesak* does not set up a clear dichotomy between opposites like the serious and the trivial, the sane and insane, straights and gays; in fact, at times the oppositional masculinities intertwine in a potential conflation.

With masculinity the battleground on which this battle of identity is fought, dominant male heterosexuality is depicted as a victim as much as an aggressor. Aksan's desire to make a great movie, in a class above the movies of Indonesia's great cinematographers (including Teguh Karya, Eros Jarot and Garin Nugroho), sets up an intriguing and very self-reflexive dialectic. Rejected by his wealthy father, Aksan has no option but to steal money from his father's safe to finance his film. Outside the diegetic levels of *Kuldesak*, the filmmakers involved in its production also struggled for several years to gain permission and to raise sufficient funds. Of course, the permissive political climate following Suharto's fall fostered boldness, creativity and experimentation. According to van Heeren (2002a),

The unexpected fall of Suharto enabled this film to reach movie theatres throughout Indonesia in November 1998. Reformasi was reaching its peak, and many restrictions on film production and exhibition were not being applied. Its rebellious production and fresh contents and techniques set Kuldesak apart from both the films produced by an earlier generation and from the everyday soap operas on television. The press...often highlighted its 'non-Indonesian' features.

The 'non-Indonesian features', although not exactly uncommon in Indonesian cinema, were almost certainly inspired by American Generation X filmmakers, such as Quentin Tarantino and Robert Rodriguez. Indeed, Generation X icons such as Tarantino and Nirvana's lead singer Kurt Cobain are recurring motifs throughout the movie. For example, the purpose of the hold-up in the VCD store is to get one of the girls' favourite movies, Tarantino's *Pulp fiction*. Snatches of dialogue are pure Tarantino and, at one point the robbery scene's soundtrack is the American rockabilly music ubiquitous in *Pulp fiction*; in the background is a giant poster advertising Tarantino's *Reservoir dogs*. We mustn't forget that, like Aksan and Aladin, Tarantino worked in a video store before he began making films (Bernard 1995). Elsewhere, we see books such as the *The Gen X reader* (Rushkoff 1994) and Generation X filmmaker Robert Rodriguez's *Rebel without a crew: or how a 23-year-old filmmaker with $7,000 became a Hollywood player* (1995) conveniently placed.

The self-parody mentioned above plays an important aesthetic and ideological role in *Kuldesak*, all the while confirming Jameson's theories about the shallowness and pastiche of popular culture in the postmodern era (Jameson 1985). I will discuss the self-parodic and self-referential aspects of the film in more detail shortly. The main point to make here is that, unlike Tarantino, Aksan does not succeed. Why not? According to the way he is portrayed, he deserves to fail. As a symbol of heterosexual Indonesian masculinity, Aksan is quite forgettable. Indeed, he is little more than a cardboard cut-out or an actor on the stage. Meek and anonymous, he is depicted as an unrealistic dreamer. He pays the ultimate price for these character flaws; in the hold-up he is shot accidentally and speaks not an angry word. 'I just wanted to make a film...I just wanted to make a film you know...' are his dying words.

In stark contrast, triumphant film critics proclaim that the four young filmmakers involved with *Kuldesak* did not fail like Aksan (*Kompas* 1998c). In the five or so years after *Kuldesak*'s release, they quickly became leading filmmakers, producing one box-office success after another. Key films in this period include *Petualangan Sherina* (The adventures of Sherina) (2000), *Jelangkung* (2001), *Pasir berbisik* (Whispering sands) (2001), and *Ada apa dengan cinta?* (What's up with love?) (2002). Although it wasn't a huge financial success, the critically acclaimed *Eliana Eliana* (2002) also involved members of the *Kuldesak* quartet. On the whole, the images of men and masculinities encoded in these films are understated and revealing. Masculine themes include the absent father (*Pasir berbisik*), the ups and downs of contemporary father–son relationships (*Eliana Eliana* and *Ada apa dengan cinta?*) and the sense of aimlessness and alienation of the emerging post-New Order generation of Indonesian men (*Jelangkung*). Nonetheless, considering the negative portrayals of men in several other films appearing in the period after the demise of the New Order regime, such as *Daun di atas bantal*, *Telegram* and Aria Kusumadewa's *Beth* (2001)[2], questions might well be asked about the presence of a misandric world view in post-New Order cinema.

Interestingly enough, when discussing his film *Eliana Eliana* at the Melbourne Indonesian Film Festival in October 2002, Riri Riza observed that 'some critics have said that all the male characters in my films are weak. To some extent this is true. But aren't we all weak?'. To test the veracity of this statement, we need not look too far beyond *Kuldesak*. By analysing the film's other strands, I gather below more evidence to show that, in terms of many of its gendered representations, *Kuldesak* really does live up to its dictionary definition, glimpsed late in the movie, as a cul-de-sac—a dead-end street. I argue that Aksan is not the only male heterosexual 'hero' to hit a humiliating 'dead end' in the struggle to fulfil his potential and that Aladin and Ceki are not the only deviant masculinities that rupture the dominant gender discourse.

Grunge and madness: resisting symbolic violence

The strand depicting Andre, a long-haired, hard-rocking metal fan, also presents a view of dominant masculinity under attack. Paradoxically, Andre can be considered as an embodiment of a subversive discourse of *maskulinitas* and of Indonesia's dominant elite. He is, after all, a spoilt rich kid with too much money and time on his hands. On his birthday we learn from a message on a telephone answering machine that his mother is flying off to Tokyo for a business meeting; Andre is told to use his credit card for anything he needs. In the background, we see cable TV, complete with video player and remote control. We soon learn that Andre, despite his wealthy background, is no goody two-shoes. For example, his cluttered room is decorated by huge posters of Kurt Cobain and James Dean. When he does wear a shirt, it is a Cobain T-shirt, beneath a Cobainesque cardigan. The grungy hard rock of an Indonesian Nirvana tribute band is blaring out of the stereo. Nose-rings, long unkempt hair and heroin shoot-up scars complete the picture. Later, after Andre drunkenly celebrates his birthday at a bar for heavy-metal fans, we witness his reaction to a cable broadcast (in English) announcing the suicide of Kurt Cobain. This particular moment in history—5

April 1994—is arguably one of *the* defining moments of Generation X. It is also a defining moment for Andre; he commits suicide not long after.[3]

It could be argued that the close association between Andre and Kurt Cobain is perhaps the point at which *Kuldesak* most successfully resists the symbolic violence of New Order patriarchy. To some extent Andre's flight into the world of grunge and heavy metal, inspired, no doubt, by a sense of anxiety about his own behaviour and societal expectations of what he is meant to be as both a man and an Indonesian citizen, subverts the very constructions of categories such as gender and sex. By escaping dominant masculinity and the potentially threatening demands of feminism, Andre presents a rebellious Cobain-like model of alternative masculinity. The grunge rock of the early 1990s, spearheaded by Nirvana, is characterised by a specifically male adolescent narcissism; it was very much concerned with finding a way to define one's masculinity. According to Lay (2000:235),

> Even if Grunge rockers like Nirvana's Kurt Cobain were not explicitly presented as a new kind of male rock persona, they have nonetheless come to impersonate the new type of man, torn angrily between hegemonic masculinity and the "new men" of the 1970s, and, most of all, the unreachable ideal man of the "post-feminist" era, incorporating all extremes, the macho and the softie.

Lay is speaking of the American context here, but the parallels with the contemporary Indonesian context are self-evident. More importantly, does Andre's alternative masculinity à la Cobain *really* subvert the centrality of patriarchal order? Or does he fall into the same trap as some feminists, whose subversions against the masculine status quo are produced and restrained by the structures of power through which emancipation is fought and are, therefore, just as likely to perpetuate the social relations of domination between the sexes (Bourdieu 2001)? The fact that Andre is written out of the script, without any rational explanation, suggests that the latter holds sway here. However, as with the portrayal of Aksan, the self-reflexivity of Andre's strand of the film suggests that the makers of *Kuldesak* are indeed searching furiously for a way to undermine the constructions and patterns that produce and reproduce patriarchal domination.

In what way is Andre's strand self-reflexive? To answer this, we must return again to one of the film's dominant motifs, the hierarchy between dominant heterosexual masculinity and its deviant other. Shadowing Andre's straight characterisation and his unchallenged position as the narrative centre, we find the mad soothsayer, Hariolus. Andre has known the hunchback Hariolus for many years; each time they meet on the street, Hariolus tells Andre's fortune. Andre is not totally convinced; he even believes that bad luck is sure to follow every encounter with Hariolus. When Hariolus predicts that Andre will find a package after his night out that will irrevocably change his life, Andre is intrigued, but ultimately dismissive of his jovial, happy-go-lucky friend. The keen insight inspired by the synthesis of madness and animalism in Hariolus, who has an owl perched on his shoulder, is in stark contrast to Andre's rebel-without-a-cause urban angst.

Significantly, the self-reflexivity embedded in this strand of the movie lies in the pivotal figure of Hariolus. Played superbly by Indonesia's leading hip-hop rapper at the time, Iwa K, Hariolus, whose haunt is outside a local supermarket, presents some of his predictions in rap. At one point we see a close-up of Hariolus laughing maniacally directly underneath a neon 'K' sign—no doubt an 'in' reference to the actor's real-life Iwa 'K' persona. It is significant that, in analysing Iwa K's influential cameo, one is reminded of Foucault's treatise on madness, where madness 'insofar as it partook of animal ferocity, preserved man from the dangers of disease; it afforded him an invulnerability, similar to that which nature, in its foresight, had provided for animals' (Foucault 1988:75). If Andre's ambivalence and suicide can be used to mirror the uncertainty surrounding the status of the Indonesian male, then Iwa K's fluid identity (half-actor/half-rapper, half-mad/half-genius) can be used as an alternative trope of *maskulinitas*. Even if his character does not totally subvert the underlying structures and mechanisms of masculine domination, Iwa K, at the very least, symbolises the masculinity of the margins, providing us with a self-conscious symbolic rupture. This has, of course, been the social role of madmen, buffoons, fools and clowns throughout the history of mankind. Indonesia is no exception; the prestige of the shadow-theatre clown-servants such as Semar and his sons Gareng, Petruk and Bagong is such that they are often considered the guardians of truth and justice.

In the other strands of the movie, madmen also play an important role. In the next narrative to be discussed, the rape and kidnapping of Lina, we are confronted with the antithesis of Hariolus's good-natured madness—the insanity of the New Order businessman and gangster boss, Yakob Gamarhada. I argue that, contrary to the other strands of *Kuldesak*, it is femininity, a traditional adversary that threatens the hegemonic masculine centre in this strand. I also argue that, if Yakob Gamarhada can be compared to the dominant patriarchal figure of the New Order era, Suharto, in the post-New Order era, traditional models of hegemonic masculinity appear to be monolithic dinosaurs.

Violence and masculinity

As this chapter's epigraph suggests, Bourdieu insists that men are also prisoners and insidious victims of the dominant gender regime. Specifically, the problem with exalting manliness lies not only in its tacit encouragement of violence, but also in its dark side—'in the fears and anxiety aroused by femininity' (Bourdieu 2001:51). This is particularly relevant when we consider the many men of *Kuldesak* in search of a sense of masculine identity. In *Kuldesak* all of the dominant males have a point of vulnerability, be it Aksan's need to prove himself by making a movie or Andre's obsession with Kurt Cobain. Both of these points of vulnerability can be linked with the search for a sense of manliness or male identity. In Lina's strand of the movie, it becomes apparent that Yakob Gamarhada's point of vulnerability is his thirst for domination, especially over young women. Paradoxically, it is this vulnerability that leads him into a world of violence—against women in particular—where he can utilise visible signs of *maskulinitas*, such as subservient henchmen and high-powered handguns.

The climax of *Kuldesak* is a smorgasbord of shooting and bloodshed. In an analysis of the various images of masculinity in *Pulp fiction*, Brandt (2000:85-6) observes the following:

> The constant gun shooting that characterizes male behavior in *Pulp Fiction* points simultaneously to the defense of masculinity through the hard-boiled heroes and to the "homoerotic" associations of the images of bodily penetration that are so common in the action genre.

One could easily apply a similar analysis to *Kuldesak, although* several important modifications must be made. First of all, in each case where a dominant male (Aksan, Andre, Gamarhada) finds himself on the wrong side of a bullet, his model of masculinity is, apparently, not worth defending. Secondly, in *Kuldesak* it is women shooting men (mostly) and men shooting women and not, as in *Pulp fiction*, men shooting men. In this sense the gun shooting can be more closely associated with *feminist* incursions of the male body. When Lina is kidnapped, she breaks free and, after arming herself with a handgun, she has little hesitation in shooting several gangsters, culminating in the death of Gamarhada himself. For Gamarhada, death comes as a punishment for his sexual perversion. His death is also a site of liberation for Indonesian women as a whole. It is no coincidence that his blood-splattered body falls down on top of an Indonesian–English dictionary, conveniently opened to the page listing 'kuldesak'. At this point, one could argue that Gamarhada's 'dead-end' model of hegemonic masculinity is no longer tolerable.

Despite Lina's heroics, her victory does little to successfully challenge male domination, as she was forced to fight Gamarhada on his terms. By using a handgun, Lina misrecognises the tool of her own physical and symbolic violence and thus reinscribes her domination. It is no coincidence that feminists seldom refer to violence as a justifiable means of creating a new gender order. Nevertheless, through the use of parody, Lina brings to light the New Order's key mechanism through which the domination of Indonesian women, and

Indonesian people as a whole, was perpetuated—physical aggression. In other words, by wielding a handgun so skilfully and effectively and magically surviving a hail of bullets unscathed, Lina caricatures the chief legacy of New Order patriarchy—violence as a legitimate mechanism of domination. As if to emphasise this point, one of Gamarhada's gangsters goes cross-eyed staring at Lina's oncoming bullet, just before it hits him between the eyes. The parody is heightened by the fact that this image is in slow motion, followed by what sounds like splattered brain sloshing onto the ground. But does parody truly expose the flawed notion of masculinity that lies at the basis of male identity politics, especially in the case of the New Order patriarchy, propped up as it was by the power of the shotgun? Parody, as Dowell and Fried (1995:4–5) observe, is a double-edged sword, as it also 'protects and reinforces the very "norm" it seeks to disclose'. Thus, while Lina's segment of the movie might exaggerate and parody male violence, this parody of male violence is almost indistinguishable from old-fashioned heterosexual paranoia, where trying to prove one's manliness in response to the feminine threat is merely a reflection of an insecure sense of masculine identity.

Homosexuality and identity

The last strand of *Kuldesak* to be discussed concerns Dina's relationship with her homosexual neighbours, Budi and Yanto. The significance of this strand lies in the status of homosexuality in contemporary Indonesian culture. Dede Oetomo (2001) observes that from the 1980s the Indonesian media began to highlight, and sensationalise, homosexuality. According to Oetomo, this media focus, together with the drive against HIV/AIDS in the 1990s, has ensured that there is a new understanding of gender and sexuality in contemporary Indonesia. In the few years following the fall of Suharto, however, homophobic attacks were on the increase, just as homosexual groups were becoming more visible (Boellstorff 2004). *Kuldesak* depicts this pattern. The fact that this film's depiction of homosexuality includes the first man-to-man kissing scene in the history of Indonesian cinema is surely a reflection of the growing visibility of the Indonesian gay movement. This scene was deleted when the film was released in Indonesia, a reminder that, in spite of a new openness towards homosexuality, homophobia runs deep. Budi is attacked twice in the film by homophobic youths, both times as a direct consequence of his sexuality. After one of the attacks, Yanto decides to abandon both Budi and Jakarta. He is obviously shaken by the attacks. Yanto's return to the village is a literal embodiment of the process of hegemonic exclusion labelled by some Western film scholars as 'symbolic annihilation' (Hanke 1992) and referred to by Bourdieu (2001) as 'invisibilisation'.

Ultimately, Yanto's challenge to the New Order's hetero-normativity is doomed to failure. He appears to believe that perhaps his heterosexual persecutors are correct—that his sexuality is deviant and he must, therefore, escape the shame and humiliation that his sexual experience and orientation entail. His return to his family is also a rejection of the urban gay lifestyle, where friendship has replaced the familial bonds underlying the conservative morality of Indonesia's heterosexual society. Because for many gay people friendship is also kinship, Budi, in losing Yanto, loses a sense of family.

The fact that the homosexual element of *Kuldesak* is ultimately subject to societal 'invisibilisation' suggests that the traditional views of 'deviant' homosexuality versus 'dominant' heterosexuality are posited and endorsed. Even when the gay couple is on screen, expressions of sexuality, apart from their much-discussed kiss, are either rather chaste or kept off-screen; Budi and Yanto remain mute about their feelings for each other and their gayness. Having said this, it could also be argued that Budi's friendship with Dina is an act of symbolic subversion. One problem with defending this argument is that the subversive characteristic of Budi's friendship with Dina is not immediately recognisable, especially after Yanto abandons Budi. When Dina attempts to comfort Budi, he angrily turns on her, telling her that she is just living in the *dunia khayalan* (dream world) of the Max Mollo TV show. Like so many other characters in this film, Dina's normality is challenged by her obsession with the bizarre antics of Max Mollo, a particularly deviant representation of *maskulinitas*. Mollo is a live-wire TV personality and pantomime artist who uses an exaggerated form of Indonesian to liven up his act somewhat. From time to time Mollo appears in the cinema at which the besotted Dina works and they conduct a silent, but touching, romance. Budi, however, attacks Dina because she reminds him of Yanto, a person not willing to face reality. But not long after that, the two embrace each other, emotionally and chastely.

It can be argued that Budi and Dina blur the line between gay and straight, thus hinting at the possibility of a deeper assimilation of gay culture into dominant Indonesian society. More importantly, the subversive nature of the scene lies in the fact that the couple are no longer defined in terms of their sexuality; they are two people who love each other in their own way. They are also two broken people. Their dreams are shattered. However, through their self-awareness they develop new understanding of their personal realities. Budi, for example, alludes to his traumatic childhood and voices his doubts about Yanto. In the last scene of the movie Dina rejects her cinema job and parodies Max Mollo, which is as cathartic as it is subversive. In this sense, the warm reconciliation between Budi and Dina is not only an act of symbolic subversion, but also an attempt to fight normative gender ideologies on an even deeper level.

By refusing to submit to the dominant norm, as Lina and the mad Hariolus refused, Dina and Budi go beyond a mere symbolic break. They challenge not only the status quo, but also their own internalised repression. Just as the madness of Hariolus is a site of perception and insight and Lina's capture and subjectification is a site for parodic subversion, Budi's homosexuality and Dina's obsession with Max Mollo are transcended and transformed. This is not to say that any of these characters totally escape their domination, their madness or their homosexuality, or even want to. Rather, by undergoing self-reflexive representational transformation to varying degrees, they no longer accept the symbolic violence of patriarchal domination as an undisputed natural category. In the context of late New Order Indonesia, this could possibly be viewed as an important step towards generating a more liberated sense of social order.

Conclusion

Just as the Indonesian nation found itself deep in crisis in the years following the fall of Suharto, the Indonesian man as a constructed category has also found himself in a period of fluidity. Cultural icons, like the film *Kuldesak*, suggest that the contemporary image of the Indonesian male straddles outdated and archetypal images of the Indonesian man and alternative or non-traditional masculinities. The alternatives, as seen in recent fiction, television advertisements and cinema, are contradictory and ambiguous.

Contradiction and ambiguity do not, however, appear to be entirely negative characteristics. This chapter has suggested that even apparently dead-end models of masculinity, such as Andre, the grunge rebel, are encoded as symbolic breaks with the dominant image of Indonesian heterosexual masculinity. Furthermore, even when contrasted unfavourably with Andre, the mad Hariolus is also able to undermine dominant heterosexual images of the Indonesian man. Despite many contradictions and the paradoxes of self-reflexivity, these symbolic ruptures are extremely important, as they highlight and question the outdated nature of conservative patriarchal stereotypes, such as the New Order thug Yakob Gamarhada, as well as the physical and symbolic violence involved in establishing and perpetuating patriarchal dominance. Through questioning gendered power, *Kuldesak* both refuses and challenges the New Order's monolithic and patriarchal consciousness, the imprint of which will no doubt affect Indonesians for many years to come.

Finally, the contradictory and hybrid nature of Indonesian maleness says much about the realities of contemporary Indonesian life. With the fall of Suharto, the disappointment of leaders such as Habibie, Gus Dur and Megawati and the acute, social, economic and security challenges faced by the current President at the time of writing, Susilo Bambang Yudhoyono, it appears that the days of a unifying, all-conquering, male hero in the mould of Sukarno, who often likened himself to the heroic Bima or Gatotkaca of the *wayang*, are long gone. However, with the opening up of a sense of democratic space for Indonesian filmmakers, and for all Indonesians in fact, new voices can be heard. The multiple perspectives and ideological contradictions of deeply political films such as *Kuldesak* reflect what is so exciting and daunting about Indonesia today—the emergence of so many identities that have been suppressed for too long.

It remains to be seen whether discussion of Indonesian male identity will play a key role in Indonesia's ongoing social, cultural and political renegotiation. In the meantime, it is time to emphasise the social and political significance of asking 'the man question', which involves questioning dominant forms of *maskulinitas* and gender oppression. As I have demonstrated throughout this book, the man question must be firmly ensconced in the political sphere as much as in the cultural sphere. It is for this reason that the discussion in the next chapter, which focuses on representations of the masculine and feminine in a selection of the cinematic expression in the years following the fall of Suharto, is bookmarked by the demise of the New Order and the subsequent culture of widespread social decay and political disorder.

Notes

1   My thanks to Amelia Fyfield for this observation (personal communication, October 2002).

2   *Daun di atas bantal* depicts the bleak lives of male urban street kids in Yogyakarta, who are victims and perpetrators of violence. Their fear and mistrust of each other and their yearning for a mother's love highlight their lack of confidence in the male domain, not to mention their failure to develop an adult sense of masculinity. *Telegram* depicts a rough-and-ready journalist haunted by his wife's death, yet in the midst of his sorrow he is reinvigorated by the innocent presence of his adopted daughter. This does not, however, transform him from a 'bad man' to a 'good man'; despite his sense of responsibility, he is promiscuous, moody and prone to irrationality. *Beth*, a love story set in a mental institution, is overrun by evil, insane or psychotic male characters. The women, on the other hand, appear to be merely innocent victims. This is a somewhat polarised description, however, and there are notable exceptions.

3   Laine Berman observes that Andre's suicide foreshadowed the suicide of the actor who played him, Ryan Hidayat, also known as Dayat. According to Berman, Dayat was also a heavy intravenous drug user who, just like Kurt Cobain and just like his character in the film, really did commit suicide, although the positive reviews the film has received never mention these uncomfortable, real-life facts (personal communication, August 2002).

chapter five

Men, violence and horror:
the films of Rudi Soedjarwo

If we consider how readily the audience accepts where femininity equals victimhood and masculinity equals rape and murder, we have to conclude that this version of masculinity should have a government warning label.

Klaus Rieser (2001:390)

In discussing recent Indonesian cinema in the context of the demise of Suharto's New Order regime and Indonesia's current social and political transformations, important questions can be asked. To what extent has cinema benefited from the crumbling of censorship? Have the new freedoms merely led to a greater freedom to depict scenes of violence and degradation? Dodging for the moment the issue of censorship, which has not had a substantive impact on post-New Order cinema, I would suggest that recent films focusing on masculine behaviour draw attention to an endemic culture of violence, masculine violence in particular, in post-authoritarian Indonesia. Boellstorff (2004) refers to this propensity to real-life violence as an important indicator of an emergent 'masculinist cast' in contemporary Indonesia. To be more precise, for Boellstorff, the rise of a masculinist cast is in response to 'political homophobia', a politicised conflict between heterosexism and homosexuality.

I would suggest that, although Boellstorff's ideas are seductive, the extent of the politicised conflict between heterosexism and homosexuality is overstated.[1] I would argue that, historically, hetero-normative masculinity in Indonesia has been far more sensitive to the threat posed by non-normative women and women's groups. There are similar claims for contemporary American manhood, which is widely believed to be suffering from decades of insecurity in the face of rabid feminists and overbearing womanhood (Faludi 1999, 2007). In the United States and in the West generally, the threat posed by sexual minorities such as gays and transgender/transsexual men is almost nonexistent. Yet I am sufficiently intrigued by the notion of a masculinist turn in Indonesia to draw upon Boellstorff's theoretical anthropology. This chapter uses Boellstorff's arguments as a means to examine the cultural logic of violence, emotion and masculine behaviour in some of the most popular movies of one of Indonesia's most prolific Generation X filmmakers, Jakarta-based Rudi Soedjarwo.

This chapter consists of three key sections: a summary of key developments in Indonesian cinema post-*Kuldesak*; an analysis of the configuration of masculine emotion and violence in Rudi Soedjarwo's *Mengejar matahari* (Chasing the sun) (2004) and *9 naga* (9 dragons) (2006); and a discussion of a horror film made by Soedjarwo in the same period, *Pocong 2* (Shrouded 2) (2006), which provides a means of exploring his equally popular representations of masculinity in the horror genre. I should state from the outset that Soedjarwo's films, despite their many good qualities, are not necessarily to my taste. I was even compelled to walk out of a cinema in Bandung towards the end of a sold-out screening of *9 naga*, much to the dismay of my companions. Even by the low standards of the genre, *Pocong 2* is quite horrid. My personal response is irrelevant, however, as films are primarily for audiences, not critics. Each of these films has attracted impressive box-office figures and VCD sales throughout Indonesia, generating as many favourable reviews as negative ones. Beauty, as they say, is in the eye of the beholder.

Cinema in the post-New Order era

Recent developments in Indonesian cinema cannot be considered separately from the euphoria associated with the fall of Suharto's authoritarian regime, which ushered in a much more open political climate and the relaxation of media restrictions in Indonesia almost overnight. The impact on Indonesian cultural and artistic expression was immediate and profound. For example, several years before Suharto's resignation, Indonesian cinema had virtually died, with barely a handful of films emerging between 1993 and 1998. As indicated in the previous chapter, with the success of *Kuldesak* in 1998, a new generation of Indonesian filmmakers was inspired. Since 1999, dedicated communities of independent filmmakers have produced numerous short films. An impressive array of film festivals, film screenings and workshops have been established throughout the archipelago; admirers of Indonesian cinema have congregated on many blogs and Internet chat forums. Numerous film websites and magazines, such as *detikhot, Kineforum, Rumah Film* and *F: Majalah Film*, devoted to the discussion of Indonesian cinema and Indonesian filmmakers, have emerged.

The social and critical impulse of Indonesian cinema has remained undiminished in the post-Suharto era. According to the editors of *Culture and society in New Order Indonesia* (Hooker & Dick 1995:2), 'Many of Indonesia's artists feel that their art is only of value if it expresses the feelings of society and communicates with it'. As a result, during the New Order era Indonesian artists worked hard to communicate directly with their audience, creatively engaging with issues of social and political significance. They have continued to do so in the years after the demise of Suharto's regime. Filmmakers, particularly independent and short filmmakers, have consistently explored issues of relevance to Indonesian society in recent years. In mainstream cinema issues of interest have included, among many others, teenage sexuality and domestic abuse (*Virgin* (2005)); urban drug culture (*Gerbang 13* (Gate 13) (2005); *Detik terakhir* (Final moments) (2007); *Radit dan Jani* (Radit and Jani) (2008)); underworld crime gangs (*9 Naga*, (2006)); corruption (*Ketika* (When) (2005)); *Kejar Jakarta* (Chasing Jakarta) (2006)); homosexuality and queer culture (*Arisan!* (The gathering) (2003); *Jakarta Undercover* (2005); *Brownies* (2005)); *D'Bijis* (2007); *Merah itu cinta* (*Red is love*) (2007) and *Coklat stroberi* (Chocolate strawberry) (2007)); the aftermath of the tsunami in Aceh (*Serambi* (Verandah) (2006)); and polygamy, as described in Chapter One. The willingness to tackle topical issues, however, does not guarantee the financial or critical success of a film. Indeed, filmmakers, like all Indonesian artists, are regularly held to account for aesthetic shortcomings. For example, according to one review of the award-winning *Ketika*, 'If only this film had some half decent production values and direction up to the standard of cinematic release, this would be one of the candidates for the best-ever films made in Indonesia' (Mahendra 2006).

Another interesting trend has emerged: many of Indonesia's cinematic releases are also appearing as novelised versions. Leading bookseller and publisher Gramedia is now doing a roaring trade in this respect, particularly with novelised versions of the dominant form of recent Indonesian cinema, the teen comedy. Soon after the release of easily forgettable teen flicks such as *Brownies* (2005) or *Jomblo* (The Bachelor) (2006), novelised versions appeared, feeding increases in box-office sales and lucrative DVD and VCD sales. From time to time film scripts have also emerged, such as *Ada apa dengan cinta? sebuah skenario* (What's up with love? a screenplay) (Prananto 2002), or *Eliana, Eliana* (Rusdi & Riza 2002). These screenplays, some of which include introductions, analysis and interviews with the filmmakers and writers, open up new understandings of Indonesian cinema. For instance, in the case of the published script of *Eliana, Eliana*, the text reveals the fascinating process by which the film emerged from the kernel of an idea to a rough draft and then through several more drafts, eventually blossoming into a fully-fledged script. The script of *Ada apa dengan cinta?* also reveals the wide gap between the script and the final polished product on the cinema screen and DVD.

In terms of numbers, in 2005 more than 50 films were either released or produced (Rahman & Agusta 2005) and in 2006 and subsequent years this pattern was repeated. Cinema has clearly benefited from the crumbling of censorship.

But new threats to the freedom of expression have cast an unwelcome shadow over the development of mainstream and independent cinema. In 2006 key Indonesian actors and filmmakers, such as Deddy Mizwar and Eddy Iskandar, expressed their concern over the nature of the proposed anti-pornography legislation (Hazmirullah 2006). Others may well have been privately despairing at their inability to represent realistic depictions of sex and sexuality in the immediate context of the bill. Just as relaxation of Indonesia's media restrictions promised unfettered depiction of one of the most taboo topics in contemporary Indonesia, self-censorship has again intersected with censorship. Although the bill was not passed in its initial form, the culture of censorship and self-censorship appears to be all-pervasive, ten years on from the New Order, with the state still playing a key role. For example, leading young filmmakers Riri Riza and Mira Lesmana were forced to contend with the cutting of over a dozen scenes in their sprawling 2007 road movie, *3 hari untuk selamanya* (3 days for forever), by the anachronistic Board of Film Censorship (*Suara Merdeka* 2007). Strangely enough, according to the leading actor in the film, Indonesia's most popular movie star Nicholas Saputra, most of the offending scenes included images of marijuana smoking, or, more precisely, the *preparation* of marijuana cigarettes, rather than the actual smoking of marijuana.[2] An incestuous sex scene, however, was uncut.

Extraordinarily, other films, such as the commercially successful *Arisan!*, have managed to depict oral sex and homoerotic kissing without censure. Why have these scenes been left uncut by the censor? Was it because *Arisan!* was produced in the brief historical window of opportunity between the departure of Suharto and the furore associated with the anti-pornography legislation? This may well have been the case, but an important factor might be the historical tolerance of alternative sexualities in Indonesia. Murtagh (2008), for example, suggests that depictions of transgender, gay and lesbian characters in Indonesian cinema have a long history, with many sympathetic representations from the New Order era onwards. Since 2002 there have been about 20 films representing gay and lesbian sexualities and, according to one blogger 'the inclusion of a gay or lesbian character has almost become an essential ingredient for success in Indonesian movies' (Murtagh 2008). The largest queer film festival in Asia, Jakarta's annual Q!Film Festival, is now in its seventh year and has spawned similar smaller events in Yogyakarta and Bali (Maimunah 2008)

An additional point worth making is that there are a number of relevant thematic directions in the recent boom in Indonesian cinema. One of the most dominant genres of recent Indonesian cinema, as mentioned earlier, is teen comedy (Hanan 2008). The enduring popularity of this genre is no doubt inspired by the reputed two million viewers and subsequent financial success of *Ada apa dengan cinta?*. Apart from Hanan's (2008) analysis of teen films, Western observers have tended to focus on other themes. From a broad feminist perspective, a handful of critics have welcomed the emergence of women filmmakers in Indonesia and the growth of films specifically devoted to women's issues (Sen 2005). Consider, for instance, a film such as Nan Achnas's haunting and evocative *Pasir berbisik* (Whispering sands) (2001). In Indonesia this low-budget film was a flop at the box office, but it has enjoyed critical acclaim and international recognition. More importantly, it has been analysed and celebrated as an example of a film written and directed by a woman, about women, starring well-known women actors (including Christine Hakim and Dian Sastrowardoyo) (Sen 2005). The film is probably aimed at a female audience too. Other critics, such as Katinka van Heeren, have tended to focus on the post-New Order cycle of horror films (van Heeren 2007) and the business of film production, distribution and consumption (van Heeren 2002b). My interest, for this book, lies in some thematic aspects of Indonesian cinema that may have been overlooked, such as cinematic representations of violence and the masculine.

A 'new masculine cast'

Boellstorff (2004) argues that an unprecedented series of violent acts against homosexual Indonesians from 1999 onwards indicate the emergence of what he terms 'political homophobia'. For example, on 11 November 2000, about 350 homosexuals and *waria* (transvestites) gathered in Kaliurang, a mountain township to the north of Yogyakarta, for an evening of artistic performances and fashion parades. The gathering was seriously disrupted by the arrival of about 150 men in white headdresses, scarves and robes to signify their connection with radical Islam. Carrying knives, machetes and clubs, they arrived in a convoy of jeeps and motorbikes and claimed to be members of the Gerakan Pemuda Ka'bah (Ka'bah Youth Movement). They verbally and physically assaulted many of those present, smashed windows and destroyed tables and chairs, injuring at least 25 people. No-one was charged over the incident. Boellstorff views violent acts, such as this one, that are directed at public events where homosexual men are attempting to stake a claim in Indonesia's civil society, as a masculinised response to a homosexual threat. 'Homophobic' is perhaps another way to describe such acts. This type of state-sanctioned homophobia, according to Boellstorff, indicates that Indonesia may be gaining 'a new masculine cast', where male-to-male sexuality is perceived to be a threat not just to normative masculinity but indeed to the nation as a whole.

I argue that Boellstorff's analysis is overstated on several counts. First of all, while a large number of men from the Gerakan Pemuda Ka'bah movement certainly did gatecrash the gay and *waria* fashion parade, they left quickly, according to some reports. More importantly, in a show of support the following year, Gus Dur attended the event, provoking one of the organisers to jokingly thank the GPK for providing the extra free publicity. We also need to consider that, in general, in the years immediately preceding the publication of this book there have been few attacks on homosexuals and transsexuals and, while some would disagree, there is a broad tolerance of homosexuality and queer culture as a whole. As mentioned above, the many recent films depicting alternative sexualities, as well as the popularity of queer film festivals since the demise of the New Order are testament enough to this.

One might also question the need to make the sudden leap from threatened normative masculinity to an imminent crisis of nation. The answer to this, presumably, lies in the relationship between gender and politics in postcolonial Indonesia. There is a substantial body of scholarship suggesting that notions of the ideal Indonesian citizen, particularly from the New Order era onwards, have been closely tied into heterosexual gendered ideologies. The New Order state went to great lengths to inculcate the ideal citizen-family structure, where people were indoctrinated to accept that a 'happy and healthy' nuclear marriage was the ideal. The effect of the happy and healthy nuclear family indoctrination was to create a narrow vision of heterosexual masculinity and femininity as the foundations of society. Because it is through marriage and heterosexuality that the gendered self and nation has been articulated, 'in the new Indonesia, men who publicly appear to make improper choices threaten this gendered and sexualized logic of national belonging' (Boellstorff 2004:470).

In response to this, I argue that male-to-male sexuality is not the only threat to normative masculinity, or indeed to the nation. An equally strong argument can be made that women who fail to fit the model of the faithful housewife pose a similar threat to both normative masculinity and the nation. This notion is not new. Suryakusuma, for example, observed that the backlash against sex, drugs and prostitution in the mid-1990s was the sign of an authoritarian regime under threat:

> In the midst of the spate of social, economic and political crises, the clampdown on the sex industry is the easiest, the most sensational and the most hypocritical as it does not touch the fundamental root of social unrest: violence, manipulation and injustice, all of which are condoned, even carried out, by the state (Suryakusuma 1994:18).

This attitude persists in the post-New Order years, giving rise to the anti-pornography furore, not to mention the new kinds of censorship and the growing culture of hardline Muslim agitation.

The argument that the ongoing trauma of the Dutch colonial era lies at the heart of the masculinist turn in post-Suharto Indonesia has already been presented in earlier chapters. As Pramoedya and many others have suggested, the repression of the New Order was thoroughly colonial in nature, and many strategies of authoritarianism and surveillance were inspired by the Dutch colonial government (Maier 1999; McGlynn 2000). Indonesia's post-authoritarian masculine psyche, therefore, has scars dating back to both the colonial and postcolonial eras.

Meanwhile, the recent boom of men's lifestyle magazines in Indonesia, quite apart from the release of several films that tentatively explore definitions of *maskulinitas*, suggests that media agents and advertisers have been quick to capitalise on the commercial potential of Indonesia's still-beating masculine heart. Many magazine and newspaper articles demonstrate that unabashed discussions of men and men's practices are now underway. The number of articles written from a male perspective about women's issues is also increasing and there have been several important films by male filmmakers focusing on women, such as Riri Riza's *Eliana, Eliana*, Hanny Saputra's *Virgin* and Hanung Bramantyo's *Perempuan berkalung sorban*. This trend, I believe, is suggestive of some Indonesian men's pro-feminist attempts to challenge patriarchal gender relations and construct non-patriarchal subjectivities and practices.

By understanding the world of Indonesian men or, at the very least, representations of Indonesian masculine behaviour in recent cinema, we can also better understand the literalist Muslim segment of the population and the anti-*Playboy* and anti-pornography lobby in particular. Although he is primarily considering the solipsistic context of political homophobia, Boellstorff suggests that it is useful to consider emotions such as *malu*, which he identifies as being similar in meaning to the Javanese *isin* or Balinese *lek*, because a sense of *malu*, or rather masculine inferiority, indignation or humiliation, may well be at the heart of the matter.

It should be emphasised that Boellstorff is referring to the feelings of *malu* of normative or 'straight' men (and their vision of the Indonesian nation as normatively male) in response to the sense of threat and embarrassment posed by homosexual activists. However, feelings of nationalised and masculinised *malu* can be engendered by other groups, including women and the West. I would argue that *malu*, in terms of it being a 'nationalized intersection of manhood and emotion' (Boellstorff 2004:481), need not be limited to the threat posed by non-normative or non-heterosexual men. Indeed, sex between men poses little threat to the centrality of patriarchy, which, in spite of its historical accommodation of gay men, is far more concerned with the dilemmas of heterosexuality. Instead, in Indonesia a sense of *malu* can be more broadly engendered by the West and Western men, and has been, to some extent, since the social, political and gendered incursions of the Dutch colonial era. As discussed earlier, the sense of threat posed by progressive women, particularly by undomesticated or overtly-sexual women in, has been equally profound. In the next chapter I argue that, in certain contexts, even overt heterosexuality, if for some reason or another it is perceived to be *ngisin-isini* or *memalukan* (shame-inducing), can be perceived as a threat to normative masculinity.

Malu, according to Boellstorff (2004:469), also has a proper rejoinder:

the potential for the nation to be represented by non-normative men challenges a nationalized masculinity, enabling what has long been understood to be a normative response to *malu*—namely, the masculine and often collective enraged violence known in Indonesian as *amok*. By definition, *amok* is always a public act.

Again, Boellstorff's argument, which is based on the perceived conflict between normative and non-normative men, can be expanded to include the possibility of other disruptions to the normative masculinist national discourse. As already outlined, women, the West and even *Playboy* magazines have the potential to emerge as much greater symbolic ruptures to the post-Suharto vision of the nation than homosexuals. After all, many films depicting homosexual relationships and alternative sexualities have emerged in Indonesia, especially since the demise of the New Order regime. The salient point to be made is that these films did not provoke the violent reactions associated with the homosexual gatherings beginning in September 1999 or, to the best of my knowledge, even a single demonstration.

Once the threat posed by non-normative Indonesian men is expanded to encompass other threats to Indonesian public and political culture, Boellstorff's ideas make a great deal of sense. In a snapshot of early post-New Order Indonesian cinema, we can see the signs of a dialectical relationship between shame and recklessness. In films such as *Kuldesak*, *Tato* (Tattoo) (2001), *Gerbang 13*, *Radit dan Jani* and especially Rudi Soedjarwo's *9 naga*, we witness essentially decent men tending towards reckless behaviour in response to the shame and internalised rage associated with poverty, powerlessness and anger, with little care for the consequences to themselves or their families. By briefly examining Rudi Soedjarwo's *9 naga*, I suggest that this deplorable pattern, when viewed in terms of Boellstorff's theories of emotion, becomes understandable, even if it is not unique to Indonesia and even if it cannot be condoned. Before discussing *9 naga*, I examine briefly an earlier film by Rudi Soedjarwo, *Mengejar matahari*, which combines mawkish sentimentality with a weak script and clumsy plot, interspersed by episodes of appalling violence. More than one film critic has observed that the style and themes of *9 naga* and *Mengejar matahari* are quite similar (Diani 2006; Pattisina 2006; Rahman 2006), so a comparison between the two seems logical.

Rudi Soedjarwo's *Mengejar matahari* and *9 naga*

Mengejar matahari revolves around the bonds of friendship among four boys who have grown up together in one of the poorer suburbs of Jakarta: Ardi, Apin, Damar and Nino (Winky Wiryawan, Udjo, Fauzi Baadilla and Fedi Nuril). Since they were young boys growing up in run-down apartments a few blocks from each other, they have played a game—racing each other around the blocks, chasing the sun (*mengejar matahari*). The film focuses principally on the boys as teenagers, when they are forced to confront the neighbourhood ruffians, a group of *preman* led by the heavily-tattooed Obet (Ade Habibie). Ironically, the group of friends—depicted with lighter skin perhaps to emphasise the tacit understanding that they are 'the good guys'—are no strangers to violence and intimidation. Damar and Ardi beat each other senseless over a girl, Rara (Agni Arkadewi); Damar savagely punches one of Obet's henchmen as a warning; and Damar, Ardi and Nino are involved in an extremely violent clash with Obet's gang after Obet knifed Apin. The violence is not limited to clashes between the boys and Obet's gang. Throughout the film, Damar, who grew up without a father, treats his mother appallingly. He is unable to restrain himself from shouting at her in anger each time she questions his violent behaviour and, it is evident by the time of the film's unfortunate climax—Damar's incarceration for his revenge-killing of Obet—that she has no control over him and perhaps never did.

Ardi is also prone to violence within his family home, albeit a strain of passive aggression. The film goes to great lengths to reveal the tension between Ardi and his retired police-officer father. Ardi's father is a harsh disciplinarian who wants his son to follow in his footsteps. Unfortunately, Ardi is an aspiring artist and has little interest in joining the police force.[3] They pass each other wordlessly in the narrow steps outside their apartment, or manoeuvre around each other uncomfortably inside the claustrophobic apartment. This uneasy silence is broken by episodes when Ardi is either lectured or harshly berated by his father for his delinquent behaviour. Ardi's response is to burn with rage, to cry in shame and to make crude artistic caricatures of his father, whom he depicts as a fire-breathing ogre dressed in a police uniform. Later, he unleashes his passive aggression by playing a key role in the street fighting outlined above. Somewhat worryingly, Indonesian film critics have tended not to raise concerns over the appalling amount of violence in the film; the fact that the so-called 'good guys'—Ardi, Damar and their friends—are just as prone to violent acts as their *preman* foes is also not questioned. Instead, critics tend to highlight plot flaws, the poor dialogue, the mordant soundtrack, inconsequential roles for women, that actors in their mid-20s play teenagers, and other absurdities. Consider the following telling review by the *Jakarta Post* reviewer Hera Diani (2004):

…all four of the men are too old for their parts. Many other aspects of the film do not make sense. It is hard to believe that teenage boys living in a slum area can afford to buy their friend a brand new videocam. And while we expect some silly, macho stuff from testosterone-charged teenage boys, we instead get Ardi crying in his room after a row with his old man. We listen to sage words of wisdom that are so sentimental and mushy that nobody would believe a 16-year-old youth would say such things. Worse still, the story abruptly ends every time Rara walks in. The absurdities build to a climax as the film fast forwards to the future, with Ardi coming home smiling, wearing a police uniform.

Soedjarwo was not discouraged. After making another movie, *Tentang dia* (About her) (2005), he quickly began work on *9 naga*, a project similar to *Mengejar matahari*, which he hoped would help him move beyond his highly lucrative teenage coming-of-age films into a film for adults depicting adult themes, particularly masculine themes.

Although not a sequel to *Mengejar matahari*, *9 naga* is also devoted to the portrayal of the relationships among urban men and their involvement in criminality. The film's emphasis on the twin themes of masculinity and violence was inadvertently advertised well before it was released. In December 2005 the Board of Film Censorship publicly expressed concern over two aspects of *9 Naga*'s eye-catching poster—the movie's provocative slogan and the dominant and provocative image of a shirtless Fauzi Baadilla (who plays Lenny in the film). The offending slogan, '*Manusia terbaik di Indonesia adalah seorang penjahat*' (The best Indonesian is a criminal), was considered to verge on incitement to violence and criminal behaviour. Furthermore, given the large number of law-abiding Indonesian citizens, it was deemed patently untrue. The image of Baadilla was controversial because it revealed his navel and a tuft of pubic hair above his low-slung jeans. As a result, there were unsubstantiated rumours that the film would be banned, rumours the Board of Film Censorship strenuously denied (*Kompas* 2005). Another rumour suggested that the media furore was little more than a publicity stunt aimed at generating interest in the film (Yordenaya 2005). Eventually, the offending slogan was removed from the posters and the section revealing Baadilla's nether regions discretely deleted (Dian 2005).

The irony is that, despite the poster's gangsterish tagline and image of a shirtless rough-and-tumble Baadilla, the movie failed to live up to expectations and was panned by some critics: 'Turns out it's a snoozefest melodrama that runs at a snail's pace and has no connection whatsoever to its title and tagline' (Diani 2006). Other critics, however, poured praise on the film. Consider the following comments from Leila Chudori (2006):

The thing is, when was the last time you emerged from a cinema after watching an Indonesian film which made your heart so proud? When was the last time you discussed an Indonesian film continuously all night? *Ibunda*? *Tjut Nyak Dhien*? *Nagabonar*? *Ada apa dengan cinta*? I'm sure it has been a long time. [*9 naga*] is the next film that will lead to endless discussion, contemplation and thought. Ah, as it turns out Indonesian cinema still has a pulse. Rudi [Soedjarwo] has fulfilled his promise to nurture it.

The film was also screened at the prestigious Rotterdam International Film Festival, and has been shown on Australian cable television.

9 naga revolves around Marwan (Lukman Sardi), Donny (Donny Alamsyah) and Lenny (Fauzi Baadilla), three childhood friends turned hit men living in an urban slum in Jakarta. The three friends have now grown up and they rail against their harsh new realities. Donny wants to come clean and plans to open a silk-screen shop. The others also struggle with inner turmoil, torn between the need to make a decent living, the need to live up to childhood loyalties and the need to face the demands of their new family situations. Ultimately, the key thematic impulse underpinning the film is relationships—relationships between men in particular.

Yet the masculine relationships in this film are inscribed in the same way as the shirtless Baadilla poster—as defensive, passive and emotionally and sensually deprived. Each man abhors being a hit man, but each is unable to break free. They are also unable to resolve their feelings of guilt and hopelessness. Their daily lives and relationships are consequently empty and banal. Donny, for instance, has his soccer-playing brother to divert his attention, but the relationship between the two brothers is passionless. Later Donny is accidentally shot and killed by Marwan, so in one sense his suffering is relieved. For his guilt-ridden partners in crime, there is no relief. Lenny has an insipid love affair with an inexpressive and uninteresting Batak girl who is unable to speak Indonesian; for most of the film Lenny is unable to summon the courage to address her. More importantly, Marwan, the main character of the film, has a loving wife, Ajeng (Ajeng Sardi), and a son, but his relationships with them are strained. Although moments of intimacy are shared, many words are left unspoken. This is in stark contrast to when he is with his male colleagues. Indeed, out in the streets in the company of his colleagues he is quite animated. Interestingly, he frequently calls them *bencong* (faggot) if they suggest that they would prefer to be with their girlfriends or at home with their families. From this habit alone we can see that in Marwan's homophobic world anything less than a display of *gagah* or virile *maskulinitas* is positively gay.

Meanwhile, beyond providing a steady income of dirty money, Marwan makes little effort to improve his home life. Indeed, he refuses to reveal where he disappears to every evening. He also fails to explain why he returns home agitated and drunk, with a pocketful of cash. His disabled wife asks him repeatedly to take his son to be immunised; he makes little effort to do so. Later, when confronted outright for his inaction, he sullenly refuses to help and his passive aggression and melancholy increases as the film goes on. Marwan's internalised rage, it is worth noting, mirrors the behaviour of other fictional characters examined in this book, such as Pramoedya's Minke, Ayu Utami's Wis and *Kuldesak*'s Andre.

It could be argued that Marwan's family is a microcosm of a shift in dominant forms of *maskulinitas* in Indonesia. But Marwan is unwilling to let the femininity of his wife control his masculinity, albeit an increasingly embattled sense of masculinity. His melancholy and his closedness to his wife and child are underpinned by the weakening of traditional gender roles among struggling families eking out an existence in metropolitan slums. On the one hand, he is expected to support his family financially, which he does. Yet on the other hand, it is necessary for him to do more, especially as his wife is in a wheelchair. Instead, he spends long periods of time sleeping in, moping around the house or arguing. Oddly enough he has many redeeming qualities that suggest that he might even *want* to do more, including his wry sense of humour, fleeting moments of deep affection for his wife and his obvious love for his child. Respected film critic, Leila Chudori (2006), observes:

> The husband-and-wife scenes between Marwan and his wife, Ajeng, are deeply intimate, deeply sweet, and deeply bittersweet. Their bedroom dialogue (ranging from everyday things such as the discovery of a strand of grey in Ajeng's hair to the problem of their child's immunisation) flows realistically, a realism which hasn't been offered by Indonesian film-makers since the passing of Teguh Karya.

Yet there is no indication that Marwan's redeeming qualities are underpinned by an open attitude to alternative forms of employment and *maskulinitas*. Therefore, his descent into the depths of violent criminality and theft at the conclusion of the film—supposedly so that his family can afford to move out of the city and live in a nice house outside Jakarta—is depressingly predictable. It is also a damning indictment of the marginalisation of men in Indonesia's urban environment, where shifting gender patterns inspired by social, political and economic change mean nothing in the face of the endemic shame and hopelessness of crippling poverty. This also highlights the fact that for many Indonesian men, if not the majority, their masculine dominance has assumed a benign and uncontested form. What is worrying about this is that it suggests that masculine violence—be it domestic, political or religious, personalised or nationalised—appears set to continue unchecked in a country that is already racked by violence, on screen and off screen. Unfortunately, Soedjarwo's subsequent forays into the horror genre reiterate the violent impact of hegemonic masculinity. As we shall see, hegemonic masculinity in Indonesia, where *maskulinitas* equals rape and murder and femininity equals monstrosity and victimhood, is itself something of a horror show.

Horror and the violence of hegemonic masculinity

At the same time that *Mengejar matahari* and *9 naga* were released, Rudi Soedjarwo produced one of Indonesia's most notorious horror films, *Pocong 2* (2006). It was the sequel to *Pocong*, also produced in 2006 and banned by the Board of Film Censorship, apparently because it was so sadistic (Kartikawati 2006). The controversy over *Pocong* was used as a clever 'marketing gimmick to promote its successor, *Pocong 2*, which cheekily put up 'Scarier than the banned *Pocong*' as its poster tag line' (Iwan 2008). The marketing strategy paid off and the film had decent audiences. Some of the reviews were quite positive. According to Rizal Iwan (2008):

> *Pocong 2* garnered acclaims as a clever and heart-pounding scare that brought modern Indonesian horror to a new level. Rudi's by-then usual use of natural settings, non-ambitious lighting and handheld camerawork—as a part of the low-budget, express filmmaking movement he introduced with his previous film *Mendadak Dangdut* (Suddenly Dangdut)—worked to the film's advantage by giving its terrors a sense of immediacy and realism. Monty Tiwa's witty, well-written script breathed fresh air in to a genre that seldom paid serious attention to storytelling, and steered the film to break out from the clutter of revenge-from-the-grave plot cliches.

Some film-goers have claimed that it is Indonesia's all-time best and scariest horror movie:

> This movie is freakin scary. after the exams, my MT teacher showed us this movie during MT periods. i can confirm to anyone that i've never screamed this loud while watching a horror movie in my life. seriously, for me, this ghost, the POCONG is very scary & in this movie, its face is really,really scary & not as fake as one can see in some horror movies.i really salute the producer & director of this movie as they've really scared the living daylights out of me & my friends. Great job guys & for those who;ve yet to catch it, please do.i can guarantee u won't regret it. (Sweetnarah 2008)

Others have described its weaknesses in terms of production and plot. The following response is instructive:

> They do not come any more mediocre than "Pocong 2", Rudy Soetjarwo's [sic] very crude and painfully amateurish movie. So basic was this movie, in terms of plot, casting and execution, you would be tempted to dismiss it within the first 20 minutes if you are after those perfectly-shot Korean or Japanese horrors. With it apparently filmed within seven days, you have to give it to Rudy—"Pocong 2" is so incredibly bad, it's actually good! (Cinema Online 2008)

The two main characters of the movie are Maya (Revalina Tamat) and Andin (Risty Tagore), sisters living together after the death of their parents. With the help of Maya's fiancé Adam (Ringgo Agus Rahman), they decide to rent accommodation in a deserted apartment block. The building is haunted by a ghostly monster covered in a white shroud, traditionally known as a *pocong*. Andin is the first to be terrorised by the monster and becomes extremely unwell. Eventually Maya consults a *dukun* (shaman) to solve the mystery. In order to elicit the underlying cause of the monster's appearance, the *dukun* gives Maya the power to see in the supernatural realm. But his intervention makes things much worse because, with her new powers, Maya suddenly begins seeing monsters everywhere.

Most reviewers highlight the role of the *pocong*, which is certainly the film's obsession. *Pocong 2* does not venture far beyond one episode of the *pocong* terrorising Maya and her sister after another. There is a belated attempt to add a back plot to the film, once Maya decides to find out why the *pocong* is manifesting itself in her life. As it turns out, the *pocong* is the embodied spirit of a teenage girl who was raped, beaten and buried alive several years earlier. Her vengeful brother, who is insane, also inhabits the apartment block. Despite the *pocong*'s ability to pop up unannounced when it is least expected, the most horrific aspect of the movie for me is the rape–revenge theme. The movie begins with the incredibly brutal capture, rape and murder of the teenage girl whose spirit becomes the *pocong*. Later, the *pocong*'s monstrous presence is a warning to Maya and Andin that another rapist is on the loose. The warning is misunderstood and in a nightmarish denouement Andin is raped and kidnapped. Eventually she is rescued just as she, covered in a white shroud, is about to be buried alive.

There is no doubt that this movie is violently misogynistic, and I would argue that it reinforces Indonesia's patriarchal order.[4] First of all, as in many horror movies around the world, female sexuality is punished in *Pocong 2* and femininity is equated with victimhood. This seems to be because the three main female protagonists in the film, Andin, Maya and her boss, a philosophy professor, exhibit a lack of traditional femininity and a surplus of masculine attributes. Andin, for example, has an androgynous name and she is *nekad*—she smokes, drinks and attends parties. It is implied that she is sexually active. As a result, the chaste older sister Maya blames Andin's horrific experiences with the *pocong* on delusions arising from her shameful (*memalukan*) behaviour. Ultimately, Andin becomes catatonic—a 'perfidious symbol of frigidity' (Rieser 2001)—before being raped. Like the monster, she is abandoned, humiliated and destroyed. The viewer has no choice but to empathise with what is called in horror discourse the 'final girl', Maya. But Maya, in the mould of the final girl, is similarly victimised for not following patriarchal terms of sexuality and behaviour. Indeed, Maya is also punished for her *nekad* progressiveness; as an assistant lecturer, she is sexually harassed by two lewd male students. The initial viewing of the apartment is also instructive. While her hapless boyfriend is defecating in the toilet in full view of the *pocong*—a truly revolting scene of 'horrific humour' which is common in Indonesian horror (Heider 1991)—Maya jumps the gun by choosing the questionable accommodation without consultation. Thus Maya oversteps the boundaries of conservative feminine behaviour and, in the masculinised logic of the film, is thoroughly deserving of what happens later.

Maya's supervisor, a philosophy professor played by respected actress Henidar Amroe, is also punished for her failure to follow the heterosexual contract. She is punished for her success as an academic and failure as a mother. She walks with a serious limp and late in the movie it is implied that this is closely connected with the death of one of her children, a daughter; once Maya can see in the supernatural realm, she sees the spirit of the dead daughter entwined around her mother's leg, thus causing the disability. It is also worth noting that Maya colludes with her supervisor to analyse the *pocong* phenomenon by pseudo-philosophical means. Their use of rationality, as opposed to using tradition, mysticism or religion to 'fight fire with fire', does not seem to be a normative feminine response to the ordeal. Rather, in a country where rationalism was linked with the pragmatic and pro-Western rationalism of the Suharto regime, to fight the supernatural through philosophy takes on a masculinist tone. After all, many government ministers have complained about the irrationality of Indonesian horror on TV and in film, its promotion of superstition and its lack of educational value. In the New Order era, there were concerns that these factors might hamper the dominant discourse of the New Order state, the development of Indonesia into a modern nation (van Heeren 2007).

Masculinist or not, whatever method Maya uses to save her sister and herself, she is doomed. Consider the alternative mode of action; by allowing her two over-sexed students to take her to visit a *dukun*, Maya deals with the haunting in a way that maintains Indonesia's conservative gender system. In other words, by consulting a *dukun*, a paragon of traditional masculine power, Maya's non-traditional femininity is disavowed and subordinated to the patriarchal social system. Paradoxically, Maya suffers from not being feminine enough in one way and not being masculine enough in another. As McLarty points out: 'Contemporary horror seems doubly dependent on images of the feminine for its postmodern paranoia: it simultaneously associates the monstrous with the feminine and communicates postmodern victimization through images of feminization' (McLarty 1996:234, quoted in Rieser 2001:387).

Secondly, as far as I can tell the *pocong* of Soedjarwo's *Pocong 2* is assigned feminine attributes and is thus an example of the 'monstrous-feminine' (Creed 1993). Many of the monsters populating the post-New Order horror boom are marked as biologically female, including most of the *hantu* (ghosts) and *kuntilanak* (ghostly witches) of *Jelangkung* (2001) and its sequel *Tusuk Jelangkung* (Penetrating Jelangkung) (2003); *Suster ngesot* (The dragging nurse) (2007) and its sequels; and *Terowongan Casablanca: Kuntilanak merah* (The Casablanca tunnel: the red witch) (2007). The monstrous-feminine is displayed in Soedjarwo's predecessor to *Pocong 2*, as well as its sequels, *Pocong 3* (2007) and *Pocong vs kuntilanak* (Shrouded vs the witch) (2008). The latter film, modelled on *Freddy vs Jason* (2003), presents us with a feminised parody of the clash between two male icons of American horror, Freddy Krueger and Jason Voorhees. Soedjarwo's most recent film, *40 hari bangkitnya pocong* (40 days of the shrouded's resurrection) (2009), continues the lucrative *pocong* franchise.

Unlike Western horror, Indonesian horror appears to be dominated historically by the monstrous-feminine. Since *Ratu Ular* (The Snake Queen) in 1972, horror has dominated New Order cinema (Heider 1991; van Heeren 2007) and, in my opinion, feminised monsters have dominated the genre.[5] This is demonstrated amply by the title of *Ratu Ular*, not to mention many others titles such as *Pembalasan Ratu Laut Selatan* (Revenge of the Queen of the South Sea) (1988), *Bangunnya Nyai Roro Kidul* (The awakening of Nyai Roro Kidul) (1985), *Putri kunti'anak* (The witch's daughter) (1988) and *Kisah cinta Nyi Blorong* (The love story of Nyi Blorong) (1989). Titles such as these suggest that Indonesian horror, from the New Order onwards, is dominated by a semi-feminised discourse. The monstrous femininity represented by Soedjarwo's *pocong* is deeply emblematic of Indonesian horror as a whole. There are also many feminine signifiers in *Pocong 2* that situate Soedjarwo's work firmly in the global horror tradition. For instance, there are enveloping maternal signifiers, including: images of *vagina dentata* (represented by the sinister lift doors to the apartment, which rarely open and, when they do, are a source of distinct unease); the intrauterine setting (represented by the cavernous apartment building); the dangers associated with the lack of the maternal (represented by Maya's ineffectual mothering of her little sister after the death of their parents, as well as the rapist whose mother, father and sister were sadistically murdered); and feminine men (represented by Maya's toilet-sitting boyfriend, who does nothing to protect Maya from the unwelcome sexual advances of other men and is also hopelessly ineffectual in dealing with the terror Maya and Andin face). Soedjarwo's use of monsters with non-normative feminine attributes, however, ensures that we must treat his work within the cultural logic of Indonesian horror.

At this point we can ask: Is the post-1998 horror cycle reactionary, in the sense that it portrays the normative male identity as being under attack from non-normative femininity? In other words, is the most recent obsession with the monstrous-feminine possibly a pro-feminist artistic 'corrective' of contemporary Indonesia's masculine cast? After all, as the *dukun* in *Pocong 2* helpfully explains, a *pocong*'s presence is nothing more than a manifestation of the supernatural realm attempting to correct disorder in the physical realm. Some have argued that cycles of horror movies occur at times of heightened social and political decay or instability (Carroll 1990; Gladwin 2003), thus reinforcing the *dukun*'s explanation. Certainly the post-New Order horror cycle reflects the deep social malaise associated with Indonesia's chaotic, post-authoritarian political culture, not to mention the crippling effects of the nation's ongoing economic disorder. Such an analysis is uncontroversial in the Indonesian context. But does the monstrous-feminine add something new to the 'horror cycle = sociopolitical instability' equation? After all, like Soedjarwo's *pocong*, Indonesian women have suffered more than most and have much more to recuperate. Men have their own difficulties, of course, but women have more. As Dorothea Rosa Herliany says about her aims as a poet: 'I prefer to stand up against oppression. It just so happens that women are the ones who are more oppressed' (Herliany, quoted in Nurrohmat 2007b:70). At a stretch, one could also argue that the spate of movies depicting feminised monsters wreaking havoc is evidence of the Indonesian feminine's backlash against the humiliations and oppression of colonialism, patriarchy and masculinised state power.

But I would be reluctant to push this line of analysis too far. First of all, most of those writing and making horror films are men who write and film from an undeniably male gaze and point of view. For instance, in *Pocong 2* and many other similar horror films, we rarely see the horror unfolding through the eyes of the female protagonists. This serves to distance the male viewer from the terror and to objectify, or even humiliate, the female protagonist in distress. As Rieser (2001:384–5) observes of the slasher film:

> One might even propose that male spectators do not identify in a straight-forward way with the female protagonist (in the sense of feeling to be her) but rather empathize with her. Witness, for example, that the gaze of the camera is only sometimes with her (and even more rarely through her eyes), while at other times "her" point of view is subverted by shots that are looking down on her, huddled and shivering in a corner (a camera angle of central importance, it seems, since it is reproduced numerous times on posters and video jackets). Thus, the film lets a male spectator feel her terror, but it remains nonetheless a female who serves as the site/sight of terror.

Similarly, in *Pocong 2* we watch the monstrous creeping up on Maya and Andin; the monstrous does not creep up on us, the viewers. Soedjarwo ensures through audiovisual techniques that it is the sisters, rather than the viewer, who are offered up to the monster.

Secondly, adolescent males constitute the majority of the Indonesian horror audience. Extending Rieser's argument, the male viewers presumably *enjoy* objectifying not only the female protagonists but also the monstrous (in *Pocong*'s case non-hegemonic femininity) and then expelling the monstrous, thus ultimately reinforcing heterosexual masculinity. Thirdly, anecdotal evidence suggests that the financial backers behind the horror genre are predominantly male businessmen, interested in little more than a good financial return. The mixed quality of the many horror films churned out over the last ten years or so attests to this fact. Finally, and most importantly, Indonesia's traditional myths and legends have long objectified female sexuality. Protean archetypes of monstrous witches, sorceresses, goddesses and ghosts have been embodying the dangers of unleashed female sexuality for centuries, as part of a traditional, conservative and patriarchal social order. These archetypes became part of the official discourse for New Order ideals of womanly behaviour—or rather for what was *not* the feminine ideal. Hatley discusses the ways in which the New Order state's conservative, family-centred gender ideology was built upon longstanding cultural forms:

> The archetypal ideal of wifely fidelity and devotion embodied in traditional forms of theatre in figures such as Sita and Sumbadra was recalled in novels of the 1970s and 1980s in female protagonists explicitly modelled on these prototypes. Popular films represented both the seductive allure and lethally dangerous power of the contrasting figure of the autonomous, sexually assertive woman. Nyai Lara Kidul, mythical queen of the South Sea, for example, appeared briefly as a voluptuous sex goddess before transforming into a hideous fanged hag reminiscent of Rangda, the widow-witch of Balinese dance-drama, emblematic of the frightful power of female sexual energy uncontrolled by male order (Hatley 2002b:131).

They say that when mud is thrown, some will stick; Sears (2007a) has observed that women in Indonesia, and Javanese women in particular, have a reputation for being uncouth, uncontrolled and overly passionate. In other words, beneath a refined veneer in the manner of the *wayang*'s virtuous feminine figures such as Sita and Sumbadra lie the potential horrors of a dormant Nyai Roro Kidul or Rangda.

It is safe to say that contemporary images of the debased feminine are closely associated with masculine fears and masculine attempts to control female behaviour and reinforce heterosexual masculinity. As we have seen in the discussion of the female protagonists of *Pocong 2*, horror films of post-New Order Indonesia can hardly be considered as pro-feminist projects. It seems unlikely that monstrous femininity could be considered as a feminine response to the shame and humiliation of historical, political and domestic repression. It is far more likely to be a manifestation of the rage of normative masculinity and the monstrosity beyond that rage.

Conclusion

This chapter has discussed the violent tendencies of heterosexual masculinity in post-New Order Indonesia, where male violence can almost be considered as a normative response to the shame and humiliation of poverty, unemployment and associated feelings of hopelessness. By analysing several films by Rudi Soedjarwo, I have also highlighted the worrying nature of conservative representations of gender. Of greatest concern is Soedjarwo's violently misogynistic 'horrid horror' including the low-budget *Pocong* and *Pocong 2*, of which the latter was released in top-end cinemas. As discussed, in films of this ilk, women on the whole are victimised and progressive femininity is violently punished. Soedjarwo's horror conflates hegemonic masculinity with rape and murder and femininity with monstrosity. I have suggested that these might be common themes in the Indonesian horror genre, which is experiencing a spectacular boom in the post-authoritarian era in the cinema and on television (Arps & van Heeren 2006; van Heeren 2007).

It is important to note that other commentators have not categorised the monstrous-feminine as a dominant feature of Indonesian horror films. According to van Heeren (2007), the four distinct features of Indonesian horror films of the New Order are the presence of supernatural powers, humour, the use of sex[6] and the use of religious symbols and *kyai* (religious leaders) as protagonists. In the post-New Order period there have been minor changes to these features; new styles and new topics have been introduced and *kyai* are absent. Unlike the New Order era when horror films were shown in lower-class movie-theatres (complete with cigarette smoke and live bats), newly released horror films are now shown in top-end air-conditioned cinemas (van Heeren 2007). More importantly, the biological gender of the monsters or supernatural entities populating the genre is not discussed. Van Heeren and others may not have noted the monstrous-feminine in their analysis because, as Heider (1991) observes, Indonesian horror films have closely resembled the Indonesian folk-legend genre, which dramatises traditional legends or folktales. As a result, traditional folk beliefs and the presence of supernatural entities, witches, ghosts, ghostly sorceresses and ghouls such as *kuntilanak*, *hantu* and *pocong* are ubiquitous and unquestioned in horror films. More importantly, the close links between femininity and the supernatural were firmly established in myth and legend, long before the emergence of cinema in the archipelago. As demonstrated in this chapter, the link between monstrosity and the feared power and potency of female sexuality has been an important aspect of these links.

Throughout Indonesia's recent history, the monster has traditionally appeared as a double for the woman, an eruption of the normally repressed sexuality of the subservient and civilised female. Thus, many of the post-1998 cinematic monsters are merely the latest in a long line of mythical and folk legend archetypes embodying the dangers of unleashed female sexuality, including Rangda, the horrific widow-witch of Bali, and Nyai Roro Kidul, the terrifying Javanese goddess of the South Seas. In the New Order era, images of the debased feminine were closely associated with attempts to control female behaviour and reinforce heterosexual masculinity. This was an important element of the state's attempts to engender patriarchal order and, thus, social and political order. In the post-New Order period, as I have argued here, images and narratives of the monstrous-feminine are little more than updated dramatisations of archetypal gender tropes designed to rejuvenate patriarchal order, which has long been conflated with social order. The next chapter, which analyses a recent literary furore, will continue the horror theme. As we shall see, Indonesia's latest horror cycle—and its complex relationship with sex, gender and religion—has manifested itself in the poetry of Binhad Nurrohmat.

Notes

1   In his analysis of political homophobia, Boellstorff is clearly writing in an exploratory mode, and thus it could be argued that he is not 'overstating' anything.

2   Nicholas Saputra, 2007 Melbourne Indonesian Film Festival, 6 October 2007.

3   Aspects of this fictional father–son relationship might well mirror the relationship between Rudi Soedjarwo and his own father, Anton Soedjarwo, a retired high-ranking police officer.

4   This analysis is inspired by Klaus Rieser's essay on masculine violence in Western 'slasher' films (Rieser 2001).

5   Anecdotal evidence supports this conclusion. For example, according to Indonesian film scholar Dina Listiorini, 'actually it's not only horror films, even in Indonesian *sinetron* (soap opera) the criminals are women. What I mean is the ones who are evil are women. By coincidence I've been collecting religious *sinetron* screening on commercial TV in Jakarta and broadcasting nationally...like RCTI, Indosiar and so on...and truly women are the ones who are victimised or the perpetrators of violence' (Personal communication, 29 November 2008).

6   In van Heeren's discussion, the presence of sex refers to representations of sexual activity rather than the gender of the monster: 'Sex emerged in 1970s' horror films and was used to spice up a movie. But by the 1980s and 1990s, the use of erotic elements to the level of smut and kitsch had become the main ingredient of such films. The central themes of those 'horror-sex' films were men having an affair, *tante girang* (literally 'cheerful aunt'; a pushy woman of loose morals), rape, and promiscuity. Sex was used not only in horror films but was part of a wider trend of Indonesian films from the 1970s that capitalized on its selling point. However, it was only in horror films that sex was fairly explicit' (van Heeren 2007:213).

chapter six

Scandal, transgression and the politics of the erotic: the poetry of Binhad Nurrohmat

> If we treat the carnivalesque as an instance of a wider phenomenon of transgression we move beyond Bakhtin's troublesome *folkloric* approach to a political anthropology of *binary extremism* in class society. This transposition not only moves us beyond the rather unproductive debate over whether carnivals are politically progressive or conservative, it reveals that the underlying structural features of carnival operate far beyond the strict confines of popular festivity and are intrinsic to the dialectics of social classification as such.
>
> Peter Stallybrass and Allon White (1986:26)

Teeuw, in his canonical textual analysis of modern Indonesian literature (1996), attempts to sum up the general situation in Indonesian literature between 1965 and the late 1970s. Although he contends that a great deal has gone on and that there is a wide interest within Indonesian society about what goes on within Indonesian literary circles, he bemoans the irrelevant position overall of literature and the lack of genuine involvement of Indonesian writers in the nation-building project. The only thing worth noting, it appears, was a literary scandal:

> It is perhaps by no means a coincidence that the literary issue which has drawn by far the most interest from Indonesian society at large in the period under discussion has been what Jassin has styled the *heboh sastra*, or literary sensation, of 1968, which dragged on well into the seventies (Teeuw 1996:65).

The sensation in question refers to the publication and reception of Kipandjikusmin's infamous short story, 'Langit makin mendung' (The darkening sky) (1968). The Kipandjikusmin scandal occurred after earlier controversies, including the storms of objections over AA Navis's short stories 'Robohnya surau kami' (The collapse of our prayer house) (1955) and 'Man Rabbuka' (Who is your Lord?) (1957), reprinted in *Antologi lengkap cerpen AA Navis* (Fanany 2005). In each case significant numbers of conservative Muslims launched spirited attacks on the authors, condemning their stories and the magazines in which they were published. In response, artists and intellectuals—many of them Muslim—defended the authors and their backers, and campaigns were launched in defence of literary and artistic freedom.

Teeuw and others have noted that each of these episodes has very little to do with the aesthetic qualities of the stories in question. Rather, the controversies highlighted the need felt by Islamic groups at the time to stake their claims for social and political relevance. Given the frequency with which radical Islamist groups have recently turned their violent attentions to artists and the arts, is a similar pattern occurring in post-New Order Indonesia? I would argue that Indonesia's present culture of censoriousness is uncannily similar to the brief historical period in which Jassin's literary furore occurred. For this reason, this chapter will examine Jassin's case briefly, as a means of introducing the latest literary sensation to hit Indonesian shores—the awarding of the inaugural KAKUS-Listiwa award for the worst writing of 2007 to the young, ethnically Javanese, Jakarta-based poet Binhad Nurrohmat for his second collection of poetry, *Bau betina* (The smell of women) (2007a). The KAKUS-Listiwa episode and accompanying furore occurred soon after *Bau betina* was unsuccessfully nominated for the prestigious Khatulistiwa Literary Award 2007.

The episode raises several questions about the production and reception of writing in Indonesia, including: How free is Indonesia's new freedom of expression, particularly literary expression? Now that state censorship has come to an end, has censorship in Indonesia really ended or merely taken other forms? Finally, what do literary scandals or mock awards tell us about the nature of writing in Indonesia? In answering these questions, this chapter also responds to Teeuw's pronouncements about the state of Indonesian writing in the late 1960s and early 1970s.

Evidently Teeuw takes a dim view of the Jassin furore and has no interest in what a literary scandal might tell us about that period of Indonesian history. For Teeuw, the Kipandjikusmin sensation appeared to be much ado about nothing and, if anything, merely evidence for the declining relevance of Indonesian literature. In the post-authoritarian context, however, could a literary sensation be possibly regarded as an indication of the opposite—the increasing relevance of literature in Indonesia's public discourse? On first glance the answer to this question would be that this is not the case. Nowadays unruly demonstrations by Islamist groups are almost never directed at authors and literary journals. Although some writers have provoked heated criticism from Muslim fundamentalists, contemporary targets for mob justice and legal prosecution include rock stars, *Playboy* editors, Islamic sects and artists and their models. Yet writers and their texts still play an important role in Indonesia's lively cultural discourse. Literature, as a fundamental element of Indonesia's national culture, has long been highly regarded, even if few Indonesians actually read novels, short stories or poetry collections.

Despite the importance of the questions raised by KAKUS-Listiwa award, this chapter will argue that the controversy surrounding the KAKUS-Listiwa award need not be considered as a barometer of the health or relevancy of writing in Indonesia. To re-examine the perennial occupation of writers and critics alike, that is, the health or otherwise of modern Indonesian literature, would be missing the point. Rather, I see the KAKUS-Listiwa as yet another example of a kneejerk response to a sense of masculinised *malu* or humiliation. In this chapter I argue that emotions such as shame and embarrassment have unequivocally underpinned the KAKUS-Listiwa and other gendered literary scandals, especially in recent years. As suggested previously in this book, normative masculinity in Indonesia has been quite sensitive to the symbolic threats posed by other categories, including non-normative masculinity, undomesticated femininity and the monstrous-feminine.

I argue that Binhad Nurrohmat's poetry has also invoked a sense of threat to normative masculinity, as demonstrated by the condemnations of socially conservative male critics. In my opinion the perceived threat has emerged from Binhad's poetic engagement with the realms of transgression and taboo, encompassing the politics of the erotic and representations of normative and non-normative masculinities. Concurring with Bodden's analysis of the condemnation of Djenar Maesa Ayu's post-New Order fiction which focuses on the sexual adventurism of the Indonesian elite and middle class (Bodden 2007), I argue that the critical condemnation of Binhad's poetry reveals strong continuities between the post-authoritarian era and the New Order, particularly in the area of what is morally acceptable and what is not, a form of moral 'binary extremism', as mentioned in this chapter's epigraph. Significantly, Bodden utilises Stallybrass and White's theorisation of transgression (Stallybrass & White 1986), which is, in turn, inspired by Bakhtin's theories of the carnivalesque (Bakhtin 1981). Stallybrass and White argue that Renaissance bourgeois society discursively attempted to define its own ideals of society by separating and rejecting the peasantry, the urban poor, subcultures and marginals, using a hierarchical discourse of 'high' and 'low', 'human' and 'non-human'. They assert that the cultural categories of the high and low, noble and debased and the rest were never entirely separable. Indeed, they argue that transgressing the rules of hierarchy and order in any one of these cultural domains could have major ramifications in the others.

Bodden (2007:97) argues that Indonesia has its own politicised culture of binary extremism or moral polarities:

> Modern Indonesian culture and society have, particularly since the onset of the New Order, been dominated by a state apparatus, governments, and ideologies which were informed to a considerable extent by the New Order's version of

Javanese aristocratic discourses (with an overlay of late nineteenth century Dutch bourgeois morality) of the way the world is and should be. One of the key classificatory binaries of these discourses was the distinction between *halus* and *kasar* (refined and crude, vulgar), which was also linked to notions of humanity and animality.

Although Bodden suggests that the realms of literature and cultural expression have demonstrated a healthy degree of autonomy from the state and its conservative ideologies, he also observes that notions of the lofty, refined nature of literature and art persist. Literature that is deemed to focus on sex, non-normative sexuality and representations of the lower sub-strata (of the body, of society, of place) is both desired and reviled. It is desired by middle-class consumers who have a transgressive interest or identification with the new cosmopolitanism and representations of sex and sexuality, a desire bred in part by New Order repression. It is reviled by the more socially conservative commentators 'who try to police and reinforce demarcations between high and low, polite and vulgar' (Bodden 2007:99) by claiming that such literature is *kasar*, or more commonly, vulgar. This 'bifurcated reaction', to borrow Bodden's terminology, has ensured that the books of female writers such as Djenar Maesa Ayu and male writers such as Binhad Nurrohmat are transgressive on multiple levels.

This chapter is arranged in three sections: a discussion of literary scandals in postcolonial Indonesia, as inspired by the observations of Teeuw; an analysis of the KAKUS-Listiwa scandal and its significance; and a discussion of representations of masculinities, horror, religion and the politics of the erotic in Binhad's literary output. The last of these three sections is an attempt to understand why Binhad's critics have been so vociferous. As in other chapters, the main discussion in this chapter is framed by Bakhtin's literary theories, particularly by his research on the transgressive nature of the carnival. In this respect I shall allude again to Stallybrass and White's theorisation of transgression (1986). I should also state from the outset that Binhad's erotic poetry, like Rudi Soedjarwo's films, is not exactly my cup of tea.[1] Questions of personal taste aside, Binhad's poems and their critical reception express something of the cultural zeitgeist of the post-New Order era and, therefore, deserve critical attention.

Heboh sastra: the case of Kipandjikusmin

Kipandjikusmin, like AA Navis, was a Muslim author. Unlike Navis, Kipandjikusmin was virtually unknown when his writing caused such a storm. His third published short story ensured that his name became immortalised in the modern Indonesian literary pantheon. Published in the August 1968 issue of *Sastra*, 'Langit makin mendung' provoked a negative reaction in various locations. First of all, a group of Muslims in Medan reacted angrily to the story and threatened legal action. There were similar reactions in several cities in Java, including Jakarta. A significant number of newspaper articles on the story and its negative reception appeared. There were even demonstrations. As Soenjono Dardjowidjojo (1974) observes, the Ministry of Religious Affairs was forced to issue a press release denouncing the publication of the story. Eventually the editor of *Sastra*, HB Jassin, was taken to court for publishing the offending story. According to Dardjowidjojo (1974:ii), 'The pressure from the community was so strong that on October 22, 1968, Kupandjikusmin made a public appeal requesting that *Langit Makin Mendung* be considered non-existent'. It was the last story he ever published.

Jassin, meanwhile, under threat of legal prosecution from an Islamic youth organisation, withdrew the offending edition of *Sastra*. His troubles intensified in 1970 when the Attorney-General took up the case and Jassin was summoned to appear in court. He was found guilty of insulting the religion of Islam and given a suspended gaol sentence. Jassin, however, refused to accept this sentence and took his case to a higher court. No further official decision was made; Deakin (1976) suggests that the court action was merely a temporary expedient to soothe ruffled emotions. Jassin heard nothing further and never revealed the true identity of Kipandjikusmin.

Kipandjikusmin's precise identity remains unclear to this day. Most commentators agree that Kipandjikusmin was a nom de plume. Some have argued that Kipandjukusmin was a pseudonym for Jassin himself, although this is extremely unlikely, as there is evidence that a number of writers were acquainted with Kipandjikusmin who was rumoured to be a young student from Yogyakarta. According to Deakin (1976), his real name was Sudihartono and his nom de plume was interpreted as being constructed from the phrase 'Kibarkan panji-panji komunisme' (Unfurl the banners of communism). If this interpretation is accurate, it was undeniably provocative to choose a name such as this just a few years after the anti-communist massacres of 1965.

Kipandjikusmin's perceived links with communism were hardly discussed. Instead, his tenuous links with Christianity, because of his years of schooling at a Catholic high school, were amplified. As a result, in the early 1970s a bizarre book analysing 'Langit makin mendung' from an Islamic perspective appeared. Written by a conservative Islamic theologian, Nazwar Sjamsu (1971), it consists of 167 pages of denunciation in which the author supports his case with pages of quotes from the Koran, in both Arabic script and Indonesian. For the majority of the readers ostensibly offended by 'Langit makin mendung', the most offensive aspect of the story lies in Kipandjikusmin's personification of God, which was said to be a violation of Islam. According to Dardjowidjojo (1974:ii),

> Kipandjikusmin was considered to have done even more harm by writing in a style referred to as *sembarangan*, that is, a style in which an author presents serious matters in a casual and careless manner. The dialogues between God and Prophet Muhammed, God's wearing old-fashioned gold-rimmed spectacles, the collision between Prophet Muhammed's vehicle and the Russian sputnik, plus some other points in the story were considered an insult to the Moslem religion in general and the Moslem followers in particular.

Sjamsu went further than this, claiming that by insulting and discrediting Islam the story promotes Christianity. In contrast, Jassin (1970) argued that the controversy was an overreaction, as the personification of God in 'Langit makin mendung' never aimed at offending Muslims because Kipandjikusmin's story was, first and foremost, fiction.

Ironically, over the years Kipandjikusmin's story has assumed legendary status, culminating in a book entitled *Pledoi sastra: kontroversi cerpen* Langit makin mendung *Kipandjikusmin* (A literary defence: the controversy of Kipandjikusmin's *The darkening sky* short story) (Dahlan & Hermani 2004). This collection republishes all four of Kipandjikusmin's short stories, including the infamous story that made his name, together with an extensive selection of essays on the 'Langit makin mendung' furore, most of which were written in the late 1960s and early 1970s. Also included is Jassin's lengthy legal defence oration, in which he highlights the fictional nature of 'Langit makin mendung' and defends Indonesian artists' right to free speech and creativity. We will see later in this chapter the manner in which this story is revered to the present day, its link with Binhad Nurrohmat and how similar episodes have continued to occur in Indonesia.

That *Pledoi sastra* emerged in the year 2004 is suggestive of a willingness to debate the role of censorship in Indonesia's literary history. Although the editors might not admit it, this retrospective turn was most probably inspired by continuing threats to freedom of expression in the post-authoritarian era. We shouldn't protest too much though, as a book such as this probably would not have been allowed to appear in the New Order era. Once again we are witnessing Bakhtinian dialogism in action. On the one hand, *Pledoi sastra* underlines once more the authoritarianism of the New Order and the cultural and religious sensitivities of the late 1960s in particular; on the other, this book reminds us of the present-day context of post-authoritarian Indonesia, with its army of cultural police. It is a dialogue involving the Kipandjikusmins of the New Order and also the Kipandjikusmins of today. As we shall see in the next section, it seems that cultural vigilantes—mostly men, of course—enjoy nothing more than a good literary scandal.

Literary sensations in the post-New Order period

Importantly, in the years following the resignation of Suharto and the demise of the New Order regime, there have been very few literary furores. Among the few literary sensations worth noting are questions surrounding the authorship of Ayu Utami's *Saman* (1998) and, more recently, Herlinatiens' literary representation of lesbian sexuality. As with the scandal experienced by Kipandjikusmin, the emergence of these sensations has allowed a number of unleashed societal energies to bubble to the surface. In the post-authoritarian context, these energies include deep-seated masculine fears of progressive femininity, the envy of mostly male Muslim intellectuals and the frustrations of Islamist-inclined organisations.

For much of 1998, hostile questions were raised as to the 'true' authorship of *Saman*. According to Hatley (1999:450), there were allegations that the text was 'in fact the work of a well-known *male* author'. Indeed, some felt that the close relationship and similar literary styles of Ayu and her mentor, Goenawan Mohamad, were reason enough to question the novel's authorship. After all, both were based in the Teater Utan Kayu literary community in Jakarta and there were even rumours of an affair between the two (Bodden & Hellwig 2007). Questions were also raised, particularly by men, over whether a woman could write so well in a male narrative voice, as Ayu did in much of *Saman* (Aveling 2007). During interviews Ayu seemed to be out of her depth at times. Hatley (1999:450) observes: 'Interviewers quiz her about particular references, from shadow puppet figures to botanical names of plants, and suggest that her conversation is somehow abrupt, in contrast to the fluent flow of her written work'. Nevertheless, questions about whether Ayu wrote her novel with any assistance were soon put to rest by indignant denials. According to Aveling (2007:20), most readers, especially women readers, felt that the unsubstantiated accusations were 'condescending and insulting'. Yet the fact that these remarks were aired so publicly and gathered so much momentum was reason enough for some to regard the rise of Ayu and other women writers like her as being deeply threatening. This was especially so in a thoroughly patriarchal society where the old restrictions, taboos and myths of womanhood remain (Hatley 1999).

Later, the publication of *Garis tepi seorang lesbian* (The margins of a lesbian) (Herlinatiens 2003) incited some controversy because of the novel's representations of lesbianism, not to mention Herlinatiens' background (Marching 2008). Herlinatiens (Herlina Tien Suhesti) was pictured on the back cover of the book wearing a *jilbab*, or veil for Muslim women. Lesbianism, it was argued, is immoral in Islam and Muslim writers such as Herlinatiens should be denounced for suggesting that one could be both a Muslim and a lesbian. Also worrying to their critics, the works of Herlinatiens and Ayu Utami featured unabashed representations of female sexuality. This theme has become de rigueur for almost all young women writers of note in the post-New Order period; besides Ayu and Herlinatiens, writers such as Djenar Maesa Ayu, Dewi Lestari, Nova Riyanti Yusuf, Ratih Kumala and Nukila Amal have all examined female sexuality in great detail, to the extent that this stream of writing has even gained its own pejorative label, *sastra wangi* (perfumed literature).

Adding fuel to the flames, critics, most of them male, have commented that the theme of female sexuality is little more than a marketing ploy (Marching 2008). In response, some critics have taken umbrage at any mention of the *sastra wangi* label, whether it be positive or negative (Guillermo 2007). Women writers have been largely ambivalent. Indeed, some women writers, including writers often linked to the *sastra wangi* brand, have stated publicly that they would prefer to distance themselves from the *sastra wangi* debate. Dorothea Rosa Herliany, for instance, has observed on a number of occasions that, although her poems refute patriarchy and discuss female sexuality, she is not a feminist and has never been a part of the *sastra wangi* stream. Indeed, Herliany has argued that her poetry is about much more than gender (Campbell 2002; Nurrohmat 2007b). By the same token, it is important to point out that there is no question that men are under attack in Dorothea's poetry. The poem 'Buku harian perkawinan' (Wedding diary) (Herliany 2001:24–5), for example, contains the following lines:

> When I married you, I never promised to be faithful.
>
> In fact, you agreed to be my slave.
>
> …
>
> Run as far as your man's feet can carry you, husband!
>
> Hide between your mother's thighs.
>
> *ketika menikahimu, tak kusebut keinginan setia.*
>
> *engkau bahkan telah menjadi budak penurutku.*
>
> …
>
> *berlarilah sejauh langkah kejantananmu, lelaki!*
>
> *bersembunyilah di antara ketiak ibumu.*[2]

This poem, spectacularly rejecting Indonesia's traditional notion of 'masculine power and female subordination' (Aveling 2001b:viii), is addressed to the narrator's husband. 'The husband', however, could just as easily be read in terms of men in general. Furthermore, the original Indonesian is '*lelaki*' which can be translated as 'man'. According to Aveling, Dorothea's 'writing presents a full-blooded, determined woman, demanding far more than mere complementariness: she wants equality, and perhaps *dominance*' (Aveling 2001b:ix). Perhaps not just equality and dominance in the bedroom and kitchen, I would add, but in society more generally, where males have long ruled supreme.

Dorothea's poetry and the relatively mild-mannered debates about the motives of young post-New Order women writers have appeared in the shadow of the increasing frustrations of primarily male Islamist-inclined elements of Indonesian society. Coupled with the uproar associated with the Danish cartoons and *Playboy*, the failed anti-pornography legislation of 2006 gave rise to popular fears about the return of censorship, self-censorship and the Islamisation of Indonesian society, culture and politics. As intimated in the previous chapter, the extent to which Indonesia's new freedom of expression is free needs to be interrogated.

The present political climate is clearly driving towards opening the media market. Since the fall of Suharto, the Indonesian media have seen an unprecedented boom and have become increasingly open, with only modest curbs on the freedom of expression (Sen & Hill 2000). Yet the political imperatives of post-Suharto politics have often turned out to be contradictory and chaotic. Moreover, there is often a considerable cultural lag between political implementation and social acceptance. For example, even if publication permits are no longer required and top-down censorship is no longer permissible, a new kind of censorship, sometimes involving private individuals and organisations, is alive and well, as demonstrated by the high-profile cases outline above. Furthermore, a strain of symbolic censorship was evident in the furores surrounding *Saman* and *Garis tepi seorang lesbian*—in the court of public opinion, where judge and jury consisted of male critics, many of them Muslim.

There have been other cases of censorial interference, involving both state and non-state agents, since Suharto's resignation. These include the banning of school history books examining the massacres of 1965–66 (Indoprogress 2007); the arbitrary censorship of selected cinematic releases (CCT 2007; Clark 2008a; Kartikawati 2006); protests against the production of certain cinematic projects (FPI 2008); the prosecution of leading fine artists and their models on indecency charges (Dirgantoro 2006); the prosecution of well-known rock musicians on blasphemy charges (Libforall Foundation 2006); the arbitrary banning of theatre productions involving some of Indonesia's most renowned playwrights and actors (ACI 2007; Forum Pembaca Kompas 2008); and several artists who have been outspoken in their opposition to the anti-pornography law have had their houses attacked (Hatley 2007). Although not an example of direct censorial interference as such, it is in the context outlined above that Binhad Nurrohmat was awarded the inaugural KAKUS-Listiwa Award of 2007.

Bau betina and the KAKUS-Listiwa Award

The KAKUS-Listiwa Award might have been welcomed merely as a practical joke, easily forgotten if it had not been taken so seriously by all parties concerned. The award was given under the aegis of Boemiputra, a literary community based in Tangerang, a satellite city west of Jakarta. Boemiputra's award notification, appearing on various newsletters and email listings, appeared to have been written tongue-in-cheek: 'To Binhad Nurrohmat we express Congratulations for the Poorness of Your Book! May your work in the future be a positive addition to the nation and its people'. The other nominees for the worst literature of 2007, all poets, form a who's who of contemporary Indonesian poetry: Soni Farid Maulana, M Fadjroel Rahman, Todung Mulya Lubis, Joko Pinurbo, Isbedy Setiawan ZS, Acep Zamzam Noor, Acep Iwan Saidi, Zen Hae and Amien Kamil.

A key reason for the furore caused by the award caused was that some observers felt it was not only a highly personal attack on Binhad but also, and more importantly, a slur on poetry itself and the prestigious Khatulistiwa Literary Award (KLA), Indonesia's leading literary award since it was established in 2001. As its organisers state, the KAKUS-Listiwa is a 'bentuk ejekan bagi Khatulistiwa Award' (a form of mockery of the Khatulistiwa Award). The first and most obvious hint that this might be the case lies in the naming of the mock award; 'KAKUS-Listiwa' (TOILET-Listiwa) is a humorous *plesetan* (pun) on *khatulistiwa* (equator). Secondly, Binhad's collection of poems *Bau betina* was one of the KLA nominations for Indonesia's best book of poetry for 2007. Binhad's nomination for the KLA and his subsequent win in the KAKUS-Listiwa was quite clearly a thumb on the nose to the organisers and jury of the KLA.[3] Thirdly, the prize money for the KLA is Rp 100,000,000 (approximately $US10, 000), quite a large sum by Indonesian standards. Mocking this extravagance, the KAKUS-Listiwa Award was Rp 100—barely 10 cents and equivalent to a public toilet's entry fee—and a trophy in the shape of a miniature toilet.

Richard Oh, spokesperson for the KLA, sensibly kept out of the debate. But Binhad was not reticent. After being alerted to his award via emails in late November 2007, Binhad entered the fray with his own succinct yet widely disseminated message. The use of capitals in the message, I would argue, highlights Binhad's ebullient mood at the time:

DEAR FELLOW BELIEVERS,

IT IS TRULY TOUCHING THE MANNER IN WHICH THEY ADORE ME. I REGARD THEIR TOILET AS THEIR VALENTINE'S ROSE FOR ME.

REGARDS,

BINHAD NURROHMAT (Nurrohmat 2007c)

The 'they' to whom Binhad refers are the writers and cultural activists connected to Boemiputra, including outspoken poets Wowok Hesti Prabowo and Saut Situmorang. The award ceremony was held in a public toilet in Ciceri in downtown Serang, Banten. The so-called ceremony was documented by a series of photos of the trophy being allegedly handed over to Binhad (or rather Binhad's stand-in, as he was in Jakarta at the time). It is worth noting that directly beneath the fake congratulatory handshake is a filthy toilet-bowl, above which a large poster of the cover of *Bau betina* hangs on the wall. Evidently a measure of artistic flair had gone into the occasion. Binhad was invited to attend the ceremony but was reported as being unable to make it. Binhad, however, asserts that he would have been more than willing to appear, so long as he received a proper written invitation. Keen to participate in a substantive dialogue, he had even prepared a speech for the occasion. The invitation never arrived, so the speech was never given.

Some commentators called for a statement of the KAKUS-Listiwa selection criteria. There were also calls for some sort of critical explanation of why *Bau betina* was considered the worst of the worst. As poet and critic Hasan Aspahani (2007) asks, 'how bad is *Bau betina*? Where are its shortcomings? Why is it considered poor? If the questions above are answered I think the Kakus-Litiwa [*sic*] will provide a huge contribution in improving Indonesian literature'. No information about the identity of the judging panel and their key judging criteria was released, so Aspahani's questions remain unanswered. Meanwhile, although unimpressed by the award, Binhad did eventually receive the trophy in the mail. It is presently gathering dust on a shelf in his modest office at his Jakarta residence.

In the midst of the KAKUS-Listiwa furore Binhad's colleagues were generally supportive. Consider the following words from fellow writer and poet Asep Sambodja (2007):

Any award whatsoever given to a writer or a work of literature needs to be humbly received by the winner. Whatever honour is given to the work, whether it is the worst work or the best, either way it can be said that the book has grabbed the reader's attention. The book in question has succeeded in influencing its readers. A good or bad label is relative. Consciously or unconsciously, the existence of Binhad Nurrohmat and even *Bau betina* has been brought to the public's attention. So congratulations to Binhad Nurrohmat. History has observed that the short story 'Langit makin mendung' was denounced and disparaged by its readers, yet even to this day it is still being discussed. As we are all possibly aware, in the late-1960s many short stories were written, but the only one that is still being talked about up until the present day is 'Langit makin mendung'. This is precisely because it was denounced. So, once more, congratulations to Binhad! Power to you sir!!!

Sambodja's reference to 'Langit Makin Mendung' is important, as it flatteringly locates Binhad's *Bau betina* in the pantheon of Indonesian literary history. Sambodja's comments perhaps also justify the manner in which I have introduced and analysed the KAKUS-Listiwa controversy—in terms of Jassin's notion of *heboh sastra*, coined in response to the 'Langit makin mendung' controversy. Although the actual awarding to the KAKUS-Listiwa was not in itself a denouncement of Binhad, members of the Boemiputra literary community commented widely on about their hostile intentions in making the award. Consider the following taunt by poet Saut Situmorang (2007): 'Ha ha ha…I bet his publishers are regretting like hell now giving in to all his desperate pleas to publish that rubbish!!! Ha ha ha…' With colleagues like this, who needs enemies?

In a wide-ranging interview in December of the same year (Triyana 2007), Binhad responded to his critics. Asked about the critical reception of *Bau betina*, Binhad is dismissive:

Critics never talk about texts properly. They only claim that this or that work is terrible or poor and so on, but they don't provide analysis. Take my work *Bau betina* for example. I doubt that they would provide us with their colourful critical responses if they had actually read it. I'm certain that they haven't read it. I don't have a problem if it is analysed with whatever conclusion, as long as it is analysis. But if they are just making accusations, whatever the judgement, be it good or bad, trashing or praising, I don't accept it. It's all rubbish, that sort of thing. If it's analysis, whether positive or negative, I'll accept it.

Referring to the organisers of the KAKUS-Listiwa, Binhad was asked if he felt judged: 'No. I think the problem here is not about writers judging others, but rather more to do with the unhealthy condition of Indonesian literature'. For Binhad, modern Indonesian literature is unhealthy primarily because of the lack of depth and direction amongst Indonesia's army of part-time literary critics. Critics and writers, he argues, seem more concerned with criticising the author of a work rather than analysing the work itself ('yang jadi masalah saya kira bukan sastranya, tapi sastrawannya'). This particular complaint has long been heard amongst Indonesia's tight-knit literary circles. But on this occasion, Binhad believes his colleagues have stepped over the line: 'This is the very first time in our literary world that an award for the worst piece of literature has been awarded by fellow writers. Before in Nazi Germany there was an award given for poor literature, but it was the authorities who awarded it—politicians—not fellow writers'.

It would be quite understandable if Binhad felt the need to pack up his computer and close up shop. But this is not the first time Binhad has been critically attacked. His first collection of poems, *Kuda ranjang* (The bed horse) (2004), was withdrawn from sale at Gramedia, Indonesia's leading bookstore, ostensibly because of concerns over its explicit treatment of sexuality. But Indonesia has a strong erotic tradition. As Creese and Bellows (2002:386–7) observe, 'There is a considerable corpus of literature in the manuscript traditions of both Bali and Java that can be broadly defined as erotic, that is, as primarily concerned with the sensual and sexual'.[4] Instead, I would argue that the effective banning of *Kuda Ranjang* was more a kneejerk response to a heated debate led by senior literary figures, some of whom regarded the poems as being vulgar and pornographic (Muhammad, D 2006). Binhad was unswayed, and indeed began editing a collection of essays documenting the resulting polemic.

According to Binhad, the furore surrounding *Bau betina* was little more than an extension of the *Kuda ranjang* polemic. For him, dealing with controversy is like water off a duck's back:

> The aim of literature is to be written. Whether there's someone out there who is willing to publish it or not is unimportant. There's no doubt that someone out there will read it. Take the *Babad Tanah Jawi* for instance, it was never published, but nowadays it can be read. Before I used to have a dream that supposing my poetry couldn't be printed, or published, I could just post my poems on the sides of city buses, or on city walls. Because I think the most important thing is how to get them written in the first place. A few of my poems in the past were regarded as poor, as lacking in quality. Just like Chairil Anwar who was once completely ignored. But then there was an HB Jassin who had a contrary opinion of Chairil's works, and thus now he is read today. Perhaps later, in a few generations to come, my poetry will be read. So I write not just for today, but for the future, for the future generations (Triyana 2007).

But shouldn't one also be writing for today, to match the tastes of today's audience? 'Ah, that's just wishful thinking. If the worth of a work of art was measured by the masses then everything I said above would be meaningless. Try placing a work by Picasso in the middle of the street and I bet you'd have comments like what sort of painting is this? Rubbish art'.

It would be tempting to regard the KAKUS-Listiwa as a reflection of the increasingly 'democratic' nature of post-authoritarian Indonesia. After all, is it not an example of participative democracy in action, where the common man has his say? Binhad scoffs at such a suggestion:

'My understanding of democracy is not like this. This is the product of an unhealthy literary system. It's a bit rich to link it with democracy. Even to place it alongside comedy is too good for it. It has more to do with a reflection of an unhealthy situation' (Triyana 2007).

Again, by raising the question of poor criticism—criticising the writer rather than their writings—Binhad reiterates his view of the KAKUS-Listiwa episode as an example of the rotten state of modern Indonesian literature. There is nothing democratic, he argues, with criticising a work of art because one does not happen to agree with the personal qualities or politics of a particular artist. As suggested earlier, this 'playing the man rather than the ball' style of criticism has been endemic in the history of modern Indonesian literary studies, and is not a recent phenomenon.[5]

The section that follows analyses the KAKUS-Listiwa, not so much as a function of the perceived shortcomings of Indonesian literary critics but rather in terms of post-authoritarian Indonesia's increasingly widespread culture of puritanism and censoriousness. I begin this analysis by making a few preliminary comments on the aesthetic nature of Binhad's poetry, seeking possible explanations for the storm of controversy it has provoked.

Binhad's poetry: aesthetic considerations

The style of Indonesian in *Bau betina*, although challenging for the average Indonesian citizen, is eloquent, lyrical and innovative and not archaic or stilted in any way. The language is also explicit and physical and, as Bakhtin observes of the poetry of Rabelais, obsessed with the lower body. The content is provocative and semi-pornographic; the collection comfortably straddles the borderline between highbrow and trash. References to sexual intercourse, penises, vaginas, ejaculation, clitorises, testicles, nipples, buttocks and pubic hair abound. It can be argued that this 'discourse of transgression', to use Stallybrass and White's terminology (1986), reflects the manner in which Binhad's poetry evokes the extremities of the base. As in the transgressive works examined in Bakhtin's literature of the carnival and in Stallybrass and White's text (1986), the poems of *Bau betina* concentrate on representations of the lower strata; topics explored include murder, promiscuity, prostitution, abortion, rape, infidelity, masturbation and urban poverty.

The exploration of the debasing 'low', coloured by its language of impurity and corporeality, is certainly a persistent characteristic of Binhad's oeuvre. The first stanza of the first poem of Binhad's first collection of poetry, 'Berak' (which can be variously translated as 'Having a shit', 'Taking a dump', 'Taking a crap' or 'Going to the toilet', depending on how explicit or euphemistic one would like to be), sets the tone[6]:

> Your nice anus
> every morning spreading over the toilet bowl
> patiently awaiting your shit.
> Your penis is as wrinkly dull as the neck of an old hunch-back
> shyly peeking out at the pile of shit
> squeezing out of the brown cheeks of your backside.
>
> *Anusmu yang bagus*
> *saban pagi mengangkangi mulut kakus*
> *yang tak bosan menunggu tahimu.*
> *Zakarmu sekuyu gelambir leher jompo*
> *bungkuk dan malu-malu*
> *mengintip puing tahi*
> *terjepit bongkah coklat bokongmu.*

For some senior critics Binhad's unashamed representation of openings, orifices and lower regions of the body (including the mouth, anus, buttocks and genitals) is reprehensible. For instance, established poet Taufiq Ismail does not rate Binhad's work as literature at all. In his eyes it is nothing more than pornography (Muhammad, D 2006). For others, Binhad has been regarded as 'perusak moral bangsa' (a destoyer of the nation's moral values); one reader claimed 'Menjijikkan membaca puisi kamu!' (It was revolting reading your poetry!) (Muhammad, D 2006). Others mention that Binhad's poetry is not only sexually explicit, it borders on misogyny. According to Muhammad (2006), the title of Binhad's first collection, *Kuda ranjang* (*The bed horse*), is instructive:

> From the choice of title alone, it seems we can already imagine the sexualised and transgressive nature of the work that the writer intends to reveal. The word "horse" is a symbol of masculinity. Borrowing the terminology of Marianna Amiruddin (*Media Indonesia*, 8/8/04), horses symbolise the "authenticity of the masculine". Then, it is connected to the word "bed". Is it not the case that the bed is also the site of women's disempowerment? In other words, if or when a man manages to coax a woman to enter his bed, then it is the man who is considered to have won, and the woman, vanquished, is defeated.

Binhad's second collection can be viewed in a similarly combative manner. Alternative 'against-the-grain' readings are also possible. *Bau betina* can be translated as 'The smell of bitches', as *betina* is a collective noun referring to bitches or female animals. But when *betina* refers to humans, as it does here, it is undeniably derogatory. In Binhad's poetry *betina* is a recurring metaphor for the feminine (just as horses in Binhad's poetry denote the masculine). Indeed,

in order to ensure that this connection is direct and unambiguous, the cover of
Bau betina, designed by Tisna Sanjaya, has an image of a woman disrobing
in a forest, underlaid by an image of a pair of bestial eyes. Unlike the positive
association between men and horses in *Kuda ranjang*, the correlation of women
and wild animals in *Bau betina* is sinister, derogatory and degrading; it reminds
us once again of the monstrous-feminine dominating the Indonesian horror
genre, as discussed in the previous chapter. My translation of *Bau betina*, 'The
smell of women' is, therefore, quite possibly excessively euphemistic and the
product of an against-the-grain reading of Binhad's verse.

We can play similar deconstructionist games with other elements of the
collection. Consider the final poem in the *Bau betina* collection, 'Permohonan'
(A request):

> God,
>
> give me
>
> women.
>
> Women,
>
> give me
>
> god.
>
> *Tuhan,*
>
> *beri aku*
>
> *perempuan.*
>
> *Perempuan,*
>
> *beri aku*
>
> *tuhan.*

Like much of Binhad's poetry, this particular poem can be read in at least two
contrasting ways. First, as a prayer, it can be read as a pared-down expression
of spiritual and emotional longing. Yet, it could be argued that the prayer also
betrays a misogynistic attitude. The first stanza suggests that women are mere
pawns in God's eyes, freely available upon request. The second stanza implies
that, for the narrator, women are, at best, ornamental and, at worst, just a means
to a male spiritual end. I do not claim appropriate expertise to judge the literary
merit of Binhad's poem. Nevertheless, pragmatically speaking, it seems to me
that this prayer is not unlike most prayers delivered every day, the world over,
from believers and non-believers alike. Are not most prayers self-serving,
delivered through a similar tunnel vision of self interest? Who indeed has never
sent up a little prayer requesting the appearance of a knight in shining armour

or a beautiful princess in order to live happily ever after? Binhad deserves our respect for eloquently voicing the thoughts that most of us dare not speak.

Ultimately, one could analyse each of the *Bau betina* poems in this way. One could put forward either a positive or negative reading, depending on one's inclination or interpretive agenda. Indeed, Binhad's poetry has polarised Indonesia's army of writers and literary critics. As with Rudi Soedjarwo's films, there are as many negative reviews appearing as there are positive ones. As an alternative to this somewhat schizophrenic approach, I would suggest that Binhad's poetry should be allowed to enter the dialogue. In the poem 'Tak ada Messiah sudi ke bordil' (There's no Messiah willing to visit a brothel) (Nurrohmat 2007a), Binhad depicts the world of brothels and prostitution as a liminal zone, a site where men and women transgress any number of social and spiritual taboos. Interestingly enough, this poem's depiction of the world of prostitution echoes the themes of one of Rendra's most famous poems dealing with a similar leitmotif, 'Bersatulah pelacur-pelacur Jakarta!' (Prostitutes of Jakarta unite!), a stanza of which was quoted in Kipandjikusmin's 'Langit makin mendung'. The standout line in Binhad's 'Tak ada Messiah' is particularly relevant to this discussion, as its poetics are as much metafictional as political:

> A CITY WITHOUT A BROTHEL
> IS LIKE A HOUSE WITHOUT A TOILET!
> *KOTA TANPA BORDIL*
> *ADALAH RUMAH TANPA KAKUS!*

I would argue that this line suggests that, even if Binhad's poetry is supposedly 'bad' (in the same way that brothels and toilets have negative connotations), it has a role to play in the field of Indonesian literature and in the ongoing Indonesian nation-building project. After all, wouldn't good poetry without bad poetry be just like a house without a toilet? Ironically, this line also pre-empts, or perhaps even inspired, the toilet trophy that would be later awarded to its author.

We need to question why Binhad's poetry has caused such a furore. This is particularly so when poetry that is, arguably, equally 'bad'—or equally 'good' poetry, for that matter—has failed to capture the public or critical imagination. First of all, I would suggest that this might have much to do with Binhad's tendency to incorporate into his poetry what Bakhtin terms 'grotesque realism'. Grotesque realism, as exemplified by the cover and content of *Bau betina*, uses the body as a microcosm for the social and political domains. By embracing the body as a site for representing masculinity and transgression, Binhad's poetry has incensed self-appointed literary police and, as well shall see, provoked the popular politics of hetero-normative Islam. In this respect there are two other important factors worth discussing: the challenging thematic content of Binhad's poetry, including an overlay of horror themes and images; and Binhad's unabashed Islamic leanings, inspired by a strictly Islamic upbringing in Javanese transmigrant villages in rural Lampung, southern Sumatra. I argue that Binhad's links with horror and Islam are reflected in both the content and the aesthetics of his poetry.

Horror, Islam and the politics of the erotic

Apart from the transgressive or offensive nature of much of *Kuda ranjang* and *Bau betina*, what else has caused such a polarised reaction to Binhad's poetry? First of all, I would suggest that Binhad's poems are a brave exploration of the ongoing tensions between social decay and the politics of the erotic in the culturally specific context of a traditionally conservative predominantly Muslim society. Indeed, Binhad's focus on the more sordid aspects of human existence—especially in the context of the urban chaos of Jakarta, Indonesia's teeming capital with over 12 million people—opens a window on the stifling undercurrents of social and spiritual decay at the heart of Indonesia's chaotic political progress. One poem in particular, 'Pecah' (Broken), is a striking comment on the existential costs associated with life and living in the post-authoritarian era:

The top of my bloody head has broken off.

Tin-can lids, dead frogs, and torn underpants

are seeping out from my broken skull.

I dump the rotten overflow into the street.

My face shoots out darts of metal.

Lacerating the eyes of people passing by

and causing the sun's forehead to bleed.

The smell of blood covers my hands which are gripping machetes

which are shaking from the sharp pointy end of my heart.

Cangkang comberan kepalaku pecah.

Sobekan kaleng, bangkai kodok, dan cincangan celana dalam

meluap dari rekah tengkorak.

Kuarak ceceran busuk ke jalan.

Mukaku mengelupas selaput seng.

Mata orang lewat tersayat.

> Kening matahari berdarah.
> Amis mencemari tangan penggenggam tangkai parang
> dan berguncang dari setombak ulu hati.

Binhad's depiction of hegemonic masculinity is often associated with alienation, isolation and horrific violence, as it is in 'Broken'. In this sense, Binhad's poetic masculinities are challenges to the normative masculine ideal.

In Binhad's poetry, no masculine myth is safe from comment or critique. For example, in 'Gigolo' the male protagonist expresses his disgust at the sexual expectations placed on the contemporary Indonesian male:

> In this room I shut off the outside world
> I've had enough of them telling me to go and have sex
> or to be like someone from a cheap pornographic poster.
> The windows and door are locked
> the wild hands of lust are groping my body:
> they know I'm so thirsty and
> just a man
> an owner of an animal between my legs.
> *Di kamar ini kenyataan di luar kusudahi*
> *tak mau lagi bujuk senggama*
> *juga lagak poster mesum yang norak.*
> *Pintu dan jendela terkunci*
> *ganas tangan birahi menggerayangi tubuhku:*
> *telah begitu haus dan tahu*
> *aku cuma pejantan*
> *penyimpan binatang di palung kelangkang.*

Even if he did happen to take pleasure in illicit sexual activity, the protagonist reveals that it is not all that it is cracked up to be; emotions such as shame and rage are pervasive:

> Outside the room I can still feel the sharp pain of a love bite on my neck
> making me as shy as a woman
> blushing under the gaze of wandering eyes.

My bed-partner last night ran into me again in the street
she treated me like a stranger not knowing my body's smell
filling me with rage and wanting to explode my penis.

Di luar kamar masih terasa perih cupang di leher
membikin aku semalu perempuan
tersipu pelotot mata-mata liar.
Kawan seranjang semalam kutemui lagi di jalan
seperti orang asing tak pernah tahu bau tubuhku
membikinku marah dan ingin meledakkan zakarku.

On other occasions sexual relations, without the shadow of infidelity, are deeply satisfying and treated with a laconic sense of humour. Consider 'Bunting' (Pregnant), which describes the pleasures of love-making during pregnancy, both from the father-to-be and mother-to-be's perspective:

Your nightie lifted up revealingly,
your thighs glow in the lamp light
your fine pubic hair reigniting my lust, bubbling it up.
You hear his voice, you say
he sings his national anthem
and he loves peeking at the eye of your penis
every night as it flows through his narrow channel.

Dastermu tersingkap
kilat paha menyilaukan mata lampu
bulu halusmu menujah gelembung birahiku.
Kaudengar suaranya, katamu
ia nyanyikan lagu negerinya
dan girang mengintip mata air penismu
setiap malam mengaliri selokan kecilnya.

On the whole, however, Binhad's poetry depicts the act of sexual intercourse from a thoroughly masculine perspective. This discourse is dominated by Bakhtinian grotesque realism, with explicit images of penetration, orgasm and sexual fluids. Consider the following stanza in 'Gairah Farah' (Farah's passion):

All through our date I've wanted to shove my penis
into every hole and pore of your body so soft and hungry
so much so that my ecstatic fantasy engorges me
and melts me like the lava of a volcano.

Sepanjang kencan ingin kutusukkan tombak zakar
di setiap lobang dan pori tubuhmu yang lembut dan lapar
hingga khayalan asyik yang mengental di sendi
melumer seperti lahar gunung api.

Consider also the following scene in 'Gaung' (Echo), which is a logical
continuation of 'Gairah Farah':

My orgasm just keeps on going
firmly burrowing deep into the lips of the universe of your body
sending out my ejaculate throughout the world's canal
releasing my cock's saliva.
My muscles as strong as steel
penetrating hard into the folds of your sex
transmitting the flame of those hunting the creases of your body.

Syahwatku tak mau tamat
teguh menggali liang semesta tubuh
menyemburkan sperma sepanjang selokan dunia
melunaskan liur kelamin leluhur.
Kelenjar setegang kawat
menujah buncah kelangkang kesumat
menggelombangkan nyala bara pemburu palung tubuhmu.

The description in the same poem of the protagonist's sexual coming-of-age
is similarly focussed on what Bakhtin (and Stallybrass and White) would regard
as the literature of the debased or 'lower strata':

My first wet dream
a flash flood of ejaculate immersing the bedroom floor
waking me up in the dead of night
and my eyes wide open worrying until dawn
pushing off my underpants glistening gold.

Mimpi basah pertama
banjir bandang sperma pembenam lantai kamar
membangunkanku di tengah amis malam
dan mataku berkobar cemas sampai pagi
melorotkan celana dalam berkilat keemasan.

Women's bodies are also frequently objectified, and several poems are written from the perspective of a voyeur, including 'Dua fragmen' (Two fragments):

The woman bathes her body in solitude in a wooden bath-tub
from the base of her neck to around her buttocks.
Bubbles of soap hang on the ends of the forest between her legs
a foreign valley its walls covered in moist moss.
Perempuan itu menggosoki tubuhnya sendiri di kulah
dari pangkal leher dan berpusar di gundukan pantat.
Gelembung sabun bergantungan di ujung-ujung belukar
di sebuah lembah asing bertebing lumutan lembab.

Meanwhile, in terms of his representations of the masculine, Binhad's poems do much more than reveal the grittiness of sexual intercourse. Other poems question the lifestyles and sexual practices of Indonesian men. For example, in 'Penebusan' (Atonement) Binhad shines a light on the moral degradation of the lower classes, and Indonesian fishermen in particular:

(A fishing boat returns from the open sea
having tamed the threat of waves and the pitch black of night
fulfilling the prayers of wives and children in remote villages
loaded up with sack-loads of pungent fish, the men's skin drenched in sweat,
a swagger in their steps, victorious over their gamble with fate.
At the noisy fish market
the day is still long and lengthy
ripe for staying up all night gambling,
inhaling the odor of cheap arak wine,
and getting wasted in brothels for nights on end.
Then, back to gambling with fate).

(Kapal nelayan pulang dari perburuan
seusai menaklukkan parang gelombang dan pekat malam
mengabulkan doa anak dan istri di kampung pesisir
bersama berkarung ikan amis, keringat lengket di badan,
dan langkah gagah memenangi pertarungan nasib.
Di halaman pelelangan ikan yang riuh
hari masih panjang dan jauh
demi suntuk di rumah judi, menghirup bau arak murahan,
dan terkapar di kamar pelacuran bermalam malam.
Kemudian kembali bertarung).

In poems such as 'Perompak' (Pirate), Binhad frames the typically macho masculinity of *preman* in terms of casual violence and misogyny:

The hands of time have carved a cross sign on two shoulders:
hills of flesh used as a weapon to strike fear into the hearts of hundreds of foes.
Only the sea, wilder than ever, is what he loves and only the sea stirs him.
The dry blood of his foes on his ship's deck makes him chuckle,
"murder is a tough job".
Hundreds of brutal duels have made his skin rough.
Arak wine has deadened his senses
excoriating the aroma of the thighs of hundreds of ravished women
and forgetting the blood of his enemies spilt at the point of his dagger.

Taring usia menggores tanda silang di dua pundak:
bukit daging penumpu kibasan senjata ke jantung ratusan lawan.
Hanya laut kelewat ganas yang dicintai dan mereguk mata air birahi.
Darah musuh kering di geladak membikin tergelak,
"pembunuhan adalah kerja keras."
Ratusan duel brutal membikin kulitnya kasar.
Arak menyengat tali syaraf
merenggut harum paha ratusan perempuan jarahan
dan lupa ceceran darah lawan di sekujur kelewang.

I would suggest that the men of Binhad's poetry are not all depicted as paragons of masculine virtue—far from it. As the stanzas quoted above suggest, Binhad's masculine heroes might be more correctly categorised as anti-heroes, not unlike Pramoedya's Minke, Ayu Utami's Wis/Saman, *Kuldesak*'s Andre and Soedjarwo's Marwan.

In many poems, alongside the chronically embattled male anti-heroes are over-dependent lovers. Many couples appear to be bunkered down, locking themselves away from the harshness of everyday realities. Consequently, there are many aubades, where lovers resist the rising sun of daybreak and the jangling of alarm clocks, make the most of public holidays, or, in the absence of their lover, miss the smell of freshly-brewed tea. In juxtaposition to this, the recurring imagery of wild animals, trees, forests, lakes and the sea can be regarded as a symbolic reflection of a repressed desire to escape from the harshness of urban living. No wonder, then, that so many of Binhad's poems are imbued with the themes of lovers nostalgically yearning for the peace of contemplation, poetry, love-making and laughter. One poem, 'Gay', set in the distant streets of Paris and revolving around the impressions of a couple of homosexual lovers, is an extension of this theme. This poem also reveals Binhad's willingness to explore alternative sexual/gendered subject-positions. In the meandering 'Hermafrodit' (Hermaphrodite) he even explores a hermaphrodite subject-position.

It is also worth noting that Binhad's poems have a flowing style, a distinctive embodiment of his examination of the politics of the erotic. Consider 'Sundal' (Whore), where a strong sense of physicality pervades:

> Days of endless passion
> our clothes placed to one side
> as we rub the walls of a mossy cliff
> the roots of a cactus seeping out sap
> the travellers' horse neighs
> making your nipples and clitoris quiver
> for a season, until it ends
> as the candles melt.
>
> *Hari-hari melulu birahi*
> *melorotkan lilitan lapisan kain*
> *menggosoki sisi tebing berlumut*
> *urat akar kaktus meneteskan getah*

kuda musafir meringkik

menggeletarkan ujung puting dan kelentit

hingga satu musim garing

bersama lelehan batang-batang lilin.

This bustling vision of the erotic is all the while overshadowed by the title of the poem. The sexual escapades alluded to above are deeply evocative, but are, nevertheless, between a prostitute and her client and limited in time. The references to a mossy cliff, cactus sap, a horse's neighing and melting candles are also distinctive of Binhad's poetry, foreshadowing the spiritual and sexual isolation of the lovers, trapped between the physical pleasures of love-making and the moral bankruptcy of their undeniably commercial transaction. The polarising tensions between agony and ecstasy, the heavenly and the sordid, nature and the metropolis, are recurring themes in Binhad's poetry. Indeed, Binhad's upbringing in a number of transmigrant villages in rural Lampung and his later move to Java and Jakarta in order to sustain a modest income as a poet and writer might well explain his comfortable references to nature, not to mention his ambivalent attitude towards the city. As the old saying goes, you can take the boy out of the country but you can't take the country out of the boy.

The pervasive sense of spirituality as well as spiritual isolation embodied by Binhad's protagonists might also reflect the influence of Binhad's years of religious training in rural Islamic boarding schools, as well as the abiding influence of his ethnically Javanese parents. But it is important to note that Binhad's protagonists can be actively spiritual without necessarily being Muslim. Consider the following scene in 'Perempuan film Amerika' (A woman from an American film):

"Are you a religious man?"

The man laughs at the serious question.

"I grew up in a poor and pious Catholic household.

I occasionally went to church at the end of the week

and every now and then I drink whisky after I masturbate."

The woman bursts into laughter.

Her mouth is full of smoke

just like after a revolver has fired a round.

"Even though I don't like whisky I'm no longer a virgin

let alone pious."

Both of them laugh for a moment and they understand each other.

After a kiss they agree on heading off to a certain address

and make their way across the road

and leave the dull sleepy bar behind.

"Apa kau lelaki relijius?"

Laki-laki itu tergelak pertanyaan tak lucu.

"Aku besar di lingkungan katolik miskin dan ketat.

Aku kadang ke gereja di akhir pekan

dan sesekali minum wiski seusai onani."

Perempuan itu ngakak.

Mulutnya berasap

seperti moncong pistol meledak.

"Meski tak suka wiski aku bukan lagi perawan

apalagi yang taat."

Keduanya terpingkal sesaat dan saling mengerti.

Seusai ciuman mereka sepakat pergi ke sebuah alamat

dan bergegas menyeberangi jalan besar yang kotor

meninggalkan bar yang kuyu terkantuk-kantuk.

This deep sense of the spiritual, combined with a relaxed attitude towards sex and sexuality, is much more fraught when Binhad turns his attention to the Muslim context. 'Dangdut' is a case in point. At the time it was written, *dangdut* singer Inul Daratista was creating a national furore because, according to Bodden, her '*goyang ngebor* or "grinding (literally "drilling") shimmy" *dangdut* performances won opprobrium from conservative Muslims and staunch defence from more liberal members of the Indonesian community' (Bodden 2007:120). Clearly Binhad sides with Inul:

Let's dance and celebrate our sadness together

so we can have a laugh for a moment, she suggests.

Outside they're waiting for the foot-soldiers of religion and God

who love preaching and forbidding people from happiness

like the annoying mouth of authority.

Do we have to only believe in a religion and God

who is incapable of teaching us how to sway our hips, dangdut-style?

> *Mari bergoyang merayakan kesedihan bersama*
> *agar bisa terbahak sejenak, bujuknya.*
> *Di luar sedang menunggu barisan agama dan tuhan*
> *yang gemar menghardik dan melarang orang bersenang-senang*
> *seperti mulut kekuasan yang menjengkelkan.*
> *Haruskah hanya percaya pada agama dan tuhan*
> *yang tak becus mengajari bergoyang?*

Binhad's barbed comments are undeniably directed at the vociferous foot soldiers of conservative Islam; Front Pembela Islam and the like. The spiritual imperative in Binhad's poetry might have much to do with Binhad's liberal Islamic faith and the abiding influence of his mother. Binhad's mother was an ethnically Javanese transmigrant from Banyuwangi, East Java, who made a living in rural Lampung selling fabric material in village markets. Among other things, including tending to a modest clove plantation with Binhad's father, she taught Arabic and Islamic studies to young children in several Muslim village schools in Lampung (Clark 2007). Binhad has followed his mother's lead, tutoring his fellow students at several Islamic boarding schools and attending the famous Krapyak *pesantren* in Yogyakarta.

Often, in the interludes between fleeting episodes of carnal pleasure, Binhad's poetic characters are haunted by images of horror. There are several dimensions to this phenomenon. First of all, many of Binhad's protagonists seem haunted by a vague and faceless sense of threat, randomly emanating from the outside world. This threat is aesthetically manifested in everyday objects, sometimes in the form of a poster on the wall, sometimes in the slashing of rain against a windowpane, and at other times by the ring of a phone or the alarm of a clock. In 'Melawat' (A visit) the sense of threat, embodied by a rusty nail, is closely connected to an atmosphere of decay:

> In this house the strong odor of your panties is no longer.
> The crooked nail is still stuck in the wall
> getting rusty in the same old place:
> aiming to poke itself into my eyeball.
> The toilet bowl is covered in mould
> and the rim of the bath-tub is covered in moss
> intending to swap love with filth.

Di rumah ini tak ada lagi bau amis pakaian dalammu.
Paku bengkok itu masih tertancap di tembok
berkarat di tempat yang sama:
ingin menusuk bola mataku.
Lobang kakus rusak dililit akar jamur
dan bibir kulah ditumbuhi lumut
hendak menukar cinta dengan kejorokan.

On one level, the atmosphere is emblematic of a failed romantic relationship. On another level, the decrepitude inscribed must also be regarded as a reflection of a much broader societal malaise, which I would argue is closely related to the political and economic travails gripping post-authoritarian Indonesia. This leads me to my second point. As revealed in 'Hibernasi' (Hibernation), contemporary Indonesia is often depicted as a nightmarish world, where marginal economic progress has coincided with a morass of social decay. Although the narrator's tone is unmistakably one of disgust, the shadow of extreme criminal violence is treated casually, almost matter-of-fact:

The neighbour's neck was torn apart by robbers
a disgusting old pedophile violates the vagina of a teenage girl:
also nothing.
Here everyone dies,
just stupid hopeless rubbish.

My friend is just a sordid dream
turning into my new foul-smelling world.
Souvenirs and books, warm chats and sexual pleasure have long gone.
In my blood there is now a foul mixture
of rivers of corpses of murderers and rapists.
Rifles and spears floating as well, rusted.
No-one knows about my painful cries
echoing darkness throughout the new world.
My steps are the crawls of a suffering man
alone in an ancient desert.

Leher tetangga digorok rampok

jompo bengis menujah vagina gadis ingusan:

juga cuma nihil.

Di sini semua mati,

sampah tolol sia-sia.

Kawanku cuma mimpi sialan yang menjelma tengik dunia baruku.

Kenangan dan buku, obrolan hangat dan nikmat birahi telah minggat.

Di darah melarut amis sungai mayat pembunuh dan pemerkosa.

Bedil dan tombak terapung di sana hingga berkarat.

Tak ada yang tahu serak rintihku menggaungkan hitam dunia baru.

Langkahku rangkakan kaki manusia siksaan

sendirian di gurun tua.

Thirdly, in 'Penunggu Malam' (The nightwatchman) and in many other poems in Binhad's first two instalments of what is intended to be an erotic trilogy, the images of horror echo the post-New Order cycle of horror dominating Indonesian cinemas and televisions. Unlike the horror genre in Indonesia's visual media, however, the monstrous in Binhad's poetry does not seem to be marked as either masculine or feminine. In the following stanza in 'Penunggu Malam' the horror is unique and understated:

A shard of rusty metal

stabs into the ends of your leather shoes

when hundreds of days dawned

chasing you and driving you out

until your nerves were shot.

The shreds of a rabbit corpse under your fingernails

are glowing with the light of hundreds of fire-flies

when the lights are dimmed and the day draws to a close.

Runcing patahan lonjoran besi karatan

menyobek ujung sepatu kulitmu

ketika ratusan siang bangkit

memburu dan mengusir kau

hingga serabut syaraf kepalamu hancur.
Sayatan bangkai kelinci di kuku jari tanganmu
menyalakan cahaya ratusan cahaya kunang-kunang
ketika lampu surut dan hari pekat.

As demonstrated by the stanza above, clearly the monstrous in Binhad's poetry is not limited to ghosts, zombies and the like. Nevertheless, ghosts and demons do occur. Unlike the recurring monstrous-feminine of Rudi Soedjarwo and his colleagues in the cinematic horror genre, there are doubts about the gender assigned to Binhad's monsters. In this sense, I would argue that Binhad's monstrosity represents the repressed in Indonesian society as a whole. Binhad's horror is also transgressive, as it is emblematic of the horror that lurks beneath the surface of Indonesian society, thus challenging the state's pretensions to political stability and economic improvement:

A power pole
a filthy sewer
a muddy road
have memorised your dirty sexy talk all night long
and hundreds of ghosts
with enraged leeches crawling out of their eyes
haunt you
every time the rain falls.
Tiang listrik
selokan busuk
jalanan becek
hapal kata-kata cabulmu sepanjang malam
dan ratusan mata hantu penuh lintah marah
mengincar kau
setiap kali hujan turun.

My fourth point is, as I have explained, that Binhad's attempts to write about socially risqué themes with such an arresting narrative force have been eclipsed by vociferous protests over the so-called 'vulgar' content and colourful language of his work. Indeed, well before the KAKUS-Listiwa furore, Binhad's poetry was negatively linked with a number of other so-called 'vulgar' post-New Order writers, including male Muslim writers Sofa Ihsan and Moammar Emka. Emka wrote the best-selling *Jakarta undercover: sex 'n the City* (2003), which has been described as 'a reportage exposé of the extravagant and decadent sex practices of wealthy Jakartans' (Bodden 2007:119). Binhad has also been linked to the Teater Utan Kayu literary group and young women prose writers of the *sastra wangi* stream, who, as explained above, have also written about sex and sexuality in an explicit and up-front fashion. It is important to note that, although Binhad has many social and professional interactions with artists and critics aligned with several groups, he maintains a measured distance from all of them.

My fifth point is that, unlike most of the *sastra wangi* writers, who are not Muslim, Binhad's unabashed Islamic leanings have provided extra ammunition for his detractors. In print form, Binhad has developed his own unique and innovative style of poetic delivery; all of his poems are printed right-justified. This ostensibly mirrors the manner in which the Arabic script is justified to the right, Arabic being the language of the sacred text of Islam, the Koran. Binhad has also published poems in Arabic, reinterpreting verses from the Koran (Nurrohmat 2005). This too has attracted criticism from conservative critics (Aleida 2005), who are unimpressed by Binhad's experimentation. Furthermore, it is well known that before he began writing his erotic poetry Binhad studied at a famous *pesantren* in Yogyakarta and had a strict Islamic upbringing. The fundamental irony, as well as the historical precedent, of marrying explicit sexuality with an Islamic world view has not been lost on conservative commentators (Fathuri 2005; Qurtuby 2005).

Of course, Binhad has, on the odd occasion, utilised his poetry to allude to his legion of critics. In one poem in the *Kuda ranjang* collection, 'Palu' (A hammer), the protagonist is set upon from all sides; he uses the almost mystical power of words to fight back:

> In the mudhole I read of my old body wrecked
>
> as I scrawl short sentences on an ugly city wall
>
> about the vicious tales of my accusers
>
> who have become like a herd of pigs with cocks of fire.
>
> *Di kubang lumpur kubaca tubuh lamaku hancur*
>
> *menulis kalimat-kalimat pendek di tembok kota yang jelek*
>
> *tentang kisah lempengan lidah pencecap bacin ludah*
>
> *kaum pemaki yang menjadi kawanan babi berkelamin api.*

Although this poem does not need a wealth of culturally specific knowledge to be understood, the image of the narrator scrawling messages of protest on city walls reminds us of the earlier quote from Day (2002a) in Chapter 2 about the 're-"masculinised"' *pemuda* youth of Java scrawling their revolutionary messages on doors and walls. In many ways Binhad's poetry reflects the 'anarchic spontaneity' of the revolutionary movement; it remains to be seen whether Binhad's aggressive male prowess can be considered as 'thrilling' as the militarised, liberationary, 're-"masculinised"' *pemuda*.

It is also worth noting that pigs and pork are quite abhorrent for Muslims of all persuasions; thus the metaphor of the last line in the poem above is particularly abusive. But, with an overlay of the horror discourse so ubiquitous in contemporary Indonesian popular culture, the remainder of the poem is even more transgressive. In the following stanza, the narrator's extreme response to his critical condemnation is sordid and nihilistic; in a word, *nekad*:

> I want my hand
> to turn into a hammer pounding deep into their stone chests.
> My bravery I imagine turning into a roaring monster
> or a demon lurking in solitude
> teasing leering at my dreadful turn of fate
> when I feel wracked with lust
> I'll rape an angel until a baby is born
> who teaches that love always destroys everything
> like the blows of a thousand hammers
> until my head
> splits
> flowing blood in waves
> tossing me who knows where.
>
> *Kuingin tanganku*
> *menjelma palu pelebam dada batu-batu.*
> *Jantan bayangku menjelma monster keramaian*
> *dan siluman kesunyian mengejek seringai nasib hitam.*
> *Ketika aku bernafsu*
> *kuperkosa bidadari sampai lahirkan bayi*

yang mengajarkan cinta lebih tekun meremuk apa pun

serupa hantaman seribu palu

sampai kepalaku

pecah

mengalir darah

menggelombang

damparkan aku menuju entah.

Despite Binhad's measured politeness in public, there can be no doubt about the strength of his true feelings towards his foes in Indonesia's confined literary circles. Furthermore, according to Andy Fuller, who was involved in the filming of a documentary on Binhad, despite the passing of time the KAKUS-Listiwa affair still rankles.[7] My own interactions with Binhad subsequent to this, either in Jakarta or Lampung, would confirm this observation; of course, the ongoing presence of the KAKUS-listiwa toilet 'trophy' on Binhad's office mantelpiece does somewhat soften the degree of Binhad's disgruntlement.

Conclusion

This chapter has examined the context surrounding the awarding of the KAKUS-Listiwa to poet Binhad Nurrohmat. Through an examination of the poems in *Kuda ranjang* and *Bau betina*, two collections which are intended to be part of an erotic trilogy, this chapter has revealed several dominant themes in Binhad's poetry, including religion, the politics of the erotic and *maskulinitas*. Ongoing leitmotifs include provocative images of social and spiritual alienation, horror and explicit sexuality, emblematic of the obsession with the debased in Bakhtin's earthy culture of the carnivalesque. Despite critical condemnation, Binhad's *nekad* or provocative stance has remained steadfast; he is defiant and unapologetic. In 2008, Binhad answered his critics in the best possible way by publishing yet another collection of poems, *Demonstran sexy*, a selection of witty aphorisms and pithy expressions of his laconic view of gender relations and the Indonesian sociopolitical landscape. Once again, we witness an ethnically Javanese, Java-based artist as activist, questioning dominant gender stereotypes and reconceptualising new masculine identities for a changing Indonesia.

As might be assumed, the controversies surrounding Binhad's poetry have also led to a great deal of interest in literary circles. Binhad has almost become a celebrity on the Jakarta (and Lampung) literary circuits, with a steady flow of invitations for interviews, seminar panels and poetry readings. For example, Binhad has been invited to read his poetry at several prestigious locations, including the Taman Budaya Lampung, Bandarlampung, Graha Bhakti Budaya Taman Ismail Marzuki, Jakarta and Teater Utan Kayu, Jakarta. He has continued to be nominated for the Khatulistiwa Literary Award, most recently in 2008. Yet, as explained above, within months of the furore surrounding his first collection of poetry, *Kuda ranjang*, all remaining copies were withdrawn from sale from the shelves of Gramedia. Nowadays it is quite difficult to obtain a copy of the poems as they are out of print.

Ironically, the furore surrounding *Bau betina* has ensured that it has almost become a collector's item. Because of financial constraints, the initial print run was quite small and has not been reprinted. Unlike the incredibly popular *sastra wangi* books, which have been reprinted many times, poetry in Indonesia is not usually published for financial gain and collections are rarely reprinted. Binhad, like so many of Indonesia's artists, writes and performs not to achieve material wealth but to participate in the national conversation. Through his artistic expression, Binhad, like the other artists discussed in this book, reveals new insights and impressions on themes as far-reaching as sex, politics, religion and gender.

Notes

1   I am, nevertheless, a fan of Binhad's non-erotic poetry, including his latest collection, *Demonstran sexy* (The sexy demonstrator) (Nurrohmat 2008). This collection of poetic aphorisms and pithy poems in the manner of Rendra's famous pamphlet poems surely deserves accolades. At the very least, this collection arguably situates Binhad firmly in a long line of great Indonesian poet activists.

2   The English translation of this poem is from Harry Aveling's translation of Dorothea's poetry entitled *Kill the radio: sebuah radio, kumatikan* (2001).

3   *Bau betina* was not on the KLA shortlist. The winner was the well-known Tasikmalaya-based poet, Acep Zamzam Noor, for his collection, *Menjadi penyair lagi* (Becoming a poet again) (Noor 2007). Ironically, Acep's collection was also on the KAKUS-Listiwa shortlist.

4   See, for example, Aveling (1969), Anderson (1990b), Wieringa (2002) and Creese (2004).

5   Indeed, this is probably why Western observers of writing in Indonesia, such as Teeuw, Aveling, Foulcher and others, are so highly regarded within Indonesia. Western critics, it is assumed, are more objective in their analyses as they are theoretically well-read and pleasantly removed from the heat of the battle. This reification of Western scholarship, I should hasten to add, has its own problems, not least its whiff of empire.

6   The translations from *Kuda ranjang* are by me and Cucu Juwita and are published in *Binhad Nurrohmat: The bed horse (Kuda ranjang)* (Nurrohmat 2008b). I have given the Indonesian versions in italics. The translations from the *Bau betina* collection are mine and have not been published.

7   Personal communication, Melbourne, December 2008.

The question of gender has assumed growing importance in post-authoritarian Indonesia. However, 'gender' is usually used in the Indonesian context with reference to women and women's issues. The 'man question' remains unasked. Indeed, ambivalence towards understanding men and the masculine in contemporary Indonesia prevails. This ambivalence has extended to the artistic sphere, including to modern literary expression, which has only rarely examined representations of *maskulinitas*. In my attempt to get the ball rolling, in Chapter 2 of this book, I aimed to explore the link between the masculine and the biographical in the works of Indonesia's greatest novelist, Pramoedya Ananta Toer. I argued that when we consider the models of masculinity inscribed in the historical novels of Pramoedya, we must also consider the many connections with real-life male historical figures. For example, Pramoedya's *Arok dedes* (1999a) portrays the 13th-century bandit, Ken Arok, in carefully tempered shades of grey. Arok is depicted as a well-educated and spiritually enlightened leader of the people, with a cunning sense of political instinct; he is also portrayed as a ruthless strategist, a thug and a murderer. Lifting this analysis from the textual to the contextual, I explored the parallels between Arok and Indonesia's President Suharto, after discussion of the links between the male protagonist of Pramoedya's Buru tetralogy, Minke, and several historical figures, including the early nationalist figure Tirto Adhi Suryo, Pramoedya's father and Pramoedya himself.

In Chapter 2, inspired by the scholarship of Nathanson and Young in the only book on the topic, I also briefly discussed the notion of misandry in Indonesia. Nathanson and Young (2001) argue that a culture of misogyny should not be replaced by a culture of misandry, as has emerged in the West. My main observation is that, although the existence in Indonesia of a culture of misandry can be illustrated with anecdotal evidence, it is hard to measure its pervasiveness, either through direct communication and investigation in Indonesia or through the analysis of media representations. For the moment, in terms of broad societal trends, Indonesia's long-suffering women do not seem to have a contemptuous or misandric attitude towards Indonesian men.

Nevertheless, in the context of present challenges to the existing gender order, I would argue that it is increasingly important to respond to an unspoken aspect of the post-New Order process of gender renegotiation, the question of Indonesian men. If misandry is a fundamental component of this question, then perhaps it could be a topic of further exploration in the future.

In Chapter 3 I examined the notion that contemporary literary representations of *maskulinitas* are as much contradictory and ambiguous as they are subversive. This is in contrast to 'traditional' images of the *gagah* (brave) and virile Indonesian male heroes. For example, Seno Gumira Ajidarma's *Wisanggeni sang buronan* (2000) symbolically and literally rejects the archetypal male hero of the *wayang*, the *halus* (refined) womaniser and warrior, Arjuna. Instead, Seno favours a well-rounded humanised version of Arjuna's son, a sensitive, intuitive, renegade warrior, Wisanggeni. Yet, in Seno's novel, Wisanggeni's heroism is understated; despite his invincibility, he remains a marginal figure of opposition, with human limitations, feelings and desires. It is no coincidence that a similar male figure, also with the name Wisanggeni, emerges in Ayu Utami's highly acclaimed *Saman* (1998). In this novel the main male character Wis is a young and passionate Catholic priest, a man enthusiastically engaged in social and political issues. However, later in the novel he changes his name to Saman, struggles with his repressed sexuality and seriously questions his faith. Ultimately he gives up his virginity to one of several predatory female friends and, because of his over-enthusiastic social activism, he is forced to flee Indonesia in disgrace. Although Ayu's Wis/Saman is a fascinating character, one highly-regarded critic is not convinced by his psychological characterisation; he finds him to be particularly flighty towards the end of the novel (Mangunwijaya 1998).

Chapter 4 also observed the limitations of masculine characterisations in the landmark film *Kuldesak* (1998). Almost all of the male characters are beaten up, written out of the script or killed off, often at the hands of gun-bearing women. Even before these men disappear from the film, many of them are stuttering, stammering, meek and hesitant, and the masculine alternatives to these antiheroes are effeminate, clowns, villainous thugs or madmen. *Kuldesak* also portrays the sense of aimlessness and despair of Indonesia's urban youth. One key element in this equation is the lack of any male role model from their parents' generation. Significantly, one of the few older males making a cameo appearance in the film plays a key symbolic role leading up to the suicide of one of the film's main characters, the teenage Andre. After a night partying in a bar, Andre is woken on the bar floor in the morning by an old man, the bar's janitor. Without a word, the old man hands Andre a package he found on the floor, which turns out to contain a gun. Later in the day Andre hears of the suicide of his idol, Kurt Cobain, and uses the gun to commit suicide. The scene with the old man is pivotal and can be considered as an ironic comment on the changing of the guard from Indonesia's older generation of men to the latest generation of youth. The fact that the janitor, like the famous janitor in Nirvana's iconic video clip of their influential grunge anthem 'Smells like teen spirit', actually does very little and says even less points to the marginal role of older males in contemporary Indonesia.

It is also important to emphasise that the janitor's gift turns out to be a poisoned chalice; it becomes the instrument for Andre's suicide. This fact is significant, especially if we consider the film's arch-villain, the middle-aged businessman Yakob Gamarhada. In between high-powered business meetings, he spends much of the film orchestrating kidnappings, rapes and murder. When he is shot dead by his latest intended victim, it is no coincidence that his blood-splattered body falls on top of an Indonesian–English dictionary open at the page listing 'cul-de-sac'. If Gamarhada can be considered as a parody of the dominant patriarchal 'villain' of the New Order era, Suharto, then, in the post-New Order era, it should be no surprise that there is little affection shown towards older males. After all, remembering the janitor's gift to Andre, what has the latest generation of Indonesians inherited from the New Order generation of generals and bureaucrats? Patterns of authoritarianism, violence, corruption and social hypocrisy might be at the top of the list. Chapter 5, focusing on several Rudi Soedjarwo films, also examined themes of masculine violence, rape and murder in the context of social decay and political uncertainty. This chapter concluded that hegemonic masculinity is as strong as ever in post-New Order Indonesia society and culture and, as a result, misogynistic and homophobic images and narratives are rife.

Chapter 6 initially explored the manner in which the reception of contemporary fiction by young women writers has been marred by gossip and criticism of the writers, who are as contemptuous of the New Order regime as of men as a whole. When asked if her novels were deliberately critical of men in general or the military in particular, Ayu Utami replied: 'both of them—the military, and men in general'.[1] Male authors, humiliated and affronted by their exclusion from the centre stage of the post-New Order literary discourse, do not seem to be quite so prepared to overthrow patriarchal symbols. Chapter 6, however, argued that some writers, such as poet Binhad Nurrohmat, have not shied away from provoking and interrogating the masculine power of Indonesian men. Binhad's efforts have not been universally praised. Indeed, although his poetry has many fans, it is vehemently despised in some circles, as evidenced by the inaugural KAKUS-Listiwa award for the worst fiction of 2007 to his second collection of poetry. The awarding of the KAKUS-Listiwa to Binhad might, on the one hand, reveal a latent heterosexual fear of unbridled expressions of eroticism involving normative and non-normative masculinities. On the other hand, the jeers of derision levelled at Binhad and his work might just be a relatively straightforward case of professional jealousy. Binhad's cultural activism is particularly unique in the sense that he brings a transmigrant's perspective to the national conversation, as well as the perspective of a liberal Muslim. Moreover, Binhad continues to write and publish his poetry in the face of vociferous condemnation and is unafraid of reprisals from conservative critics and hardline Muslim groups who so easily take offence. This is all the more impressive when we consider the stranglehold that popular-front Islamism holds over the Indonesian government ten years on from Reformasi.

In general, Indonesia over the last decade can be described as a nation in transition; from being a populous country under the authoritarian rule of Suharto's New Order to a post-authoritarian phase, characterised by a series of weak and indecisive governments and a plethora of unleashed societal energies. Prominent among the latter are the Islamist-inclined segments of the population, frustrated by the ongoing crises in the country, the moral lassitude of Indonesia's expanding media and the global dominance of non-Islamic and anti-Islamic forces. Indonesia's replacement of authoritarian rule with liberal forms of democratic governance has also led to signs of an Islamic backlash, characterised by a widespread atmosphere of censorial interference, shame and disgust. Indonesian artists have rolled their sleeves up and pushed on regardless. Censorship, whether by state or non-state agents, has long been an integral element of Indonesia's artistic production. Some would contend that an entire generation of Indonesian artists and writers was muzzled by New Order censorship. According to Maier (1999:258) 'Suharto and his administrative apparatus have castrated a generation of writers, robbing them of their generative power, the power of being historical witnesses who could tell others about what is happening before their very eyes'. As we have seen, there is a great deal of evidence to support this view. However, this book has shown that many writers, poets, filmmakers, actors, musicians and artists were undaunted by the authoritarianism of the New Order. The fact that the post-authoritarian era has been marked by an upsurge of popular cultural expression (Heryanto 2008) suggests that a younger generation of artists has 'hit the ground running' and that censorial interference, from whatever source, is easily circumvented. It could also be argued that in many cases censorship continues to be an inspirational factor for cultural production, even in the post-authoritarian period.

Within this fluid sociopolitical context, the New Order state's homogenising conceptions of gender and gendered roles are being reshaped and renegotiated. An integral part of this process has been the need to redress, politically and legally, the many insidious consequences of the New Order's policies of containment and suppression of Indonesian women. However, it would not be controversial to say that up until now Indonesian women and Western feminist scholars seem relatively unconcerned by issues related to Indonesian men and Indonesian masculinities. This should be of no great surprise. After all, for feminists the world over, no matter what school of feminism, the needs and problems of women are their primary concern (Nathanson & Young 2001). Indonesian women have been living in a society where male rule has long been unequivocal. Indonesian women still have a great deal of catching up left to do. Meanwhile, it continues to be the case that Indonesian men have had little to say on the matter of *maskulinitas* or *kejantanan*, which is yet to be viewed as an issue of any importance. As we search for possible reasons, Oetomo provides us with a clue in his observation that, while femininity is a marked category in contemporary Indonesia, 'masculinity is unmarked' (Oetomo 2000:46).

Indonesian men have little call for interrogating the status of men and the social construction of male identity, as to all intents and purposes they have little to complain about. According to Oetomo (2000:57),

> One can make inadequate inferences, at best, about Indonesian masculinity from the criticisms voiced of inequalities between women and men. The portrait that emerges is of men always acting as heads of families and as breadwinners, operating in the public sphere, and not being responsible for the upbringing of children or the sharing of household work. In the area of sexuality, one would infer a thinly disguised "legendary" heterosexual promiscuity of men and a consistent role of men as initiators and dominators in heterosexual intercourse.

From the shallow and unrealistic macho masculinity of cigarette advertising to the overblown clichés of soap opera, Islamic film and *wayang* shadow theatre, popular cultural stereotypes perpetuate these relatively unquestioned archetypes of Indonesian hegemonic masculinity. It may not be surprising, therefore, that ambivalence to the question of Indonesian male identity prevails, even as issues and practices of gender representation have been opened up for public debate in contemporary Indonesia. But as this book has revealed, in the hands of a number of Indonesia's leading novelists, poets, playwrights and filmmakers, the interface between male identity, sex and politics has become a rich seam for artistic exploration. As Seno Gumira Ajidarma (2005) argues, contemporary cultural expression has the capacity to interrogate, deconstruct and provide an alternative to 'imagined' masculine stereotypes: 'The imagined masculinity is being debunked and in its place emerges the real man. Of course, even this is a construction—but at least it is an alternative to the dominant discourse'. By examining cultural representations of masculinities in the context of authoritarian and post-authoritarian politics, this book has highlighted some of the ambiguities and complexities of this phenomenon.

Notes

1   Personal communication, Launceston, March 2003.

Films

3 hari untuk selamanya (3 days for forever) directed by Riri Riza

9 naga (9 dragons) (2006) directed by Rudi Soedjarwo

40 hari bangkitnya pocong (40 days of the shrouded's resurrection) (2009) directed by Rudi Soedjarwo

Ada apa dengan cinta? (What's up with love?) (2002) directed by Rudi Soedjarwo

Arisan! (The gathering) (2003) directed by Nia Dinata

Ayat ayat cinta (Verses of love) (2008) directed by Hanung Bramantyo

Bangunnya Nyai Roro Kidul (The awakening of Nyai Roro Kidul) (1985) directed by Sisworo Gautama

Berbagi suami (Love for share) (2006) directed by Nia Dinata

Beth (2001) directed by Aria Kusumadewa

Brownies (2005) directed by Hanung Bramantyo

Coklat stroberi (Chocolate strawberry) (2007) directed by Ardy Octaviand

Daun di atas bantal (Leaves on a pillow) (1998) directed by Garin Nugroho

D'Bijis (2007) directed by Rako Prijanto

Detik terakhir (Final moments) (2007) directed by Nanang Istiabudi

Eliana Eliana (2002) directed by Riri Riza

Freddy vs Jason (2003) directed by Ronny Yu

Gerbang 13 (Gate 13) (2005) directed by Nanda J Umbara

Jakarta Undercover (2005) directed by Lance

Jelangkung (2001) directed by Rizal Mantovani

Jomblo (The bachelor) (2006) directed by Hanung Bramantyo

Kejar Jakarta (Chasing Jakarta) (2006) directed by Adhitya Mulya

Ketika (When) (2005) directed by Deddy Mizwar

Kisah cinta Nyi Blorong (The love story of Nyi Blorong) (1989) directed by Norman Benny

Kuldesak (Cul-de-sac) (1998) directed by Nan T Achnas, Mira Lesmana, Rizal Mantovani, Riri Riza

Mendadak dangdut (Suddenly dangdut) (2006) directed by Rudi Soedjarwo

Mengejar matahari (Chasing the sun) (2004) directed by Rudi Soedjarwo

Merah itu cinta (Red is love) (2007) directed by Rako Prijanto

Pasir berbisik (Whispering sands) (2001) directed by Nan T Achnas

Pembalasan Ratu Laut Selatan (Revenge of the Queen of the South Sea) (1988) directed by Tjut Djalil

Perempuan berkalung sorban (Woman wearing a headscarf) (2009) directed by Hanung Bramantyo

Petualangan Sherina (The adventures of Sherina) (2000) directed by Mira Lesmana and Riri Riza

Pocong (Shrouded) (2006) directed by Rudi Soedjarwo

Pocong 2 (Shrouded 2) (2006) directed by Rudi Soedjarwo

Pocong 3 (Shrouded 3) (2007) directed by Monty Tiwa

Pocong vs kuntilanak (Shrouded vs the witch) (2008) directed by David Poernomo

Pulp fiction (1994) directed by Quentin Tarantino

Putri kunti'anak (The witch's daughter) (1988) directed by Atok Suharto

Radit dan Jani (Radit and Jani) (2008) directed by Upi

Ratu Ular (The Snake Queen) (1972) directed by Lilik Sudjio

Reservoir dogs (1992) directed by Quentin Tarantino

Serambi (Verandah) (2006) directed by Garin Nugroho

Sri (2000) directed by Marselli Soemarno

Suster ngesot (The dragging nurse) (2007) directed by Arie Aziz

Tato (Tattoo) (2001) directed by Hanny Saputra

Telegram (2001) directed by Slamet Rahardjo Djarot

Tentang dia (About her) (2005) directed by Rudi Soedjarwo

Terowongan Casablanca: Kuntilanak merah (The Casablanca tunnel: the red witch) (2007) directed by Nanang Istiabudi

Tusuk Jelangkung (Penetrating Jelangkung) (2003) directed by Dimas Djayadiningrat

Virgin (2005) directed by Hanny Saputra

Publications

ACI blog 2007, 'Butet Kartaredjasa kena cekal', http://artculture-indonesia.blogspot. com/2007/12/butet-kartaredjasa-kena-cekal.html, viewed 28 December 2008.

Adams, Rachel and David Savran 2002, *The masculinity studies reader*, Blackwell, Oxford.

Aisenberg, Nadya 1994, *Ordinary heroines: transforming the male myth*, Continuum, New York.

Ajidarma, Seno Gumira 1997, *Ketika jurnalisme dibungkam sastra harus bicara*, Bentang, Yogyakarta.

—— 2000, *Wisanggeni sang buronan*, Yayasan Bentang Budaya, Yogyakarta.

—— 2002, 'A story about unimportant news reports' in Bodden, Michael (ed), *Jakarta at a certain point in time: fiction, essays and a play from the post-Suharto era in Indonesia*, Centre for Asia-Pacific Initiatives, Victoria.

—— 2005, 'Runtuhnya kejantanan', *Matra*, March.

Aleida, Martin 2005, '"Kuda ranjang" yang liar', Bahasa List, http://listserv. dartmouth.edu/scripts/wa.exe?A2=ind0509&L=BAHASA&P=57, viewed 28 December 2008.

Allen, Pam 2007, 'Challenging diversity? Indonesia's anti-pornography bill', *Asian Studies Review* 31(2).

Anderson, Benedict RO'G, 1965, *Mythology and the tolerance of the Javanese*, Cornell Modern Indonesia Project, Ithaca.

—— 1972, *Java in a time of revolution: occupation and resistance*, 1944–1946, Cornell University Press, Ithaca and London.

—— 1990a, 'The idea of power in Javanese culture' in *Language and power: exploring political cultures in Indonesia*, Cornell University Press, Ithaca.

—— 1990b, *Language and power: Exploring political cultures in Indonesia*, Cornell University Press, Ithaca.

—— 1990c, 'Old state, new society: Indonesia's New Order in comparative historical perspective' in *Language and power: exploring political cultures in Indonesia*, Cornell University Press, Ithaca.

—— 1996, '"Bullshit!" s/he said: The happy, modern, sexy Indonesian married woman as transsexual' in Sears, Laurie J (ed), *Fantasizing the feminine in Indonesia*, Duke University Press, Durham.

Arps, Bernard & Katinka van Heeren 2006, 'Ghosthunting and vulgar news: popular realities on recent Indonesian television' in Nordholt, Henk Schulte and Ireen Hoogenboom (eds), *Indonesian transitions*, Pustaka Pelajar, Yogyakarta.

Ashcroft, Bill, Gareth Griffiths and Helen Tiffin 1995, *The empire writes back: theory and practice in post-colonial literatures*, Routledge, London and New York.

Aspahani, Hasan 2007, '*Bau betina* dan KAKUS-Listiwa (1)', blog, http://sejuta-puisi2.blogspot.com/2007/11/bau-betina-dan-kakus-listiwa-1.html, viewed 28 December 2008.

Aspinall, Edward, Herb Feith & Gerry van Klinken 1999, 'Introduction' in Aspinall, Edward, Herb Feith & Gerry van Klinken (eds), *The last days of President Suharto*, Monash Asia Institute, Clayton.

Aveling, Harry 1969, 'The thorny rose: the avoidance of passion in modern Indonesian literature', *Indonesia* 7.

—— 1975a, 'A note on the author' in Pramoedya Ananta Toer, *A heap of ashes*, University of Queensland Press, St Lucia.

—— 1975b, 'Introduction' in Pramoedya Ananta Toer, *The fugitive*, Heinemann Educational Books (Asia) Ltd, Hong Kong.

—— 1991, 'Introduction' in Pramoedya Ananta Toer, *The girl from the coast*, Select Books, Singapore.

—— 2001a, *Secrets need words: Indonesian poetry, 1966–1998*, Ohio University Center for International Studies, Athens.

—— 2001b, 'Introduction' in Aveling, Harry (ed), *Kill the radio: sebuah radio, kumatikan*, Indonesiatera, Magelang.

—— 2007, 'Indonesian literature after Reformasi: the tongues of women', *Kritika Kultura* 8.

Bahari, Razif 2003, 'Remembering history, w/righting history: piecing the past in Pramoedya Ananta Toer's Buru Tetralogy', *Indonesia* 75.

—— 2007a, 'Between a rock and a hard place? Interstitial female subjectivity in between colonialism and patriarchy: women in Pramoedya Ananta Toer's Buru tetralogy', *Indonesia* 83.

—— 2007b, *Pramoedya postcolonially: (re-)viewing history, gender and identity in the Buru tetralogy*, Pustaka Larasan, Bali.

Bain, Lauren 2005, 'Women's agency in contemporary Indonesian theatre' in Parker, Lyn (ed), *The agency of women in Asia*, Marshall Cavendish, Singapore.

Bakhtin, Mikhail 1981, *The dialogic imagination: four essays by MM Bakhtin*, University of Texas Press, Austin.

—— 1984a, *Problems of Dostoevsky's poetics*, University of Minnesota Press, Minneapolis.

—— 1984b, *Rabelais and his world*, Indiana University Press, Bloomington and Indianapolis.

Barton, Greg 2005, *Jemaah Islamiyah: radical Islamism in Indonesia*, Ridge Books, Singapore.

Baskoro, LR, Munawwaroh, Marta Silaban and Rofiki Hasan 2008, 'Ancaman atas nama pornografi', *Tempo* 10(9), 4–10 November.

Bernard, Jami 1995, *Quentin Tarantino: the man and his movies*, Harper Collins, London.

Bettelheim, Bruno 1976, *The uses of enchantment: the meaning and importance of fairy tales*, Thames & Hudson, London.

Blackburn, Susan 2004, *Women and the state in modern Indonesia*, Cambridge University Press, Cambridge.

Blackwood, Evelyn 2005, 'Transnational sexualities in one place: Indonesian readings', *Gender & Society* 19(2).

Blackwood, Evelyn & Saskia Wieringa (eds) 1999, *Female desires: same-sex relations and transgender practices across cultures*, Columbia University Press, New York.

Bodden, Michael 1996, 'Woman as nation in Mangunwijaya's *Durga Umayi*', *Indonesia* 62.

—— 1999, 'Seno Gumira Ajidarma and fictional resistance to an authoritarian state in 1990s Indonesia', *Indonesia* 68.

—— 2007, 'Shattered families: "transgression", cosmopolitanism and experimental form in the fiction of Djenar Maesa Ayu', *Review of Indonesian and Malaysian Affairs* 41(2).

Bodden, Michael & Tineke Hellwig 2007, 'Introduction', *Review of Indonesian and Malaysian Affairs* 41(2).

Boellstorff, Tom 2004, 'The emergence of political homophobia in Indonesia: masculinity and national belonging', *Ethnos* 69(4).

—— 2005, *The gay archipelago: sexuality and nation in Indonesia*, Princeton University Press, Princeton and Oxford.

Booth, Wayne C 1984, 'Introduction' in Bakhtin, Mikhail, *Problems of Dostoevsky's politics*, University of Minnesota Press, Minneapolis.

Bourdieu, Pierre 2001, *Masculine domination*, Stanford University Press, Stanford.

Brandon, James R 1993, *On Thrones of Gold*, University of Hawaii Press, Honolulu.

Brandt, Stefan 2000, 'American culture X: identity, homosexuality, and the search for a new American hero' in West, Russell and Frank Lay (eds), *Subverting masculinity: hegemonic and alternative versions of masculinity in contemporary culture*, Rodopi, Amsterdam.

Brenner, Suzanne 1999, 'On the public intimacy of the New Order: images of women in the popular Indonesian print media', *Indonesia* 57.

Budianta, Melani 2000, 'Reflections on the Indonesian women's movement after Reformasi', *Asian Exchange* 16(1).

—— 2003, 'The blessed tragedy: the making of women's activism during the Reformasi years' in Heryanto, Ariel and Sumit K Mandal (eds), *Challenging authoritarianism in Southeast Asia: comparing Indonesia and Malaysia*, Routledge, New York and London.

Campbell, Ian 2002, 'Some developments in Indonesian literature since 1998', *Review of Indonesian and Malaysian Affairs* 36(2).

Campbell, Micaela 2007, 'Mother/non-mother: Ibuism as subtext in the literary works of Ayu Utami', *Review of Indonesian and Malaysian Affairs* 41(2).

Carroll, Noel 1990, *The philosophy of horror: or, paradoxes of the heart*, Routledge, London.

CCT (Cempaka Culture and Tourism) 2007, 'Movie industry asks court to overturn 1992 film law', http://cempaka-tourist.blogspot.com/2007/12/movie-industry-asks-court-to-overturn.html, viewed 29 December 2008

Christanty, Linda 2008, 'Pembunuhan Sultan dan sisir George Bush dalam sastra kita', *Kompas*, http://cetak.kompas.com/read/xml/2008/12/07/01153982/pembunuhan.sultan.dan.sisir.george.bush.dalam.sastra, viewed 10 January 2009.

Chudori, Leila 1998, 'Sosok-sosok dalam roman 'Saman': menyajikan hak seksual perempuan', unpublished manuscript.

—— 2006, 'Semburan Rudi, sang naga', *Tempo*, 48(34), 23–29 January.

Cinema Online 2008, 'Cinema Online's review [of Pocong 2]', Yahoo! Malaysia Movies, http://malaysia.movies.yahoo.com/Pocong+2/movie/14183/, viewed 21 March 2010.

Clark, Marshall 1999a, 'Cleansing the earth' in Aspinall, Edward, Herb Feith and Gerry van Klinken (eds), *The last days of President Suharto*, Monash Asia Institute, Clayton.

—— 1999b, 'Seno Gumira Ajidarma: an Indonesian imagining East Timor', *Review of Indonesian and Malaysian Affairs* 33(2).

—— 2001, 'Shadow boxing: Indonesian writers and the *Ramayana* in the New Order', *Indonesia* 72.

—— 2004a, 'Too many Wisanggenis: reinventing the Wayang at the turn of the century', *Indonesia and the Malay World* 32(92).

—— 2004b, 'Men, masculinities and symbolic violence in recent Indonesian cinema', *Journal of Southeast Asian Studies* 35(1).

—— 2004c, 'Indonesian masculinities: images of men in Indonesian TV advertising', *Review of Indonesian and Malaysian Affairs* 38(2).

—— 2006, 'The subversive mythologies of Pipit Rochijat, from the Suharto era and beyond', *Asian Folklore Studies* 65(1).

—— 2007, '*Bau betina*, rasa malu bangsa' in Nurrohmat, Binhad, *Bau betina*, I:BOEKOE, Yogyakarta.

—— 2008a, 'Binhad Nurrohmat: a new force in Indonesian poetry' in Clark, Marshall with Cucu Juwita (eds), *Binhad Nurrohmat: the bed horse (kuda ranjang)*, Koekoesan, Jakarta.

—— 2008b, 'Indonesian cinema: exploring cultures of masculinity, censorship and violence' in Heryanto, Ariel (ed), *Popular culture in Indonesia: fluid identities in post-authoritarian politics*, Routledge, London and New York.

Cooper, Nancy I 2004, 'Tohari's trilogy: passages of power and time in Java', *Journal of Southeast Asian Studies* 35(3).

Coté, Joost 1998, 'Tirto Adhi Soerjo and the narration of Indonesian modernity, 1909–1912: an introduction to two stories', *Review of Indonesian and Malaysian Affairs* 32(2).

—— 2005, 'Romancing the Indies: the literary construction of Tempo Doeloe, 1880–1930' in Coté, Joost & Loes Westerbeek-Veld (eds), *Recalling the Indies: colonial culture & postcolonial identities*, Aksant Academic Publishers, Netherlands.

Creed, Barbara 1993, *The monstrous-feminine: film, feminism, and psychoanalysis*, Routledge, New York and London.

Creese, Helen 2004, *Women of the kakawin world: marriage and sexuality in the Indic courts of Java and Bali*, ME Sharpe, Armonk and London.

Creese, Helen and Laura Bellows 2002, 'Erotic literature in nineteenth century Bali', *Journal of Southeast Asian Studies* 33(3).

Dahana, Radar Panca 2000, 'Memburon Batara Guru', *Tempo* 10(29).

Dahlan, Muhidin M & Mujib Hermani (eds) 2004, *Pledoi sastra: kontroversi cerpen Langit makin mendung Kipandjikusmin*, Melibas, Jakarta.

Dardjowidjojo, S 1974, 'Introduction' in Morgan, MDW (ed), *The darkening sky: an Indonesian short story*, Southeast Asian Working Paper 5, University of Hawaii.

Day, Tony 2002a, *Fluid iron: state formation in Southeast Asia*, University of Hawaii Press, Honolulu.

—— 2002b, 'Between eating and shitting: figures of intimacy, storytelling and isolation in some early tales by Pramoedya Ananta Toer' in Day, Tony and Keith Foulcher (eds), *Clearing a space: postcolonial readings of modern Indonesian literature*, KITLV Press, Leiden.

—— 2007, 'Locating Indonesian literature in the world', *Modern Language Quarterly* 68(2).

Day, Tony and Keith Foulcher 2002, 'Postcolonial readings of modern Indonesian literature: introductory remarks' in Day, Tony and Keith Foulcher (eds), *Clearing a space: postcolonial readings of modern Indonesian literature*, KITLV Press, Leiden.

Deakin, Christine 1976, 'Langit makin mendung: upheaval in Indonesian literature', *Archipel* 11.

Derks, Will 1996, '"If not to anything else": some reflections on modern Indonesian literature', *Bijdragen tot de Taal-, Land- en Volkenkunde* 152(3).

—— 2002, 'Sastra pedalaman: local and regional literary centres in Indonesia' in Day, Tony and Keith Foulcher (eds), *Clearing a space: postcolonial readings of modern Indonesian literature*, KITLV Press, Leiden.

Dian, Yulia 2005, 'Poster '9 naga' akhirnya ditutup', detik HOT, www.detikhot.com/index.php/tainment.read/tahun/2005/bulan/12/tgl/12/time/144143/idnews/496597/idkanal/229, viewed 26 February 2007.

Diani, Hera 2004, '"Mengejar matahari': no shining example of filmmaking', *Jakarta Post*, www.thejakartapost.com/yesterdaydetail.asp?fileid=20040725.O01, viewed 28 December 2008.

—— 2006, '"9 naga" all smoke, no fire', *Jakarta Post*, 15 January.

Dipayana, Arya Aji 2000, 'Wisanggeni berkelabat', unpublished manuscript.

Dirgantoro, Wulan 2006, 'Double pressure: the Indonesian art world post-Pinkswing park', *Contemporary Visual Arts + Culture Broadsheet* 35(4).

Dowell, Pat & John Fried 1995, 'Pulp friction: two shots at Quentin Tarantino's *Pulp fiction*', *Cineaste* 21(3).

Elson, Robert Edward 2001, *Suharto: a political biography*, Cambridge University Press, Cambridge.

Emka, Moammar 2003, *Jakarta undercover: sex 'n the city*, Galang Press, Yogyakarta.

Enloe, Cynthia 1990, *Bananas, beaches and bases: making feminist sense of international politics*, University of California Press, Berkeley and London.

Faludi, Susan 1999, *Stiffed: the Betrayal of the American Man*, W. Morrow & Co, New York.

—— 2007, *The Terror Dream: Fear and Fantasy in Post-9/11 America*, Metropolitan Books, New York.

Fanany, Ismet (ed) 2005, *Antologi cerpen lengkap AA Navis*, Kompas, Jakarta.

Faruk, HT 1998, 'Keindahan novel *Saman*', unpublished manuscript.

Fathuri, SR 2005, 'Kala santri masuk dunia "esek-esek"', *Syir'ah* 41(5).

Ford, Michele 2003, 'Beyond the *Femina* fantasy: the working class woman in Indonesian discourses of women's work', *Review of Indonesian and Malaysian Affairs* 37(2).

Ford, Michele and Lyn Parker (eds) 2008, *Women and work in Indonesia*, Routledge, London and New York.

Forum Pembaca Kompas 2008, 'Pementasan monolog Butet di Medan terancam batal', www.mail-archive.com/forum-pembaca-kompas@yahoogroups.com/msg31001.html, viewed 29 December 2008.

Foucault, Michel 1988, *Madness and civilization: a history of insanity in the Age of Reason*, Vintage Books, New York.

Foulcher, Keith 1981, "Bumi manusia' and 'Anak semua bangsa': Pramoedya Ananta Toer enters the 1980s', *Indonesia* 32.

—— 1987, 'Sastra kontekstual: recent developments in Indonesian literary politics', *Review of Indonesian and Malaysian Affairs* 21(1).

—— 1995a, 'Post-modernism or the question of history: some trends in Indonesian fiction since 1965' in Hooker, Virginia Matheson (ed), *Culture and society in New Order Indonesia*, Oxford University Press, Kuala Lumpur.

—— 1995b, 'In search of the postcolonial in Indonesian literature', *Sojourn* 10(2).

—— 2005, 'Biography, history and the Indonesian novel: reading *Salah Asuhan*', *Bijdragen tot de Taal-, Land- en Volkenkunde* 161(2/3).

FPI 2008, 'FPI menolak keras produksi film LASTRI', www.fpi.or.id/artikel.asp?oy=sik-24, viewed 10 January 2009.

Geertz, Clifford 2002, 'Deep play: notes on the Balinese cockfight' in Adams, Rachel and David Savran (eds), *The masculinity studies reader*, Blackwell, Oxford.

Gandhi, Leela 1998, *Postcolonial theory: a critical introduction*, Allen & Unwin, St. Leonards.Gilbert, Helen and Joanne Tompkins 1996, *Post-colonial drama: theory, practice, politics*, Routledge, London and New York.

Gilbert, Helen and Joanne Tompkins 1996, *Post-colonial drama : theory, practice, politics*, Routledge, London.

Gladwin, Stephen 2003, 'Witches, spells and politics: the horror films of Indonesia' in Schneider, Steven Jay (ed), *Fear without frontiers: horror cinema across the globe*, FAB Press, Godalming.

GoGwilt, Chris 1995, 'Pramoedya's fiction and history: an interview with Indonesian novelist Pramoedya Ananta Toer' in Herring, Bob (ed), *Pramoedya Ananta Toer 70 tahun: essays to honour Pramoedya Ananta Toer's 70th year*, Yayasan Kabar Seberang, Stein.

Gouda, Frances 1993, 'The gendered rhetoric of colonialism and anti-colonialism in twentieth-century Indonesia', *Indonesia* 55.

Graham, Sharyn 2006, *Gender diversity in Indonesia: beyond gender binaries*, Routledge, London.

—— 2007, *Challenging gender norms: five genders among Bugis in Indonesia*, Thompson Wadsworth, Belmont.

Guillermo, Ramon 2007, 'They say I'm a monkey', *Indonesia* 83.

Hamilton, Graeme 2001, 'Male bashing could prove disastrous, authors warn', *National Post*, 14 November.

Hanan, David 2008, 'Changing social formations in Indonesian and Thai teen movies' in Heryanto, Ariel (ed), *Popular culture in Indonesia: fluid identities in post-authoritarian politics*, Routledge, London and New York.

Hanke, Robert 1992, 'Redesigning men: hegemonic masculinity in transition' in Craig, Steve (ed), *Men, masculinity and the media*, Sage, Newbury Park.

Hatley, Barbara 1980, 'Blora revisited', *Indonesia* 30.

—— 1990, 'Theatrical imagery and gender ideology in Java' in Atkinson, Jane Monnig and Shelly Errington (eds), *Power and difference: gender in island Southeast Asia*, Stanford University Press, Stanford.

—— 1994, 'Stage texts and life texts: women in contemporary Indonesian theatre', *Australasian Drama Studies* 25.

—— 1999, 'New directions in Indonesian women's writing? The novel *Saman*', *Asian Studies Review* 23(4).

—— 2002a, 'Postcoloniality and the feminine in modern Indonesian literature' in Day, Tony and Keith Foulcher (eds), *Clearing a space: postcolonial readings of modern Indonesian literature*, KITLV Press, Leiden.

—— 2002b, 'Literature, mythology and regime change: some observations on recent Indonesian women's writing' in Robinson, Kathryn and Sharon Bessell (eds), *Women in Indonesia: gender, equity and development*, Institute of Southeast Asian Studies, Singapore.

—— 2007, 'Subverting the stereotypes: women performers contest gender images, old and new', *Review of Indonesian and Malaysian Affairs* 41(2).

Hazmirullah 2006, 'Film & sinetron kita semakin tak mengindonesia', *Pikiran Rakyat*, 25 January.

Heider, Karl G 1991, *Indonesian cinema: national culture on screen*, University of Hawaii Press, Honolulu.

Hellwig, Tineke 1992, 'Rape in two Indonesian pop novels: an analysis of the female image' in Locher-Scholten, Elsbeth and Anke Niehof (eds), *Indonesian women in focus*, KITLV Press, Leiden.

—— 1994, *In the shadow of change: images of women in Indonesian literature*, Centres for South and Southeast Asia Studies, University of California, Berkeley.

—— 2007, 'A dragon-shaped hummingbird: Nukila Amal's writing from the nation's margin', *Review of Indonesian and Malaysian Affairs* 41(2).

Heraty, Toeti 2000, *Calon arang: kisah perempuan korban patriarki*, Yayasan Obor, Jakarta.

Herliany, Dorothea Rosa 2001, 'Buku harian perkawinan' in *Kill the radio: sebuah radio, kumatikan*, translated and edited by Harry Aveling, Indonesia Tera, Magelang.

Herlinatiens 2003, *Garis tepi seorang lesbian*, Galang Press, Yogyakarta.

Heryanto, Ariel 2006, *State terrorism and political identity in Indonesia*, Routledge, London.

—— 2008, 'Pop culture and competing identities' in Heryanto, Ariel (ed), *Popular culture in Indonesia: fluid identities in post-authoritarian politics*, Routledge, London and New York.

Heryanto, Ariel and Stanley Yoseph Adi 2002, 'Industrialised media in democratizing Indonesia' in Heng, Russell (ed), *Media fortunes, changing times—ASEAN states in transition*, Institute of Southeast Asian Studies, Singapore.

Hill, David 1984, *Who's left? Indonesian literature in the early 1980s*, Working Papers on Southeast Asia, Monash University, Clayton.

Hill, David T 1995, *The press in New Order Indonesia*, Sinar Harapan, Jakarta.

Hobsbawm, Eric 1959, *Primitive rebels: studies in archaic forms of social movement in the nineteenth and twentieth centuries*, WW Norton & Company, New York.

Holquist, Michael 1981, 'Introduction' in Bakhtin, Mikhail, *The dialogic imagination: four essays by MM Bakhtin*, University of Texas Press, Austin.

Hooker, Virginia Matheson and Howard Dick 1995, 'Introduction' in Hooker, Virginia Matheson (ed), *Culture and society in New Order Indonesia*, Oxford University Press, Kuala Lumpur.

Hourihan, Margery 1997, *Deconstructing the hero: literary theory and children's literature*, Routledge, London.

Indoprogress blog 2007, 'Hilmar Farid: bangsa ini menjadi tawanan fantasi', http://indoprogress.blogspot.com/2007/03/hilmar-farid-bangsa-ini-menjadi.html, viewed 28 February 2008.

Iwan, Rizal 2008, 'Rudi's return to horror dashes expectations', *Jakarta Post*, 3 September, www.thejakartapost.com/news/2008/03/08/rudi039s-return-horror-dashes-expectations.html, viewed 29 January 2009.

Jameson, Fredric 1985, 'Postmodernism and consumer society' in Foster, Hal (ed), *Postmodern culture*, Pluto Press, London and Sydney.

Jassin, HB 1970, *Heboh sastra 1968: suatu pertanggungandjawab*, Gunung Agung, Jakarta.

Johns, Anthony 1972, 'Pramoedya Ananta Toer: the writer as outsider, an Indonesian example' in Johns, Anthony (ed) *Cultural options and the role of tradition: a collection of essays on modern Indonesian and Malaysian literature*, Australian National University Press, Canberra.

Kartikawati, Eny 2006, '*Pocong* 1 ditolak, *Pocong 2* siap gentayangan', detik HOT, www.detikhot.com/index.php/tainment.read/tahun/2006/bulan/10/tgl/03/time/174506/idnews/688232/idkanal/229, viewed 29 December 2008.

Keeler, Ward 2004, 'Afterword: Mangunwijaya as novelist/puppeteer' in YB Mangunwijaya (ed), *Durga/Umayi: a novel*, University of Washington Press, Seattle.

Khalieqy, Abidah El 2001, *Perempuan berkalung sorban*, Yayasan Kesejahteraan Fatayat, Yogyakarta.

Kipandjikusmin 1968, 'Langit makin mendung', *Sastra* 8.

Kitley, Philip 2008, '*Playboy* Indonesia and the media: commerce and the Islamic public sphere on trial in Indonesia', *Southeast Asia Research* 16(1).

Kompas 1998a, 'Kayam: potret realitas; Pram: integritas tinggi', 5 April.

—— 1998b, '"Saman", generasi baru sastra Indonesia', 5 April.

—— 1998c, '*Kuldesak*: keterserpihan anak muda', 5 December.

—— 2005, 'Film '9 Naga' kesandung poster dan puser', www.kompas.com/gayahidup/news/0512/13/222532.htm, viewed 13 December 2007.

Lahiri-Dutt, Kuntala and Kathryn Robinson 2008, 'Bodies in contest: gender difference and equity in a coal mine' in Ford, Michele and Lyn Parker (eds), *Women and work in Indonesia*, Routledge, London and New York.

Lay, Frank 2000, '"Sometimes we wonder who the real men are"—masculinity and contemporary popular music' in West, Russell and Frank Lay (eds), *Subverting masculinity: hegemonic and alternative versions of masculinity in contemporary culture*, Rodopi, Amsterdam.

Leuter, Estella and Carol Schrier Rupprecht 1985, *Feminist archetypal theory: interdisciplinary revisions of Jungian thought*, University of Tennessee Press, Knoxville.

Lev, Daniel 1985, 'Colonial law and the genesis of the Indonesian state', *Indonesia* 40.

Levertov, Denise 2000, 'A force in Indonesian poetry' in Paine, Ed J (ed), *The poetry of our world*, Harper Collins, New York.

Libforall Foundation 2006, 'A "musical fatwa" against religious hatred & terrorism', www.libforall.org/popculture-republic-of-love.html#Warriors_of_Love, viewed 30 October 2006.

Liddle, R William 1996, *Leadership and culture in Indonesian politics*, Allen & Unwin, Sydney.

Locher-Scholten, Elsbeth 1994, 'Orientalism and the rhetoric of the family: Javanese servants in European household manuals and children's fiction', *Indonesia* 58.

Magnis-Suseno, Franz 1999, 'Langsir Keprabon: New Order leadership, Javanese culture and the prospects for democracy in Indonesia' in Forrester, Geoff (ed), *Post-Soeharto Indonesia: renewal or chaos*, Crawford House, Bathurst.

Mahendra, Dodi 2006, '*Ketika* (2005)', Sinema Indonesia, http://sinema-indonesia.com/neo/index.php?s=Ketika&paged=3, viewed 12 January 2009.

Maier, Henk 1999, 'Flying a kite: the crimes of Pramoedya Ananta Toer' in Rafael, Vicente L (ed), *Figures of criminality in Indonesia, the Philippines, and colonial Vietnam*, SEAP, Ithaca.

—— 2002, 'Stammer and the creaking door: the Malay writings of Pramoedya Ananta Toer' in Day, Tony and Keith Foulcher (eds), *Clearing a space: postcolonial readings of modern Indonesian literature*, KITLV Press, Leiden.

—— 2004, *We are playing relatives: a survey of Malay writing*, KITLV Press, Leiden.

Maimunah 2008, 'Indonesia's Q!Film festival: young Indonesians are using an alternative film festival to promote awareness of sexual diversity', *Inside Indonesia* 93, http://insideindonesia.org/content/view/1138/47/, viewed 19 March 2010.

Mangunwijaya, YB 1998, 'Menyambut roman "Saman"', *Kompas*, 5 April.

Marching, Soe Tjen 2007, 'Descriptions of female sexuality in Ayu Utami's *Saman*', *Journal of Southeast Asian Studies* 38(1).

—— 2008, 'Herlinatiens: between lesbianism, Islam and feminism' *Inter-Asia Cultural Studies* 9(1).

Martyn, Elizabeth 2005, *The women's movement in post-colonial Indonesia: gender and nation in a new democracy*, Routledge, London and New York.

McDonald, Hamish 1980, *Suharto's Indonesia*, Fontana/Collins, Melbourne.

McGlynn, John H 2000, 'Silent voices, muted expressions: Indonesian literature today', *Manoa* 12(1).

McLarty, Lianne 1996, '"Beyond the veil of the flesh": Cronenberg and the disembodiment of horror' in Grant, Barry Keith (ed), *The dread of difference: gender and the horror film*, University of Texas Press, Austin.

McMillan, Peter 1992, *Men, sex and other secrets*, Text Publishing, Melbourne.

Medrado, Benedito, Jorge Lyra and Marko Monteiro 2001, 'Masculinities in Brazil: the case of Brazilian television advertisements' in Pease, Bob and Keith Pringle (eds), *A man's world? Changing men's practices in a globalised world*, Zed Books, London.

Millie, Julian 2007, 'We are playing relatives: a review', *Review of Indonesian and Malaysian Affairs* 41(1).

Mohamad, Goenawan 2002, 'Forgetting: poetry and the nation, a motif in Indonesian literary modernism' in Day, Tony and Keith Foulcher (eds), *Clearing a space: postcolonial readings of modern Indonesian literature*, KITLV Press, Leiden.

Muhammad, Amir 2002, 'Smorgasboard: lesson from Indonesia', Kakiseni, www. kakiseni.com/articles/columns/MDEyMQ.html, viewed 29 December 2008.

Muhammad, Damhuri 2006, 'Zikir kelamin: "ikhtiar" Binhad Nurrohmat lewat sajak', Gerbang Kota News, http://gerbangkota.multiply.com/journal/item/9, viewed 29 December 2008.

Murtagh, Ben 2007, 'Beautiful men in Jakarta and Bangkok: the pressure to conform in a recent Indonesian novel', *Southeast Asia Research* 15(2).

—— 2008, 'Chocolate strawberry: an Indonesian film breaks new ground on the subject of teenage sexuality', *Inside Indonesia* 93, http://insideindonesia.org/content/view/1139/47/, viewed 2 February 2009.

Nadjib, Emha Ainun 1998, *Saat-saat terakhir bersama Soeharto: 2,5 jam di istana (kesaksian seorang rakyat kecil)*, Zaituna, Yogyakarta.

Nathanson, Paul and Katherine K Young, 2001, *Spreading misandry: the teaching of contempt for men in popular culture*, McGill-Queens University Press, Montreal.

Nilan, Pam and Prahistiwi Utari 2008, 'Meanings of work for female media and communication workers' in Ford, Michele and Lyn Parker (eds), *Women and work in Indonesia*, Routledge, London and New York.

Noor, Acep Zamzam 2007, *Menjadi penyair lagi*, Pustaka Azan, Bandung.

Nordholt, Henk Schulte and Margreet van Till 1999, 'Colonial criminals in Java, 1870–1910' in Rafael, Vicente L (ed), *Figures of criminality in Indonesia, the Philippines, and colonial Vietnam*, Southeast Asia Program Publications, Ithaca.

Nurrohmat, Binhad 2004, *Kuda ranjang*, Melibas, Jakarta.

—— 2005, 'ketikamu' in Senggono, Endo (ed), *Maha duka Aceh*, Pusat Dokumentasi Sastra HB Jassin, Jakarta.

—— 2007a, *Bau betina*, I:BOEKOE, Yogyakarta.

—— 2007b, *Sastra perkelamin*, PUstaka puJAngga, Lamongan.

—— 2007c, 'Binhad terharu', 26 November, www.mail-archive.com/artculture-indonesia@yahoogroups.com/msg00062.html, viewed 20 March 2010

—— 2008a, *Demonstran sexy*, Koekoesan, Jakarta.

—— 2008b, *Binhad Nurrohmat: the bed horse* (Kuda ranjang) translated and edited by Marshall Clark with Cucu Juwita, Koekoesan, Jakarta.

Oetomo, Dede 1996, 'Gender and sexual orientation in Indonesia' in Sears, Laurie J (ed), *Fantasizing the feminine in Indonesia*, Duke University Press, Durham and London.

—— 2000, 'Masculinity in Indonesia: genders, sexualities, and identities in a changing society' in Parker, Richard, Regina Maria Barbosa and Peter Aggleton (eds), *Framing the sexual subject: the politics of gender, sexuality, and power*, University of California Press, Berkeley and Los Angeles.

—— 2001, 'Gay men in the Reformasi era', *Inside Indonesia* 66.

Pamudji, MS 2000, 'Mempersoalkan kembali Reformasi Wayang', *Suara Merdeka*, 22 August.

Paramaditha, Intan 2007, 'Tracing the white ink: the maternal body in Indonesian women's writing', *Review of Indonesian and Malaysian Affairs* 41(2).

Parker, Lyn 2008, 'Theorising adolescent sexualities in Indonesia—where "something different happens"', *Intersections* 18, http://intersections.anu.edu.au/issue18/parker. htm, viewed 28 December 2008.

Patterson, Annabel 1991, *Fables of power*, Duke University Press, Durham.

Pattisina, Edna C 2006, '*9 Naga*: drama-aksi yang gelap', *Kompas*, 15 January.

Pausacker, Helen 2004, 'Presidents as punakawan: portrayal of national leaders as clown-servants in Central Javanese Wayang', *Journal of Southeast Asian Studies* 35(2).

Pease, Bob and Keith Pringle 2001, 'Introduction: studying men's practices and gender relations in a global context' in Pease, Bob and Keith Pringle (eds), *A man's world?: changing men's practices in a globalised world*, Zed Books, London.

Pelras, Christian 1996, *The Bugis*, Blackwell, Oxford.

Pemberton, John 1994, *On the subject of 'Java'*, Cornell University Press, Ithaca and London.

Perlman, Marc 1999, 'The traditional Javanese performing arts in the twilight of the New Order', *Indonesia* 68.

Pipit, Rochijat K 1993, *Baratayuda di negeri antah berantah*, Humor, Jakarta.

Platzdasch, Bernhard 2000, 'Islamic reaction to a female president' in Chris Manning and Peter van Diermen (eds), *Indonesia in transition: social aspects of Reformasi and crisis*, ISEAS, Singapore.

Prananto, Jujur 2002, *Ada apa dengan Cinta?: sebuah skenario*, Metafor Publishing, Jakarta.

Qurtuby, Sumanto Al 2005, 'Agama, seks, dan moral', *Syir'ah* 41(5).

Rahman, Lisabona 2006, '9 Naga', *Kompas*, 15 January.

Rahman, Lisabona and Paul Agusta 2005, 'Many local films, but has quality improved?' *Jakarta Post*, www.thejakartapost.com/review/feat03.asp, viewed 27 December 2005.

Reeve, David 1996, 'Indonesia' in Milner, Anthony and Mary Quilty (eds), *Communities of thought*, Oxford University Press, Melbourne.

Resink, GJ 1975, 'From the old *Mahabharata*—to the new *Ramayana*—Order', *Bijdragen tot de Taal-, Land-en Volkenkunden* 131(2/3).

Rieser, Klaus 2001, 'Masculinity and monstrosity: characterization and identification in the slasher film', *Men and Masculinities* 3(4).

Robinson, Kathryn 1997, 'Indonesian women: a survey of recent developments', *Review of Indonesian and Malaysian Affairs* 31(2).

—— 2007, 'Masculinity, political power and regime change in Indonesia', unpublished manuscript.

—— 2008, *Gender, Islam and democracy in Indonesia*, Routledge, London.

Robinson, Kathryn and Sharon Bessell (eds) 2002, *Women in Indonesia: gender, equity and development*, Institute of Southeast Asian Studies, Singapore.

Robison, Richard & Vedi Hadiz 2004, *Reorganizing Power in Indonesia: The Politics of Oligarchy in an Age of Markets*, Routledge, London & New York.

Rodriguez, Robert 1995, *Rebel without a crew: or how a 23-year-old filmmaker with $7,000 became a Hollywood player*, Plume Books, New York.

Roeder, OG 1969, *The smiling general*, Gunung Agung, Jakarta.

Rusdi, Prima and Riri Riza 2002, *Eliana, eliana: sebuah skenario*, Metafor Publishing, Jakarta.

Rushkoff, Douglas 1994, *The Gen X reader*, Ballantine Books, New York.

Sadli, Saparinah 2002, 'Feminism in Indonesia in an international context' in Robinson, Kathryn and Sharon Bessell (eds), *Women in Indonesia: gender, equity and development*, Institute of Southeast Asian Studies, Singapore.

Sambodja, Asep 2007, 'Tanggapan', Artculture-Indonesia, www.mail-archive.com/artculture-indonesia@yahoogroups.com/msg00022.html, viewed 14 January 2009.

Sastrosatomo, Soebadio 1998, *Politik Dosomuko rezim Orde Baru: rapuh dan sengsarakan rakyat*, Pusat Dokumentasi Politik 'GUNTUR 49', Jakarta.

Scherer, Savitri 2006, 'Tuna karya, jilbab and cow-boy hat: youth in Suharto's Indonesia as reflected in the work of Remy Sylado and Emha Ainun Nadjib', *Indonesia and the Malay World* 34(99).

Seal, Graham 1996, *The outlaw legend*, Cambridge University Press, Cambridge.

Sears, Laurie J 1996a, *Shadows of Empire: Colonial Discourse and Javanese Tales*, Duke University Press, Durham and London.

—— 1996b, (ed.) *Fantasizing the feminine in Indonesia*, Duke University Press, Durham and London.

—— 2007a, 'Postcolonial identities, feminist criticism, and Southeast Asian studies' in Laurie J Sears (ed), *Knowing Southeast Asian subjects*, University of Washington Press, Seattle.

—— 2007b, 'Reading Ayu Utami: notes for a study of trauma and the archive in Indonesia', *Indonesia* 83.

Sen, Krishna 1994, *Indonesian cinema: framing the New Order*, Zed Books Ltd, London.

—— 1995, 'Repression and resistance: interpretations of the feminine in New Order cinema' in Hooker, Virginia Matheson (ed), *Culture and society in New Order Indonesia*, Oxford University Press, Kuala Lumpur.

—— 2005, 'Film revolution? Women are now on both sides of the camera', *Inside Indonesia* 83.

Sen, Krishna and David T Hill 2000, *Media, culture and politics in Indonesia*, Oxford University Press, Melbourne.

Shirazy, Habiburrahman El 2004, *Ayat Ayat Cinta*, Republika: Jakarta.

Sidel, John 1999, 'The usual suspects: Nardong Putik, Don Pepe Oyson, and Robin Hood' in Rafael, VL (ed), *Figures of criminality in Indonesia, the Philippines, and colonial Vietnam*, SEAP, Ithaca.

Siregar, Wahidah Zein Br 2006, 'Political parties, electoral system and women's representation in the 2004-2009 Indonesian parliaments', CDI Policy papers on political governance, No. 2, http://www.cdi.anu.edu.au/_research/2006-07/ D_P/2006_11_PPS_2_Siregar/2006_11_PPS2_WS.pdf, viewed 11 April 2010.

Situmorang, Saut 2007, 'Anugerah KAKUS-Listiwa Award diserahkan hari ini di WC UMUM', 24 November, www.mail-archive.com/artculture-indonesia@ yahoogroups.com/msg00062.html, viewed 20 March 2010.

Sjamsu, Nazwar 1971, *Mendjeladjah heboh sastra 1968: menudju titik kebenaran*, Pustaka Sa'adijah, Bukittinggi.

SMH (Sydney Morning Herald) 2006, 'Playboy Indonesia's editor-in-chief faces charges', 7 December.

Stallybrass, Peter and Allon White 1986, *The poetics and politics of transgression*, Cornell University Press, Ithaca.

Stoler, Ann Laura1995, *Race and the education of desire: Foucault's history of sexuality and the colonial order of things*, Duke University Press, Durham and London.

Suara Merdeka 2007, 'Film Riri Riza kena sensor', www.suaramerdeka.com/ harian/0702/02/bud05.htm, viewed 28 December 2008.

Sunindyo, Saraswati 1995, 'Gender discourse on television' in Hooker, Virginia Matheson (ed), *Culture and Society in New Order Indonesia*, Oxford University Press, Kuala Lumpur.

Suryakusuma, Julia I 1994, 'The clampdown on women's sex industry', *Indonesia Business Weekly* 18.

—— 2004, *Sex, power and nation: an anthology of writings, 1979–2003*, Metafor Publishing, Jakarta.

Sweetnarah 2008, 'Perfect movie 4 those really needing a GOOD scare!', Yahoo! Malaysia Movies, http://malaysia.movies.yahoo.com/Pocong+2/movie/14183/, viewed 4 January 2008.

Teeuw, A 1996, *Modern Indonesian literature II*, KITLV Press, Leiden.

Tickell, Paul 1986, 'Subversion or escapism?: the fantastic in recent Indonesian fiction', *Review of Indonesian and Malayan Affairs* 20(1).

Toer, Koesalah Soebagyo 2006, *Pramoedya Ananta Toer dari dekat sekali: catatan pribadi Koesalah Soebagyo Toer*, Kepustakaan Populer Gramedia Jakarta.

Toer, Pramoedya Ananta 1952, 'Dia yang menyerah' in *Tjerita dari Blora*, Balai Pustaka, Jakarta.

—— 1980, *Bumi manusia*, Wirya Karya, Kuala Lumpur.

—— 1981, *Awakenings*, translated by Max Lane, Penguin Books, Ringwood.

—— 1994, *Perburuan*, Hasta Mitra, Jakarta.

—— 1997, 'Sastra, sensor dan negara: seberapa jauhkah bahaya novel?' in Laksana, AS (ed), *Polemik hadiah Magsaysay* Institut Studi Arus Informasi, Jakarta.

—— 1999a, *Arok dedes*, Hasta Mitra, Jakarta.

—— 1999b, *Bukan pasar malam*, Bara Budaya Yogyakarta, Yogyakarta.

—— 1999c, *Percikan revolusi + Subuh*, Hasta Mitra, Jakarta.

—— 1999d, 'Dendam' in *Percikan revolusi + Subuh*, Hasta Mitra, Jakarta.

Triyana, Bonnie 2007, 'Binhad Nurrohmat: sastra Indonesia tidak sehat', Great Literary Works, http://greatliteraryworks.blogspot.com/2008/05/binhad-nurrohmat-sastra-indonesia-tidak.html, viewed 15 December 2008.

Utami, Ayu 1998, *Saman*, Kepustakaan Populer Gramedia, Jakarta.

—— 2005, *Saman: a novel*, translated by Pamela Allen, Equinox Publishing, Jakarta.

van Erven, Eugene 1992, *The playful revolution: theatre and liberation in Southeast Asia*, Indiana University Press, Bloomington.

van Heeren, Katinka 2002a, 'Revolution of hope: independent films are young, free and radical', *Inside Indonesia* 70, http://insideindonesia.org/content/view/391/29/, viewed 19 March 2010.

—— 2002b, 'The case of *Beth*: monopolies and alternative networks for the screening of films in Indonesia in transition', *IIAS Workshop: globalizing media and local society in Indonesia*, Leiden, the Netherlands.

—— 2007, 'Return of the Kyai: representations of horror, commerce, and censorship in post-Suharto Indonesian film and television', *Inter-Asia Cultural Studies* 8(2).

Vickers, Adrian 2005, *A history of modern Indonesia*, Cambridge University Press, Cambridge.

Vltchek, Andre and Rossie Indira (eds) 2006, *Exile: conversations with Pramoedya Ananta Toer*, Haymarket Books, Chicago.

Warouw, Nicolaas 2008, 'Industrial workers in transition: women's experiences of factory work in Tangerang' in Ford, Michele and Lyn Parker (eds), *Women and work in Indonesia*, Routledge, London and New York.

Widodo, Amrih 1988, '"Wayang" revisited: the politics of language of a New Order student', unpublished manuscript.

Wieringa, Edwin P 2002, 'A Javanese handbook for would-be husbands: the *Serat candraning wanita*', *Journal of Southeast Asian Studies* 33(3).

Wieringa, Saskia 2003, 'The birth of the New Order state in Indonesia: sexual politics and nationalism', *Journal of Women's History* 15(1).

Williams, Emily 2006, 'Indonesia's anti pornography and pornoaction bill: views from Yogyakarta', honours thesis, University of Tasmania.

Wilson, Ian Douglas 1999, 'Reog Ponorogo: spirituality, sexuality, and power in a Javanese performance tradition', *Intersections* 2.

Wulia, Tintin 2008, 'The name game: or, the years of living with no name' *Inside Indonesia*, No. 93, http://insideindonesia.org/content/view/1127/47/, viewed 29 December 2008.

Yordenaya, Ine 2005, 'Akal-akalan publikasi?', detik HOT, www.detikhot.com/index.php/tainment.read/tahun/2005/bulan/12/tgl/12/time/155939/idnews/496753/idkanal/229, viewed 15 December 2008.